ISBN 978-0-243-27852-7
PIBN 10106372

English
Français
Deutsche
Italiano
Español
Português

www.forgottenbooks.com

Mythology Photography **Fiction**
Fishing Christianity **Art** Cooking
Essays Buddhism Freemasonry
Medicine **Biology** Music **Ancient
Egypt** Evolution Carpentry Physics
Dance Geology **Mathematics** Fitness
Shakespeare **Folklore** Yoga Marketing
Confidence Immortality Biographies
Poetry **Psychology** Witchcraft
Electronics Chemistry History **Law**
Accounting **Philosophy** Anthropology
Alchemy Drama Quantum Mechanics
Atheism Sexual Health **Ancient History**
Entrepreneurship Languages Sport
Paleontology Needlework Islam
Metaphysics Investment Archaeology
Parenting Statistics Criminology
Motivational

LABOR QUESTIONS

AND

SOCIALISM.

BY

CHARLES BRADLAUGH.

———◆———

LONDON :

A. AND H. BRADLAUGH BONNER,

63 FLEET STREET, E.C.

—

1895.

2/6

LONDON:
PRINTED BY A. BONNER,
34 BOUVERIE STREET, FLEET STREET, E.C

CONTENTS.

THE

EIGHT HOURS' MOVEMENT.

BY

CHARLES BRADLAUGH.

[*Reprinted by permission from* "THE NEW REVIEW".]

LONDON:

FREETHOUGHT PUBLISHING COMPANY,

63 FLEET STREET, E.C.

1889.

PRICE TWOPENCE.

LONDON :

PRINTED BY CHARLES BRADLAUGH AND ANNIE BESANT,

63 FLEET STREET, E.C.

THE EIGHT HOURS' MOVEMENT.

THE movement, to the discussion of which this paper is confined, is the movement for limiting by statute the hours of employment in all industries throughout this kingdom to eight hours per day. To this movement, so far as it relates to adults, whether men or women, I am most decidedly opposed, on the grounds : (1) That it is not, and ought not to be, the business or duty of Parliament to fix the hours during which adults may work. There is a tendency growing, of most dangerous character, and of which this eight hours' movement is part, to look to the Legislature or to the Government to supply immediate remedies for all evils, however arising, in the struggle for existence. (2) That though the shortest hours of labor possible in each industry should be sought by, and are beneficial to, the employed, such hours of daily labor should be the subject of separate negotiation and arrangement in each industry, and such arrangements should be arrived at by mutual discussion and understanding between the employers and the organised employed. (3) That if "eight hours' labor per day" be translated to mean that no works of any description are to be conducted for more than eight hours in each twenty-four hours the giving legal effect to a prohibition of that kind would be certainly ruinous to many of the largest industries in this country. (4) That to prevent men in all kinds of labor from working more than eight hours out of twenty-four may, and in some cases certainly would, involve a serious reduction of the wages hitherto received.

I wish to be clearly understood as being thoroughly and earnestly in favor of shortening hours of labor to the lowest point consistent with the profitable conduct of each industry. I agree with Mr. Thomas Burt, one of the most loyal representatives of labor ever sent to the House of Commons, in his statement in the *Contemporary Review* that " at present in some industries the hours are scandalously and injuriously long ", and that " in nearly every case " such overlong hours " could, with advantage to everybody concerned, and with injury to none, be greatly reduced ". My opposition is to the proposal to make compulsory by statute one set of hours for all conditions of employment. Great difference of opinion exists even amongst the workers themselves as to how short a daily period of labor in each industry is possible, having regard to profitable conduct of the respective undertakings.

I suggest that one most effective way of ascertaining the least number of hours practicable in any industrial enterprise would be by the establishment, in every department of skilled labor, of co-operative production, this being undertaken either directly by the great Trade Unions, or by Workmen's Associations encouraged by trade organisations, and the capital for which co-operative production should in each case be solely or almost entirely found in shares by workers belonging to the trade, and the management of which should be appointed by the shareholding workers, as is now done in the case of co-operative distribution. Men would thus be able to verify under the most favorable conditions the cost of production ; they would know the highest profit attainable, the highest wage payable, and the period of exploitation necessary for profit. There is at present some want of clearness as to what is meant amongst the advocates of the eight hours' movement. Mr. Burt, in the article before referred to, states that " at the recent Trades Union Congresses, both at the ordinary and the international, it was abundantly evident that the workmen of the United Kingdom differ widely and radically on the question of the regulation of the hours of labor ". And the difference is not only as to the regulation, that is, whether the regulation shall be mutual or statutory, there is difference as to the number of hours. Mr. William Abraham, M.P., the official representative of the Rhondda Valley miners, has put his view with distinct precision, *i.e.*, that there should only be one shift of eight hours per day. There are others, who write and talk more vaguely, who decline to be bound by all that is involved in the extreme pronouncement of Mr. Abraham, but who do not definitively repudiate his proposal, and who avoid committing themselves in specific words. At the Trades Union Congress at Bradford, Mr. Threlfall, who represents a Labor Electoral Association, proposed an Eight Hours' Bill for coal workers and railway servants. Mr. Keir Hardie, a Scotch miners representative, moved as an amendment "that eight hours should be the maximum of labor per day for workmen engaged in all trades". Mr. Keir Hardie added a proviso "that seamen should be included in any measure restricting the hours of labor". The amendment and resolution were each in turn rejected by the delegates assembled at Bradford; but the Parliamentary Committee of the Trade Congress was instructed to take a vote of the trades on the two questions:—(1) Are you in favor of an eight hours' working day? (2) Are you in favor of it being obtained by Act of Parliament? I am not aware what answer has yet been given to these queries, but the matter will certainly come up for discussion at the next Trades Union Congress.

The matter had been previously raised for discussion amongst the Trades Unionists at their Swansea and other Congresses, and in 1887 the Parliamentary Committee was instructed "during the year to obtain a plebiscite of the members of the various Trade Unions of the country upon this important question, and whether, if approved, such reduction of hours shall be brought about by the Trade Unions themselves or by means of an Eight Hours' Labor Bill". In accordance with such instructions the Parliamentary Committee issued a circular to the various trade societies calling upon them to vote in the matter. The Parliamentary Committee assumed, and I think accurately assumed, that a general eight-hour day enforced by law would certainly lead to a general reduction of wages, for they asked the trades to declare whether they would "be willing to make the necessary sacrifice in the total week's wage which such an alteration might involve". It seems abundantly clear that if in any industry it be now the habit to work nine hours or nine-and-a-half hours or ten hours then the reduction to eight hours must involve either lower wage or increased cost of production, or perhaps both. The Parliamentary Committee's report to the next Congress does not show the result of the voting. The President of the Congress only said "that several of the skilled trades are very divided on the subject, this arising not so much from a dislike to legislative interference as from the difficulties they foresee in applying such a measure to their particular industry".

In the course of the discussion at Bradford, Mr. Wilson —who sat in the House of Commons for the short Parliament of 1886, as a representative of the Durham miners, and who produced a most favorable impression in all quarters of the House by his great ability—asked "what would become of those men who worked less than eight hours a day under an Eight Hours' Bill?". The fact being that the intelligent and well-organised miners of Northumberland and Durham have, without any help from Parliament, already reduced the hours of underground adult labor to less than the proposed eight hours' limit. From a paper prepared by Mr. Ralph Young, the very earnest Secretary of the Northumberland miners, it appears that the hours of Northumberland coal-hewers working at the coal-face are six and three-quarters, or about seven hours and a-half bank to bank, and the hours of other underground men are eight hours bank to bank. Thirty-seven years ago the hewers worked from nine to twelve hours a day. These reduced hours both in Durham and Northumberland have been the result of negotiation and arrangement between the men and the coal-owners. In reply to Mr. Wilson, Mr. Keir Hardie said "that if there were men who were working six hours a day, and men who were working twelve hours per day, it was an improvement to have them all working eight hours per day". Whether the men who have already won shorter hours without statute would quietly consent to have their day's labor lengthened by Parliamentary enactment is a point on which Mr. Keir Hardie was not interrogated.

Mr. Chapman and Mr. Kell, delegates from boot and shoe-makers, pointed out, in the discussion at Bradford, that much work in their trade was done in the workers' homes, and that "it would be obviously impossible to enforce an eight hours' limit under such conditions", and Mr. Heasleden "said that in the lace trade, which had to struggle with Continental competition, employing men

during long hours at low wages, a universal Eight Hours'
Bill would simply be destruction ". The eight hours'
movement is supported on different, and on conflicting
grounds, by differing advocates. Amongst coal miners,
where eight hours' underground work is a very full day's
labor, it has in many cases solely meant restriction of
output, *i.e.*, it is asserted that the production being large,
prices are low, and the wage is therefore low, and it is
contended that if the output were restricted prices would
be higher, and that, either under the sliding scale or
otherwise, the men would be able to exact higher wage.
It is probably for this reason that Mr. Abraham would
restrict mines to one shift of eight hours. Similar arguments — as to the limitation of production by working
shorter time per day, or fewer days per week—are used
in textile and other manufactures. If these industries
had no competitors abroad, and if the home consumption
were sufficient to maintain the industry, even then the
position would be difficult enough. For increase of cost
in every industry would mean reduction of the purchasing
power of wage. But the bulk of our manufacturing and
mining enterprise is, in the main, dependent on its export
trade. Our produce is sent to foreign countries, and has
to compete in foreign markets with foreign productions.
A restriction of output here, followed by increased price,
through temporarily securing higher nominal wage, would
stimulate increase of foreign output, until the supply
meeting, or exceeding, the demand, the lesser output at
home, though obtained at increased cost, would fall in
price to the level of its foreign competitor. Restriction of
output can only avail when those who restrict have a
monopoly of the raw material, or the sole control of the
means of manufacture. To-day, coal and iron are being
worked in all quarters of the globe, and it is no longer
possible to keep secret, and thus to control, any special
method of manufacture. Textile industries are developing
in countries where labor is very cheap, because the standard
of comfort has been very low, or because life requirements
are less costly.

Some workmen urge that if the men who are now working more than eight hours were limited to eight hours and
no more, then there would be the need for more laborers,
and that the number of unemployed would be reduced.

Mr. Thompson, a Scotch delegate, speaking at the Bradford Congress, said, "There were thousands of persons to-day who had no purchasing power, but who, if an Eight Hours' Bill were passed, would have to be employed. The result would be a larger purchasing power in the country." It is hardly needful to urge that this contention is utterly fallacious. If the amount now paid in wage is simply divided amongst a larger number of receivers, there is no increase whatever of purchasing power. If the proposition is, that though the number of hours worked would be unchanged, the workers being more numerous, higher wages must be paid, then the answer is, that if you unduly increase the cost of manufacture you will stimulate foreign competition, not only in foreign markets, but also in the home market, which market alone would be insufficient to maintain your present industries. If you succeed by protective duties in excluding foreign manufactures from your home market, you increase the price of all articles of consumption and thus reduce the purchasing power of wage.

It is contended by many that the reduction to eight hours per day would not decrease the rate of wage, and the illustration is taken of the building trade amongst stonemasons, where, with now a lesser average of hours per week, there is a higher average of weekly wage payment than with longer hours some years since; but unless greater result is attained in the lesser hours it can hardly be contended that the cost is not more, and although this might not be an entire evil, if the result, as in the building trade, were limited to home consumption, the question of cost becomes of high importance when the industry has in great part to be maintained by exportation of the result produced to foreign markets.

It is urged that there are other industries dependent on foreign demand in which hours have been shortened and in which wage has not been reduced, but in all these industries greater skill and improved appliances have been attended with increased production. This is notoriously the case in coal mines.

Mr. Threlfall writes that, "an Eight Hours' Bill has become absolutely necessary", and he pleads that "the rapid growth of the producing population—at the rate of a thousand a day—without a corresponding increase in our foreign trade", and "the development of labor-savin machinery, bring about an over-stocked labor market, with consequent poverty, misery, and destitution". The rapid growth of population can scarcely be checked by compelling those who are now subsisting by their labor to reduce their means of subsistence, unless the process is continued till the misery point is reached; and it is utterly untrue that labor-saving machinery has, as yet, permanently diminished the laborers required in any large industry in this country. If Mr. Threlfall's argument is to be carried to a logical conclusion the constant increase of laborers is to be met by a constant reduction of the hours of labor. The Bill introduced by Mr. Cunninghame Grahame, M.P., proposes to enact that " a person shall not, in any one day of twenty-four hours, be employed underground in any mine for a period exceeding eight hours from the time of his leaving the surface of the ground to the time of his ascent thereto, except in case of accident or other emergency "; and proposes " a penalty not exceeding forty shillings for each offence." This does not touch overground workers, nor does it forbid double shifts. It applies to metalliferous mines as well as to coal mines. Mr. Cunninghame Graham proposes to punish the employer, but not the employed, yet, if it is to be made an offence for an individual to work more than eight hours per day, each adult party to the offence ought surely to incur some penalty. If Mr. Cunninghame Graham considers that the man has not enough of volition to be more than a mere instrument, he rather challenges the electoral position recently given to his client. Possibly Mr. Cunninghame Graham thinks that a proposal to inflict any punishment on the men would be met by strenuous resistance.

In January, 1885, there was held for three days in the Princes' Hall, Piccadilly, under the very efficient presidency of the Right Hon. Sir Charles Dilke, a most remarkable gathering; an "Industrial Remuneration Conference ", attended by delegates from many of the most important industries in the United Kingdom, and attended also by some of the most prominent amongst capitalists and social reformers. The question for that Conference, as framed by its projector, was "What are the best means for, consistent with justice and equity, bringing about a more equal division of the daily products of industry between capital and labor, so that it may become possible for all to enjoy a fair share of material comfort and intellectual culture, possible for all to lead a dignified life, and less diffi-cult for all to lead a good life"? By the careful preliminary arrangements made by the controlling committee, some very valuable papers were secured and read, which were followed by useful discussion, and a complete report of the whole of the papers and speeches has since been pub-lished as a volume. No paper was specially devoted to the hours of labor, but many vital references were made from varying standpoints. It is to be regretted that this Conference, so useful for its free exchange of opinions, has not been followed by others. As it is, the record of its proceedings is marvellously pregnant with promise not unmixed with occasional serious warning.

In a speech by Mr. James Aitken, of Greenock, it was urged: "Is it not necessary that there should be a reduc-tion of the hours of labor so as to allow everyone to earn his own livelihood? It would certainly be better that ten men should work six hours per day and all be employed, than that six men should work ten hours a day and the other four men go about idly as paupers." This was cheered and was not then answered, but the reply is, first that if the six men by working ten hours only just earn their fair livelihood, then to take away nearly one half of their earnings will be to reduce them and their families to chronic discomfort. The four unemployed ought neither to be maintained as paupers, nor be compelled to deprive the six employed of four-sixths of their precious earnings. New sources of employment should be sought for in this, or in some other country. I believe that the land of this country might provide additional employment for many hundreds of thousands ; that emigration might relieve some scores of thousands, but I do not believe in any permanent cure for want of employment so long as there are always ten to struggle for subsistence miserably where six might thrive comfortably. This question of over-population needs to be faced, for it is not enough to share the food of six amongst ten if next generation the problem is to be the sharing the insufficiency of ten amongst six-teen. Mr. J. Burnett, now the labor correspondent of the Board of Trade, then the representative of the Amalgamated Engineers, attacking overtime, said: "Every man who works overtime four quarter days takes away a days' work from another man ". But it would be often the case that overtime would be worked under sudden pressure and the introduction of strange and casual hands for such sudden employment would sometimes be difficult, especially in highly skilled industries. The men who hang about to be called in for such occasional jobs are not usually of the most reliable class. Again, take an industry like that of the cycling manufacture which has developed at Coventry, which is apparently overworked certain months in the year and is slack at others. To forbid overtime would involve the attraction of additional population at Coventry who would be needed for the busy time only, who would even then be only partly needed, and who would have to be maintained out of the rates or driven away in the slack season.

Mr. Lowthian Bell, who read a paper at the Conference, mentioned that the introduction of the nine hours' system in a large locomotive building establishment brought up the cost of labor to the employer in the two years of 1874, and 1881, as compared with 1850, to 51·73, and 38·70 per cent respectively, and though this in no sense shows that labor was too highly paid in the later periods, it is some evidence that reductions of hours of labor involve serious increase of cost.

The workers and those who claim to be their special advocates seem to advocate, and seem now disposed to copy, the worst forms of bad legislation of past generations as to the regulation of the relations between employer and employed. Then, laws were passed to control the laborer, now, it is proposed to procure enactments to control the employer. As Professor Thorold Rogers points out, the Act of Elizabeth and the regulations of Quarter Sessions which prescribed twelve hours work a day all the year round only provoked evasion and resistance on the part of employer and employed. The natural tendency to-day is in the direction of shorter hours of labor.

Where laws for limiting hours of labor have recently been resorted to, they have achieved very little. This is illustrated by recent Transatlantic experience, and is shown by the introductory remarks on the hours of labor in Vol. XX. of the tenth Census of the United States of America. On the contrary, organisation has already had considerable effect in diminishing the number of hours worked per day.

The United States Census reporter, giving the percentages of hours worked for the quinquennial period, from 1830 to 1880, adds :—

"The small percentage reported under the eight-hour period will be noticed. Notwithstanding the agitation in favor of eight hours as a day's work, the percentage of the total number reporting this as the period of daily labor in 1880 is even less, by a small fraction, than in 1830. This does not indicate that the hours of labor have not decreased since 1830. Indeed, the table shows the contrary, there having been a marked increase in the ten hour period, and a marked decrease in the twelve to thirteen, and thirteen to fourteen hour periods between 1830 and 1880, as will be seen by the following tabulation of the percentages of the different hours of labor for the years 1830 and 1880 :—

Hours of Labor.	Percentage in 1830.	Percentage in 1880.
8 to 9	5·4	5·1
9 to 10	13·5	8·8
10 to 11	29·7	59·6
11 to 12	5·4	9·6
12 to 13	32·5	14·6
13 to 14	13·5	2·3

" The number reporting the hours of labor as ten to eleven increased from 29·7 per cent in 1830 to 59·6 per cent in 1880, more than double, while those reporting twelve to thirteen decreased from 32·5 per cent to 14·6 per cent, and those reporting thirteen to fourteen decreased from 13·5 per cent to 2·3 per cent."

In the State of New York an Eight Hours' Bill was carried in 1870, but it does not appear to have been very strictly enforced. It enacts that "eight hours shall constitute a legal day's work for all classes of mechanics, working men, and laborers, excepting those engaged in farm and domestic labor; but overwork for extra compensation, by agreement between employer and employee, is hereby permitted." The law is made applicable to the State, and to all municipal corporations, but while penalties of not less than one hundred dollars are imposed for breach or evasion of the law in State or municipal contracts, no penalty is imposed on other employers, or employed.

By the third annual report of the Bureau of Statistics of Labor for the year 1885, it is pretty clear that the trades in which the eight hours' limit is observed are few, and only those in which strong Unions exist, and the Chief Commissioner reports : " The conditions of trade are such that it is almost fruitless to attempt to adopt short hours in one State, and neglect to do so in others." Witness after witness showed that the mere eight hours' law was of little avail. Henry Emrich, cabinet-maker, said : "An eight hours' law will only be of any effect through the action of the organisations themselves ", and he added : "The only way to secure short hours is by combination in a particular trade where it is desired." A witness, an engineer, testified : "The State of Massachusetts passed a ten hours' law, and we know that work was driven out of Massachusetts into Rhode Island." This witness, who was in favor of a compulsory eight hours' law throughout the United States, was also in favor of the State feeding his family, "if the pay for eight hours was insufficient to maintain them". W. McClelland, in favor of short hours, said : " When our Union is strong enough we can bring these things into practice ourselves ", and he added : " Here is the eight hours' law, and you will find letter-carriers working ten and eleven hours; what is the use of it " ? A moulder testified : " We have got too many laws for the working man, but they are like the statuary in Central Park—dead." " I have more faith in labor organisation than I have in law." A harness-maker testified "that the Union had shortened the hours of labor without legislation," but the men worked ten hours a day, despite that the eight hours' law had existed fifteen years. Another witness, a brassworker, testified strongly in favor of an eight hours' law, but said : "I do not think it could be enforced, but I think the moral influence of such a law, and the enforcing it on the State workers would influence the others by the force of example." Edward Conkling, a painter, testified " that the reduction of hours could be better brought about by organisation than legislation", adding : "the stonecutters have proved that; President Grant said that it was impossible to enforce the eight hours' law"; the stonecutters enforced it by their organisation.

John A. Kavanagh, printer, testified: "I would make eight hours a legal day's work, but if a man wants to work fifteen hours a day I wouldn't prohibit him from doing it if he wanted to.

Q. In your judgment can a reduction of the hours of labor be better secured by legislation or by organisation of labor?

A. By organisation of labor.

Q. You think that would be the best way to accomplish it?

A. I think that is the only way to accomplish it; I don't think it can be done by legislation."

Hermann Gutstadt, cigar-maker, testified:—

Q. "Do you think the hours of labor can be shortened by legislation?

A. I do not; not effectively. I believe that the hours of labor can only be effectively regulated by labor organisations. The State is nearly powerless. For instance, we have an eight hours' law on the statute-book never enforced.

Q. You don't think it would be advisable to recommend more legislation on that subject?

A. I do not think it would be of any use to place a law upon the statute-book which cannot very well be enforced by the State."

The Fifth Annual Report of the New York Labor Bureau, 1887, contains the following passage, significant in face of the fact that the eight hours' law had been on the statute-book for seventeen years:—

" Strikes for the regulation of hours of labor during the past year have not been as frequent as formerly. The collapse of the nine-hour movement in May, 1885, seems to have had a deterring effect upon the movement, and the attempts to reduce hours of labor during the past year were confined to special industries, such as waiters and bakers, with a few others. The half-holiday movement seems to have received its strength from a tacit understanding on the part of the employers, who were willing to adapt themselves to a changed condition of affairs."

The several States have special enactments as to hours of labor, of which the following are samples. In Wisconsin:

"*Section* 1,729, *Revised Statutes.*—In all engagements to labor in any manufacturing or mechanical business, where there is no express contract to the contrary, a day's work shall consist of eight hours, and all engagements or contracts for labor in such cases shall be so construed, but this shall not apply to any contract for labor by the week, month, or year."

On April 8th, 1887, the Legislature of New Jersey enacted:—

"That twelve hours' labor to be performed within twelve consecutive hours with reasonable time for meals, not less than half-an-hour for each, shall constitute a day's labor in the operation of all cable, traction, and horse car street surface railroads, and of all cable, traction, and steam elevated railroads owned or operated by corporations incorporated under the laws of this State, for the employees of such corporations in operating such railroads."

The Massachusetts Short Hours' Movement has for its chronicler the eminent labor statistician, the Hon. Carrol D. Wright, now at Washington, and needs more lengthy treatment than space will now permit.

It must be borne in mind, in estimating the importance of the foregoing extracts, that Federal legislation on an eight hours' basis dates back to June 25th, 1868, so far as Government works are concerned. In the Fourth Biennial Report of the Illinois Labor Bureau, the Hon. J. S. Lord, in his able statement of the progress of the eight hours' movement, says:—

"May 19th, 1869, and again May 11th, 1872, President Grant issued proclamations calling attention to the provision of this law, and directing that no reduction should be made in the pay on account of the reduction in the hours of labor of those coming within the purview of the Act. Subsequently, May 18th, 1872, Congress passed an Act securing to all workmen, laborers, and mechanics in the employ of the Government between June 25th, 1868, and May 19th, 1869, full pay on a basis of a regular day of eight hours, the period covered being that between the passage of the Act and the date of President Grant's first proclamation on the subject. Notwithstanding the obvious intent of Congress to comply with the wishes expressed in the petitions of those who urged the passage of this law, the heads of departments held that in failing to repeal an Act of July 16th, 1862, requiring the wages of employees in the navy yards to conform to those in private establishments, Congress had merely established the length of a day's work for the Government and that they were bound to pay *pro rata* the same wages as those paid in private employment. This view was sustained both by attorney-General Evarts and Attorney-General Hoar, so that the effect of the law has been simply to reduce the earning opportunity of the Government employee by 20 per cent."

Desiring that the fullest and best information should be accessible, I have obtained an order of the House of Commons for a return showing all laws limiting the hours of adult labor throughout Europe as well as in the United States of America, with such statistics as are obtainable as to the working hours in each country or State, and the best information as to the enforcement or otherwise of such laws.

Believing that any attempt by Parliament to fix the hours of labor would be permanently disastrous to the best interests of the workmen themselves; fearing that many workmen are too readily allowing themselves to be misled by earnest but unpractical enthusiasts, and by reckless traders on social grievances; and noting that in some recent electoral struggles promises have been given by the candidates to vote for measures which reverse all Radical traditions, I shall give my voice and vote in Parliament to prevent any breaking down of the self-reliant spirit which puts the bulk of our population materially in advance of most European peoples.

IGHT HOURS' MOVEMENT.

VERBATIM REPORT

OF

A DEBATE

BETWEEN

Mr. H. M. HYNDMAN and Mr. C. BRADLAUGH.

(Revised by both Disputants.)

LONDON:

PUBLISHED BY

A. AND H. BRADLAUGH BONNER,

AND SOLD BY

R. FORDER, 28 STONECUTTER STREET, E.C.

PRICE SIXPENCE.

LONDON :
PRINTED BY A. BONNER,
63 FLEET ST., AND 34 BOUVERIE ST., E.C.

EIGHT HOURS' MOVEMENT.

Debate between Mr. H. M. HYNDMAN *and* Mr. CHARLES BRADLAUGH, M.P., *at St. James's Hall, Piccadilly, on Wednesday, July 23rd, 1890.*

———◆———

Mr. SYDNEY BUXTON., M.P., in the chair.

The CHAIRMAN: Ladies and gentlemen,—My duties as chairman this evening are very simple, and, looking round on the audience, I say that they will be very easy. They are to keep order, and to see fair play. (Hear, hear.) Gentlemen, in my individual capacity, I share the privilege that each one of you rejoices in as an Englishman, of having an opinion on the eight hours' question, and on every other question under the sun; but in my capacity as chairman this evening I have no opinion either on the eight hours' question or any other question, except that law and order shall prevail in this hall this evening. (Applause.) Now, gentlemen, I think it will be necessary for me to interfere only in two respects. In the first place, I shall be very stern with the speakers that they keep absolutely to the time that has been allotted to them; and secondly—and I hope you will support me in this—I should desire, as far as in me lies, to prevent any personal attacks or personal recrimination which may possibly crop up in this debate. (Hear, hear.) We are met here this evening for a public purpose. It is the desire of every one of us here this evening, I am sure, to arrive as far as we can at the truth and the justice of this question, and we all desire to do what in us lies for the benefit and the advantage of the labor question and of the nation at large. (Hear, hear.) Now, gentlemen, this debate will be watched

B 2

with very considerable interest, not only from the great
importance of the question itself, but also as possibly
creating a precedent for future action; because if the
two disputants will, as I am sure they will, meet each
other fair and square in argument and in debate, fair and
square in a way that is almost impossible, and is very
seldom done when opponents are speaking from separate
platforms, we shall find that other great questions of the
day will be similarly discussed in the way that this eight
hours' question is going to be discussed this evening, Why,
gentlemen, I should not be surprised if this mode of con-
ducting debate were to become so popular that some of our
debates in the House of Commons might be taken from
the arena of the House of Commons to the arena of a
common platform, and perhaps we may live to see the
leaders of the House and the leader of the Opposition—
(laughter)—to see Mr. Smith and Mr. Gladstone—(cheers)
—disputing questions of precedence, and questions of pre-
cedents in St. James's Hall; or perhaps we may find Mr.
Balfour and Mr. Parnell—(cheers and hisses)—debating
from a common platform the great question of Irish national government. But, ladies and gentlemen, seriously,
such a debate as this cannot fail to be of use. It throws
light on this great question. It gives food of thought for
each one of us, and it will help to show on which side the
truth prevails, and it will help the public mind to come to
a just conclusion on this question.

Now, gentlemen, it only remains for me to tell you what
will be the order of procedure, and to express the confident
hope that every one of you here will give a full, fair, and
attentive hearing to the two speakers. Now, gentlemen,
Mr. Hyndman will open the debate with the proposition
which he has submitted in writing to Mr. Bradlaugh,
which is as follows:

"That the enactment by law of eight hours a day, or forty-
eight hours a week as the maximum amount of work for adults
in all factories, mines, workshops, and businesses conducted for
profit will prove a valuable palliative of our present industrial
anarchy."

In addition to that, Mr. Hyndman has, at Mr. Bradlaugh's
request, drawn up a draft Bill embodying this proposition,
which probably most of you in the Hall now hold in your

hands. To that proposition of Mr. Hyndman's Mr Bradlaugh will propose the following counter proposition:

"That it is desirable that all wage-earners should work the smallest number of hours per day consistent with the profitable conduct of the industries in which they are respectively engaged; that the limitation of eight hours a day as the period during which an industrial establishment may be carried on may be fatal to many large industries in this country; that the hours of labor in each industry should be severally settled by conciliatory conference between the employed and employers or their representatives."

(Cheers.) Now, ladies and gentlemen, Mr. Hyndman will make his proposition, and he will speak for exactly half an hour. Then Mr. Bradlaugh will follow, also for half an hour. Mr. Hyndman will then follow Mr. Bradlaugh in a quarter of an hour's speech; then Mr. Bradlaugh will have another quarter of an hour; Mr. Hyndman will have a further quarter of an hour, and Mr. Bradlaugh will wind up with a final quarter of an hour. So that we shall have this great question debated by each speaker for the hour allotted to him, and I can only wish that many of the questions in the House of Commons were debated in such a short time as that. It would be useless to attempt after the subject has been debated in a meeting like this to vote upon it by show of hands. (Hear, hear.) No one, certainly not I, could be responsible for any accurate counting, and, therefore, we do not propose to have a show of hands in reference to this matter; and as we have come here to hear Mr. Hyndman and Mr. Bradlaugh I do not propose to accept any amendment and proposal from anyone in the Hall. (Hear, hear.) I now call on Mr. Hyndman to make his proposition.

Mr. HYNDMAN: Mr. Chairman, Friends, and Fellow Citizens, in opening this debate here to-night, with the proposition that I have formulated, and meeting the counter-proposition which Mr. Bradlangh has made in his turn, I quite agree with our Chairman that we have a serious subject under discussion—one which does affect every man and woman who is working for wages throughout this great country. The proposition you have heard, and the remarkable part of it is this, that nobody so far as I know—not even my opponent here on the platform to-night—denies in any shape or way that over-work exists

at the present time. (Hear, hear.) Furthermore, he says
that it is desirable that over-work should be limited. The
difference between us lies in how to limit it, and what
steps to take. But, before I deal with the antagonistic
view, I must first of all state what the result is of the
present system. For I see in my opponent's counter proposition that the same wording is introduced which he
introduced in his article in the *New Review*. He says,
"profitable to any industry". Now, Mr. Chairman, with
this word "profitable" we have to consider what is it that
is profitable to the people of this country? I say that if
it can be shown, as shown it undoubtedly can, that in
industry after industry—in nearly every industry in this
country—workmen and workwomen are worked to an
extent which not only is not profitable to them, but which
absolutely saps their vitality, destroys their intelligence,
and leaves them no leisure for consideration, and crushes
them down like brutes of the field, and worse—then I say
no industry is profitable. (Applause.) No industry is
profitable which can only be carried on under conditions
which mean degradation for those who practise that industry. (Great applause.) There are few perhaps who
consider what is the pecuniary value of health. That to
the community must be the most profitable industry that
can be possibly entered upon which obtains the best
possible health for every man, woman, and child in the
particular community, for in that lies the great resources
of this great country. But at the present moment what
is going on? Health is being sapped in every way, in
every trade, and not only is that so, but, to take this
question of eight hours, if you ask any medical man or
any physiologist he will tell you that eight hours a day of
continuous hard work is too much for any man. (Hear,
hear.) You cannot work a horse for more than three and
a-half to four hours a day, and any man who has tried
working with his hands seriously and hard for eight hours
a day will admit that eight hours is too much labor for
anyone to continue in health, if he carries it on day in and
day out, year in and year out. Therefore, I say the proposition I have before me here to-night is essentially a
moderate proposition, and I have rarely stood in that
position in my life of late years. (Hear, hear.) Now,
what are the effects of over-work? One of the effects is

this. I do not say that over-work is the only cause of the early decease of the working-classes, but the working-classes at this time die at just half the age of the class to which I belong—the class, namely, of those who live upon labor. The average of the working-classes of the present time is about twenty-seven years as against fifty-five for those who do not work. ("Shame!") And there is one remarkable feature in this which I hope my opponent will give his best attention to, and that is this: that so bad is this overwork for the people that during periods of depression, when the workers are not permitted to work owing to the system of industrial anarchy which at present prevails, positively the death-rate among the workers falls, although at that very time they are exposed to semi-starvation and worse. (" Shame!") That was the case during the time of the Lancashire cotton famine, when positively during that awful period the death-rate among the workers of Lancashire fell, although a cotton famine and a period of no work prevailed throughout that great county. I say that it is a very important fact. Again, let us look around upon the industrial anarchy that prevails to-day. Here you see those in Government employment at Woolwich Arsenal, at Enfield, and in the Post Office, where I was delighted to see the sweated victims have lately raised some protest against the official sweater—(loud applause)—in every one of those industries what do you find under the Government that at the very time that exceptional hours are being worked— fifteen, sixteen, eighteen, and even thirty-six hours at a stretch have been worked at Woolwich Arsenal—at that very time there have been 20,000 and 30,000, and even 100,000 unemployed men walking along the streets of London. At the very time that those exceptional hours were being worked the comrades of these men were walking the streets without the capacity to work, because they were not permitted to do so. I say, therefore, that that is practically anarchy—that one man should be overworked, and his vitality reduced, and his health destroyed, and at the same time another and quite as capable a man is going round, unable to work because he is not permitted to do so. That, I say, is practically an anarchical system. But further than that, the man who is out of work, and is not doing his share of the work of the community, is a tax on that community, and a burden on himself. (Hear, hear.) Now, we have had for years past two great opponents of this idea of limiting the hours of labor. We have had against us the political economists and the parsons. They are the secular and the sacred ministers of Mammon. (Hear, hear.) The function of the political economist is to confuse our hearts, and the function of the parson is to chloroform our intelligence. But happily, at the present time, both the one and the other are beginning to see the necessity of taking the same side with the people, and not later than last week there came forth from one of these darkest places of the earth—the study and the class-room of the political economist—a book, in which it is alleged by a professor of political economy that one of the most important things for a people to consider is the well-being of the people who work themselves—(hear, hear)—and that even if less wealth is produced by a reduction of those hours of labor which at present are so excessive, it will be beneficial to the people as a whole rather than the continuance of the present system. (Cheers.) Therefore, we no longer to-day have even the political economists as a whole against us. On the other side, I will not deal with the parsons—it is not necessary. (Laughter.) However, the point now is, what is the result of our present system? The result is this: that if you take the condition of the workmen and workwomen, their physical strength is being deteriorated by the present system. The height and the chest measurement of recruits have fallen markedly since the Queen came to the throne fifty years ago. Anyone who is acquainted with the manufacturing districts, as I have been since I was a boy, must see not only in the reports of certifying surgeons and sanitary inspectors, but from his own experience and under his own eye he can see perfectly clearly that deterioration continually going on; and in the same way the shop-girls and girls behind the bars, and women working for hire at an occupation which is exceedingly wearisome, although it does not appear to be so. What is stated in the *Lancet* and in the *British Medical Journal* and by such men as Dr. Richardson and others? They all say that work, when carried on for these long hours, this long standing behind these bars, this long work in the factory, is practically rendering the women who are

forced to take up this excessive toil incapable of producing
healthy children for the next generation. (Hear, hear.)
I say that from any point of view whatsoever a system
which not only destroys the present generation, but lays
the foundation of weakness and debility for the next,
cannot be profitable in any sense of the word, but must be
ruinous to the community at large. (Loud cheers.) Now
if this were carried on by a majority at the expense of the
minority, Mr. Chairman, I should equally contend that it
was our bounden duty to relieve the minority from this
injustice and injury that they were suffering from. I
should say that to be collective slave-drivers in that sense
at the expense of the few would be equally ruinous and
rascally. What is the case? It is not the question of the
minority being slave-driven for the benefit of the majority;
it is the majority at the present time who are being slave-
driven and injured for the benefit of a comparatively small
minority. (Applause.) Therefore, if that be so, and it is
manifest upon the very facts put forth from the Government offices, then not only as a matter of expediency, but
as a matter of the highest ethical right, we are bound at
the present time to interfere with this system. And further
it is easy to do. There is no reason why not. The power
of man over nature at this present time is almost infinitely
greater in many departments of industry than it was fifty
or one hundred years ago. In every industry in this
country the power of one man or woman to produce wealth
has been multiplied many fold during the period of the
lifetime of men in this hall. If that be the case—and we
admit it every day of our lives—why is it that the workers
alone are to have no benefit from this progress? Why is
it that they at the present time should work sixteen and
eighteen hours a day, and even longer hours in some
trades than years ago, when they are producing at this
present time far more in a few hours than they were fifty
or one hundred years ago in the longer hours? For once I
must say what I heard the other day, and I think it will
appeal to some present. There was a girl in the employment of a manufacturer who himself has what are called
Socialistic sympathies. She was making three pairs of
stockings in a day with a machine then in vogue. Another
machine is introduced whereby eight pairs of stockings
could be made in a day; and her employer said to her,

"I am going to provide you with a machine that will enable you to make eight pairs of stockings where you could only make three pairs before." The child was delighted. Her face beamed with smiles, for she thought out of this increase of eight pairs as against three she at least would derive some advantage. But he then explained to her that all his rival manufacturers would equally have the improved machines, and although she would be making the eight pairs of stockings in the same time she had previously made three, not one particle of advantage would she derive from it either as girl, as woman, or when she went down to her grave. ("Shame!") You see there is the manifest irony of the present system —harder and more intense toil; greater wealth for the community; and no benefit whatsoever, but perhaps longer hours of work, to those that produce the wealth. I say that is neither just nor expedient, and that it is worth trying to diminish, and that it should be put down by process of law. (Applause.) But now we call for the interference of the State, which means, or should mean, the organised forces of the whole community. (Hear, hear.) My opponent on this platform says that it should be, as his proposition states, by mutual agreement— (Hear, hear, and laughter)—between the shark and flying fish. I venture to think that that is impossible—(hear, hear)—and the best evidence I can give of that is the action of my opponent himself. When he wants something very important carried—and I do not deny that in certain respects what he has done in the House of Commons has been beneficial with regard to the workers—(cheers)— I say that that endeavor to extend the operation of the Truck Act—why did not he leave that to Trade Unions? (Applause.) As we pointed out in our little journal *Justice* at the time, the moment Mr. Bradlaugh very much wished to carry something which he considered for the benefit of the working classes, he dropped all his talk about Trade Unions, and at once appealed to the Legislature to enforce that which he knew Trade Unionists could not by themselves do. But he does not confine himself even to the restrictive operation of the law, but at the present moment he is sincerely desirous that the land should be cultivated, that much of this land which we see around us which is out of cultivation at the present time should have industrious people put upon it, who should cultivate it for the benefit of the community. Does he leave that to the Trade Unions? Not at all. Once more he appeals to the Legislature to compel—to compel, only think, individuals are to be compelled—to cultivate the land which at present is out of cultivation. I say, therefore, that I have a perfect right to claim my opponent on this platform as an ally of mine and the rest of us Social Democrats in this hall in this appeal to the State to interfere with the right of the individual to wrong the community. (Hear, hear.) But why did he not appeal to Trade Unionists? Because they are not strong enough to do his business. (Hear, hear.) Because Trade Unionists at the present time constitute but a small minority, unfortunately, of the working classes in this country; and, because, what is very important indeed, women are scarcely at all numbered in the Trade Unions at the present time. Their trade-unionism has scarcely begun and yet there is no portion of the community that is so much crushed by overwork at the present time as these defenceless women, and even children, who do not belong to any union at all. (Applause.) For whom then should the power of the State be called in? Why certainly for those who are incapable at the present time of defending themselves—on a more important question even than the Truck Act, or the compulsory cultivation of land. But Trade Unions have attempted to do certain things for themselves, and, unfortunately, they have to a large extent failed. I may enumerate the most important matters that they are exceedingly earnest about, and where they have failed to carry out what they have set before them. They failed to abolish piecework, although everybody who is a Trade Unionist knows they wish to put an end to it. They failed to suppress overtime, although everybody who is a Trade Unionist knows very well that the extra wages for overtime do not in any way compensate them for the extra amount they take out of themselves in that overtime. (Hear, hear.) They have not been able in any degree to limit the number of apprentices, which is a matter to which they themselves give very great attention. And also, more important than all, they have been wholly incapable of dealing with the question of the unemployed. (Applause.) Now,

then, that being so, I say that it is perfectly clear
that the trade unions are not capable of coping with this
question of the limitation of the hours of labor. The short
hours for work are in many cases completely illusory, and
overtime comes in to build up the day's work to a regular
sweating business. But not only so; where they have
won in a few cases even of late, you can see what the
result is. The question is never considered settled. If
you take, for example, the gas stokers, what happened
there? They won the eight hours' day—as they thought;
but a period came when Mr. George Livesey and the gas
stokers—(groans)—got into conflict, and what has he
done? The moment he won he reinstated the twelve
hour day. Therefore, we say that these examples show
perfectly clearly that Trade Unionism, valuable as it may
be, is insufficient to do the very thing which Mr. Bradlaugh says it is desirable to do. Now, take a case
which shows how very different it is on the other
side. The Factory Acts — although I am perfectly
aware that now and then they are evaded—and I wish
to goodness criminal punishment were imposed on
any man who breaks them in any shape or way—the
Factory Acts have, in the main, been successful, and what
is very remarkable is, as I shall have occasion to point out
later, that these very arguments that my opponent is
putting forward in the press, and is now, I presume, going
to put before you on this platform, were alleged against
these Factory Acts by the champions of the very class that
he is championing here to-night. (Applause.) But where
they have been adopted, they have been signally beneficial.
Now, at this very time, what is the case with regard to
the eight hours? The Eight Hours' Bill, as I understand
from the chairman, most of you have in your hands, and
I think you have. What do we ask, on a wider scale, but
that which the Factory Acts and other enactments have
already consecrated—the intervention of the State to limit
the power of a class to crush the people by overwork
owing to the competition that is going on? (Applause.)
What is the difficulty of the working class? Those of
you who belong to it know it perfectly well. It is absurd
to suppose you are independent. It is an illusory freedom
—a fraudulent liberty—which is held out to you. You
know very well that there is no whip of the slave driver

either so strong or so bitter as that of having to go morning after morning seeking for work, when practically there is none to be found. (Loud applause.) When, as a matter of fact, you may be underbidding your own fellows, and be called a "blackleg", because, unfortunately, wife and children are starving at home. I say that is one of the matters we distinctly hope and intend, as far as we can, shall be interfered with. And, remember, I do not, and never have, based any right or any claim upon mere majority. I should believe we were equally right if I were standing on the platform in a minority of one, as I have been on more than one question (Laughter.) But the majority on this question is growing fast. (Hear, hear.) At this very time, throughout this country, the mass of the working classes are discussing this question of the eight hours. At Southport, the other day, 70,000 miners voted solid for it ; and throughout the trade unions at the present time, if a vote were fairly taken, it is my firm belief that a large majority would go for the Eight Hours Bill. (Applause.) But we know further than that where it has been adopted it has proved to be beneficial. If you ask those who are working the Huddersfield tramway, they will tell you the eight hours measure has been a beneficial one; if you ask even a capitalist like Mr. Beaufoy, who adopted it in his workshop, he will tell you it has been beneficial to him and to his men too. If you go to Victoria, where the skilled unionists have got it, both capitalists and masters agree it has been beneficial to the community. Therefore, although there it was brought about by the combination of Trade Unions, and although in fact it has not extended to unskilled laborers and women, still I am quoting these as instances showing the benefit which arises to the people. As a matter of fact, anybody can understand the benefit. A man, instead of being worked to death, has some leisure in which to study the problems about him—to consider— what we Social Democrats most want—to consider the difficulties he is in, and the slavish position, which, at the present time, he occupies. What then are the objections to this ? First, that it will interfere with individuals. Is it not a question of slavery at the present time ? How much of individualism is left in a man who never sees his children except asleep—who has to work fourteen, fifteen, and sixteen hours a day ? (Applause.) How much of individualism has a woman who has worked for perhaps fourteen to sixteen hours behind a bar for twelve shillings a week? Or the sweated seamstress, how much has she of individuality left for anyone to crush? I say such arguments are derisive and absurd. Again, it is said it will reduce wages. Why at the present moment those who work the shortest hours are those who obtain the highest wages. What is even very germane to the matter, the plumbers who are working under a Royal Charter eight hours a day receive one penny per hour more wages than any other persons in the building trade. Again, I contend that when competition is reduced—as reduced it will be—at any rate in any trade where there is permanent employment, like railways, government employments, tramways, etc.—that the competition being withdrawn the unemployed being, to a certain extent at any rate, absorbed, wages will tend to rise because of the competition being taken away. For what is it that keeps down wages to-day? The fact that four men are competing for one man's job. (Applause.) Again, not only so, but those who are taken into work at the present time would constitute an enormous home trade more valuable than any foreign trade as any one will tell you who has examined the circumstances. Why is it that the unemployed cannot buy? Because they have no wage wherewith to buy. But if you put these men into work, certainly in railways; certainly in Government employment; certainly in omnibuses and tramways; most of which is unskilled labor; then these men would have a demand for reproductive use, and they would practically take up large portions of those commodities that now weigh on the market. Then I am told it will crush capital. Poor capital! I have generally found the capitalist uncommonly well able to take care of himself, either in this or in any other country I ever was in. I do not know why we need trouble much about crushing capital. (Loud cheers.) Again, I am told that it will ruin many industries in this country; which I take to mean that it will ruin them by foreign competition. Again I say precisely the same argument was put before us on the question of the Factory Acts. It was alleged over and over again, and it proved exactly the contrary. From the time the Factory Acts passed until the year 1871 was a period of booming prosperity, such as this or any other country has never known. I contend that if you reduce the hours of labor to eight per day the fresh machines which are now hanging on the markets would be introduced at the present time, and that that would be the danger, and not any other. For so far from interfering with our competitive force, as Robert Owen proved eighty years ago at New Lanark, short hours of labor of intelligent men are practically better than long hours of men who have no time to learn or think. (Applause.) Nor is this all. If you go to the different countries who have competition to fear, against whom are they setting up tariffs? Against the shorter hours that are worked in the English trades. You find that all over the Continent and in America. And in the neutral markets whom have we to fear? Why America, where in certain trades they work shorter hours even than our own? It is the skilled and intelligent work of America, under shorter hours, that we have to fear, far more than the long hours of Germans, Belgians, or anybody else. I would further say there is an enormous host of people who would not be affected at all by this foreign competition in any shape or way. There is the Government employment, railways, tramways, omnibuses, bake-houses, gas-works, municipal employment, dressmaking, domestic servants, servants in hotels, largely agricultural, and coal mines to a very great extent, shopmen, and shop girls; these, with those who are dependent on them, numbering something like two millions of people, adults, who would be benefited by this legislation, and who would not be affected in any way by foreign competition. At any rate, the workers are ready to run the risk. (Loud cheers.) They call for the limitation of the hours of labor, and they know perfectly well that their wages, so far from being reduced, would probably rise, and at any rate they would be compensated for any temporary drawback by the greater amount of leisure and the greater amount of freedom they would gain. At this present time the Eight Hours Bill is being demanded in every country in Europe, and that also meets the question of foreign competition. Why, when we met at that International Congress in Paris last year, what was demanded from all quarters of the earth, as a palliative merely, was an eight hour law to restrict the slave driving of to-day. And further, Mr. Chairman, as a·

revolutionary Social Democrat I say I know perfectly well this Eight Hour Bill is but a palliative, but it is a valuable one, because we know perfectly well that the introduction of better machinery may possibly bring about a larger accumulation of commodities, which will bring on crises earlier than before. We are confident of the future. With an educated and leisurely class we are sure that demands on the Government will be made; and when met will be beneficial to the whole community.

MR. BRADLAUGH: There are several points upon which it is necessary that we should be absolutely clear if any wise result is to follow this debate. The first point I ask my opponent to address himself to when he rises again, and which has been left in doubt by his speech, is whether he means that there shall be only one shift of eight hours in each industry. (Hear, hear.) That is a most important matter as affecting a large proportion of the figures which it will be my duty to lay before you. Apparently that is what he meant by his reply to my counter proposition on that point, but it is by no means clear, either from his own proposition, or from the Bill which he has drafted. Next I want to know whether he means his proposition to apply to all kinds of labor, or only to adult labor. His proposition only applies to adult labor, but the Bill applies to all kinds of labor, whether adult labor or not. It would, therefore, include all young persons as well as those who are beneath the Parliamentary age of young persons, and a most important issue will be raised upon that question. I agree that in some trades, and in occupations which are not trades, there is much over-work; but I deny that there is over-work in every occupation in this country. (Hear, hear, and expressions of dissent.) As the burden of proof rests upon my opponent, who is the challenger here, I will ask him to consider one or two occupations as to which I shall not make vague statements, but precise statements, when I deal with them, and I will show you the importance of this. You may quote a resolution of a number of men in favor of eight hours, as was quoted of the miners at Southport, either not knowing yourself, or, if you know, concealing from the audience, that the miners voted for the eight hours for the purpose of stopping output, and for no other reason whatever. If we are to discuss this on the basis of a stoppage of output, in how many trades is that to apply, and what kind of calculations have been made by the person who proposes to effect that by process of law? Shortly, remember this. The Bill and the proposition of my opponent involve a compulsory declaration that no person shall work more than eight hours per day, and may mean that no industrial establishment shall be conducted for more than eight hours a day, and I undertake to show in the last event by figures impossible of dispute, which I have here, that the bulk of the textile industries in this country would be ruined at once. (Laughter.) Yes, be ruined at once, and that the miners of Northumberland have declared that a compulsory eight hours' Bill applied to their county might make thousands of them work a longer time, and would certainly throw thousands of them out of employment. (Applause and laughter.) I do not blame you for being dissatisfied with my statement, but I would beg you to remember that as the reporter is taking a verbatim report it will be to your interest, if I am wrong, that every inaccurate statement I make should remain stamped to convict me afterwards. (Hear, hear.) I would point out to you that in the opening speech, probably from the great pressure of matter upon the opener, we have had none but the vaguest statements, and that there is no case in which we have had any statistics quoted to prove it. I would point out to you that with reference to the death-rate there has been no statement which would enable me to turn round to my opponent, and to quote statistics against him He has not said that the death-rate is increasing generally. He dare not say that. He has not said how much of the death-rate with which he has dealt applies to children under five years of age who do not work at all; and I will undertake, if he will venture to reduce his vague statements to positive allegations of fact, to meet them at once with statistics which are impossible of contradiction. (Hear, hear.) Now there is another curious thing. The speaker made a great deal of Government employments, but his proposition does not touch Government employment: it is limited to mines, workshops, and businesses conducted for profit. Probably that is only a slip of the pen; but what I complain of is that in this eight hours' question looseness of language is used all round; and at any rate if it is to be submitted to the Legislature to examine we ought at first to know what is meant by the proposition put forward. If you limit your working in mines or factories to eight hours per day, is it to be with the possibility of double or treble shifts? if not, it lies upon you to show that in each case where longer hours are worked it is possible to conduct that industry so as to find the money each week to pay the wage. (Applause and laughter.) I will tell you what I mean by " profitable " —(interruption)——

The CHAIRMAN : I really must appeal to every one of you in the audience to give Mr. Bradlaugh as patient a hearing as Mr. Hyndman received. (Hear, hear.) No one could have received a more attentive and patient hearing than the first speaker, and it is only fair that both speakers should receive an equally attentive hearing. (Hear, hear.)

Mr. BRADLAUGH : I would ask you who are in the minority in this hall—(laughter)—and who disagree with what I am saying, at any rate to be confident in the justice of your cause, and to let my impeachment of it be made clear. There was no attempt on the part of my opponent to examine carefully the terms of his proposition. He talked about industrial anarchy—when I was interrupted I was about to deal with profitable business, and I will deal with that, and go back to the point of industrial anarchy afterwards. It shows the evil of interruption, as diverting one from the argument in hand. By business conducted for profit I mean a business, the conduct of which, after recouping the cost of raw material, after recouping the outlay in the fixed plant, and other matters connected with the establishment, after providing such wage as shall ensure life to the worker—("Oh, oh!" and continued interruption, in consequence of which the sentence was unfinished[1]). I defined life and pleaded for life, and tried by reforms to make life more possible thirty years ago. (Hear, hear, and applause.) I may have stood still, but I have not changed. (Renewed applause.) I define life to the wage earner to mean reasonable subsistence for himself and those

---

[1] The words omitted should be, " would leave reasonable profit to the capital and personal enterprise required ".

of his family who are either unable to work, or insufficiently educated to work, to include leisure, not only for rest, but for education and enjoyment. (Hear, hear.) So that my definition of life would have sunshine in it, while revolutionary Social Democracy will only have brimstone and bayonets. (Cheers and groans.) How are we to test the alleged industrial anarchy which forms the main feature of the proposition which I am here meeting? It is alleged that there is more poverty to-day? Show the statistics. I have mine here, but I wait until you show them. Is it alleged that there is more disease? Our vital statistics are more complete than they ever were at any period of our history. Is it alleged that there is more crime? Is it alleged, except in relation to Ireland, in consequence of the agrarian misery that there prevails, that there is even more poverty? On the contrary, the statistics are entirely the other way. (Applause.) Now I challenge those who are dealing with the point of view of my opponent to give us, not vague statements, but actual allegations of fact which I may explain and contradict if I do not agree with them. (Hear, hear.) Then we are told— (" Oh " !)—but at any rate *you* cannot oppose this of all men in the world, for you have appealed to the Legislature. It shows that the speaker has never read, or if he has read, has conveniently forgotten the Truck Act, to which he refers. The Truck Act was directed to punish as crime frauds committed by employers on employed. (Hear, hear.) It did not attempt to regulate the relations between employer and employed, except where those relations were fraudulent, for the purpose of defrauding the employed person of the wage agreed to be paid to him. If I had been wrong in it, it would not have mattered much, nor ought these kind of charges to stand in lieu of proof of the proposition (hear, hear)—because if I had been as absurd and inconsistent as many men are who often address the public, I ought not to have my inconsistency pleaded as if it were proof of the proposition, the *onus probandi* of which lies upon my opponent here; nor does it at all apply to my proposal with reference to the compulsory cultivation of land, because in that case, rightly or wrongly (I may be wrong), my view, and my contention in the House of Commons, was, that just as upon the laboring man the criminal law imposes the duty of utilising his labor under

penalty of indictment, so on the land owners, land being
necessary to the country, my contention was that the duty
did rest upon him by law of cultivating it, so that it
might bear its fair burden of the taxation, and contribute
to employment. (Applause.) I pass those matters which
are irrelevant if they were accurate, and which are inaccurate as well as irrelevant. (Cheers and laughter.) I
will now continue to examine how it has been neglected
to be attempted to be proved that any kind of palliative
can come from the imposition of eight hours. What
would be the increased cost of production from the
diminution of the hours of labor? Not a word has been
said on that. I admit that our means of information are not
very great, but we have some, and the reckless allegation that experience proved that in every case where
the hours of labor have been shortened, the productive
labor (therefore affecting the cost of production) has
increased, has not been borne out, and we have more
than one case to illustrate it. The burden rests upon
my opponent, and if I said nothing on this it is upon
his shoulders that the whole of these facts should have
been borne to you. But we have the cases of the
Northumberland and Durham coal trade arbitrations,
carefully reported; and in the Coal Trade Arbitration for
December, 1875, which I will not burden you with quoting
at any length, unless my opponent should venture to challenge the statement of fact I am abridging from it—it
was proved by exact figures, and I have got the whole of
them taken out here, that between January, 1871, and
November, 1875, in consequence of the reduction in the
hours of labor—which I am in favor of, and have always
been in favor of—(applause)—in consequence of the reduction in the hours of labor by mutual arrangement
between the employers and the employed—(laughter)—
the cost of production, taken as if at the same rate of wage,
had been increased by 21 per cent. (Hear, hear.) And if
in any case an increase is shown, the burden rests upon the
one who says to the employer: you shall not work your
works, and to the men: you shall not work in them—the
burden rests on him before he makes the employer
criminal, and the working man without employment starving in the street—the burden rests upon him to show how
he would meet it. (Great interruption.) In a Northern

chemical works, of which I have also the figures carefully taken, in 1871, eight-hour shifts were substituted for twelve-hour shifts. In the case of the ball furnacemen, and in the case of the decomposers, the pecuniary result was an increase of 20 per cent in the wages; and the curious thing is that when bad times came the men themselves asked to go back to the old methods of working, and I will show you why presently. The speaker denounced overwork, but do you understand that his proposition is, working-men, that if some of you have been sick for three days you shall never have the opportunity of making up those three days? (Hisses.) "Starving men" and "starving women" brought cheers from different parts of the hall; but do you understand that when a man has been out of work for a fortnight they say: "Oh, you must go on starving; you shall not be allowed to fill the cupboard or the coal-cellar by extra exertion." (Applause and uproar.) Anticipating that some attempt might be made to prove some portion of the proposition, I had the whole of the facts with reference to the textile industries of the country carefully indexed. But I shall not quote them until some attempt is made on the part of my opponent; and he ought to have said to you that nearly every statistic that you can quote to-day in relation to labor, except the Foreign Diplomatic Reports, which were begun before I entered the House of Commons, you owe to my vote, and to my motion in the House, and to no other cause whatever. (Applause.) I do not want to take any other credit for that than is due to the fact that I am in a position to say that at any rate I have not tried to keep men ignorant or to delude them with vain phrases. I have tried to get for them the substantial benefits of accurate knowledge. The whole of the eight hours legislation, throughout the civilised world, and for America; the whole of the returns as to that were laid on the table of the House on my motion; and they do not corroborate the vague statements which have been incorrectly made to you by the speaker in the course of his opening speech. Nay, it is a curious thing that he spoke of the claim for eight hours from America. Well, but in a journal of which I think my opponent knows something, I find the declaration that the American matter cannot be used at all for that the eight hours cry has

" fizzled out " there. That is the language of the *Common-weal*, and I am bound to assume that at least in some respects, though not in many, these gentlemen know what they are talking about, especially when it tells against them. (Laughter.) Now, in the textile trades it is clear that the reduction means eight and a-half hours per week, and I ask my opponent to state to this assembly what is the average proportion of profit for the last twenty years in the cotton industries. If he says he does not know, he ought to know, and I will ask him whether it is the fact that in five years, ending at the end of 1889, £6,750,000 of capital, invested in the major part by working men and small middle-class men in factories in Oldham conducted under their own supervision, did not average more than 3¾ per cent. I will ask him how much less production you will have by eight and a half hours less work ? (A voice : "That is too much".) Too much! and a legislator behind me echoes the " too much ". I shall believe some of these men when I find them investing their own moneys in properties at a less rate. (Applause.) At the present moment a man may get idly and with no risk, by putting his money into consolidated stock, 2½ or 2¾ per cent. He can get, on an average, on railway and other substantial securities, something like four per cent, and we are told that he will risk his capital in industries which, though in some cases they bring great profits, always bring great risks, and in many cases enormous loss, and that he will do that for men who say that this eight hours is only the beginning, and give the illustration of the horse working three and a-half hours a day, hoping that you will be asses enough to cheer that—(cheers and laughter)—and reminding you that over and over again it is pretended that some such an amount of labor as three or four hours would be sufficient for the conduct of the industries of this country. I speak here to-night—as I shall show you before I have finished—what large numbers of working men in unions and out of unions have said. I shall not read vague speeches to you, I will give you the exact declarations that they have officially made. Now in the labor returns of Massachusetts, which Labor Bureau was the one which most enticed me to induce the Government to establish a Labor Statistical Department in this country, we have the proportion of wage to cost of production given in a large number of trades. It varies extraordinarily. It varies according to the plenteousness of raw material, and the fashion in which it is used. There is no necessity for me to go into details, for not one has been given on the other side. I ask my opponent whether he has read those statistics, which have been republished in England? If yes, how he differentiates the cost of production in Massachusetts from the cost of production here. He cannot differentiate it so that it will tell in favor of the proposition he is bound to affirm here. (Cheers.) I now pass to my own proposition. My counter proposition is that it is desirable that all wage earners should work the smallest number of hours per day consistent with the profitable conduct of the industry in which they are respectively engaged. (Hear, hear.) While it is true that eight hours in a quicksilver mine would be absurd and murderous, it is not true that eight hours is too much in every occupation. (Cries of "hear, hear", and "yes, yes".) Those of you who think it is ("You try it"), in what position are you? (Interruption.) I have worked for some of you more than eight hours per day, and at any rate the burden of the attempt at decency should be on you in my presence, even if you cannot indulge in it in my absence. I allege that the hours of working in different trades, in different industries, are more or less arduous according to the character of the industry in which the persons are engaged, and that no hard and fast rule can be made which could apply or ought to apply to all industries. My second proposition is that the limitation to eight hours per day as the period during which an industrial establishment may be carried on would be fatal to the large industries. Oh! but, says the speaker, that is an allusion to foreign competition; and he gave a large number of industries which would not be affected by foreign competition. Amongst others he took coal mines, which of all other industries of the world are more affected by foreign competition than any other in the country. They affect the iron industries, they affect the whole metal industry—I say nothing about the export trade in coal; but for a man to tell you that the coal industries of this country have no relation to our ability to put in foreign markets our produce at such a rate as will induce the foreign purchaser to take them

from us, is a monstrous proposition, which shows that he
has not even studied the question. (Cheers.) My next
contention is that the hours of labor in each industry
should be severally settled by conciliatory conference between the employers and the employed, or their respective
representatives. My opponent says, truly enough, that
the Trades Unions only represent the minority of the
artisan workers of this country. That is perfectly true;
but my proposition is not limited to Trades Unions. I
should think it was quite possible, although I am in favor
of Trades Unions and always have been all my life; and
I consider a great deal of the social improvement of the
workers has been due to the action of Trades Unions—
(hear, hear)—especially with their thrift provisions.
(Hisses.) That gentleman does not like saving; but if
my opponent dares to tell you that what he calls industrial
anarchy has prevented men from saving, I have every
figure taken down here, and will read them, as showing
the actual economies of labor. I allege that man and
man are more likely to make a fair contract with each
other—(laughter and uproar)—if they had the opportunity
of making it voluntarily than when they are compelled to
it by law. ("No, no.") No! but you had the law and
abandoned it. You say no. I do not wonder at your
being ignorant of every proposition I put forward, but I
do wonder that you do not give me reasonable opportunity
of proving the case which it is my duty to submit to you.
I say that the shorter the hours of labor the greater the
opportunity for rest, recreation, and education, and I have
already put to you my definition of what the life limit of
wage should be. Now proposition 2, that is as to the
closing of all industrial enterprises going beyond the extent
of one shift of eight hours, must be met by my opponent,
because he has quoted the Southport case, and the Southport 70,000 men agitated, as William Abrahams of
Rhondda expressly agitated, for the one shift of eight
hours and eight hours only, and they did it on the ground
of limiting the output of this country. I say that the
closing of every industrial establishment at the limit of
eight hours, if it were in any way justifiable, and I shall
submit to you presently that in no way would it be, throws
the burden on those who seek to do it by force, of the proof
that it can be done, and the industries of the country can

still be carried on. The speaker says capital can take care of itself. Unfortunately it can, but the working man cannot; and if your drive our industries to other countries of the world what will happen? There will be more hunger here. The people who talk for revolution may desire that hunger, but I who desire the peace and well-being of this country—(hear, hear, and cheers)—and that the progress which has been made during the past fifty years shall be increased and consolidated—I take these propositions, and put upon those who are on the other side the burden of at least giving one fact against me. (Applause.)

THE CHAIRMAN: I will now call on Mr. Hyndman to answer in a quarter of an hour. I really must appeal to the gentlemen in the body of the Hall not to interrupt the speakers, because it only adds to the whole length of the proceedings, and is likely to put out the speakers in argument. It is only fair that both sides should have a complete and proper hearing, and I appeal to all of you, whatever may be your individual opinions, really to give an attentive hearing to the speakers, so that we may conduct this meeting in an orderly and proper way.

MR. HYNDMAN: Mr. Chairman, Friends, and Fellow Citizens, I am surprised that my opponent should have ventured to state, after having the Bill before him which I drafted at his demand, that I did not deal in any shape or way with Government employments. I will read you the clause: "No person employed under the Crown in the United Kingdom in any department of the public service or in arsenals, small arms factories, dockyards, clothing establishments, or other industrial business, etc., shall, except in case of special unforeseen emergency, be employed for a longer period than eight working hours in any one day, or for more than forty-eight working hours in any one week". (Applause.) I think it is presuming a little, and therefore I shall not attempt to follow my antagonist here into the personal clap-trap which he has thought fit to introduce. (Cheers and hisses.) I do think it very extraordinary that with that before him at his own demand, he should have presumed—because it was presumption—to have made such a statement as that I had not formulated anything about Government service. Now, he has asked for some facts and figures, and I will give him some. First of all, he states that in a period of depression the mills in Oldham were earning 3¾ per cent. (Cries of "No, No".) I say that he stated they were earning but 3¾ per cent. (Cries of "No, No," "Yes," "Ridiculous.") I must ask, Mr. Chairman, for law in this, because it is exactly what Mr. Bradlaugh said.

Mr. BRADLAUGH: I will tell you if you wish it. If the speaker wishes it I will tell him. I said that in the Limited Liability Mills in Oldham, in which working men and small middle-class men have put in their capital, five years' experience to the end of 1889 gives on the share and loan capital of £6,750,000 a little less than 3¾ per cent.

Mr. HYNDMAN: That is exactly what I said. I will ask you, Mr. Chairman, to stop that gentleman, who cannot interrupt except for the purpose of misstatement. I would ask Mr. Bradlaugh, when he says "Supposing that eight-hour shifts were worked, where is the money to come from to employ these men?", to study Schedule D of the Income Tax Returns and to study the returns of the banks in Manchester and the banks in Oldham at the very time when this period of depression was going on, because he will find from Mr. Goschen's statement in the House of Commons—and he will find from the Income Tax Returns—that during the whole period of depression the Income Tax Returns in this country were steadily going up. And what do they amount to? £600,000,000 sterling under Schedule D, and it is calculated that the professional and non-professional classes in this country at the least figure that I have ever seen get £400,000,000 sterling for doing no work at all. Now, I say out of that may come the money—if it is money he wants—to pay the wages. But more than that. During this very period of depression he speaks of, the purchasing power of money had increased from 25 to 30 per cent through nearly the whole range of commodities. The purchasing power of incomes which had so increased had very largely increased in purchasing power all through. So I say if extra money is needed we know where to go for it. And the banks were paying 15 to 20 per cent at the very time that the Oldham mills were earning what my opponent stated. And how about the rents during that period? Were not they paid? Did not they come out of the workers in the-

same way that every other interest and profit does?
(Hear, hear.) Therefore, I say that there is absolutely
no difficulty whatever in meeting this demand of his for
further wages if shifts are worked. Now, personally, I
say this. I would not restrict the working shifts to eight
hours a day—that is to say, in the cotton industry, if
it is necessary to keep mills running. What I am
concerned about is that the workers should not be overworked. How long the machinery is worked is a matter
of perfect indifference to me. If, however, in the coal
trade, workers find it to their interest to restrict the output,
then I say that they are at perfect liberty to do that in the
same way that they restrict it to the eight hours a day at
the present time. But I am accused of stating that the
coal trade is not interfered with by foreign competition.
I never stated anything of the sort. I said that in large
part it was not affected by foreign competition, and I put
in those words not only in the speech, but I put them on
paper here—"in large part". Nor is it. Through large
districts of this country it is quite impossible for anybody
to compete in any shape or way with the English coal;
and I say further than that—which Mr. Bradlaugh is
perfectly well aware of—at the present time there are
many machines that could be introduced for coal-cutting
if the opportunity arose and the employers thought it
worth their while to do so. They do not do so. For what
reason? Because it is cheaper to employ men at the
present time than to use those machines. (Hear, hear.)
But if the coal mines were worked for the benefit of those
who worked in them it would be quite different. As to
the output of coals, let me give you a few statistics again.
What is the cost of coal when it comes out of the pit's
mouth per ton? What is it at the present time through
the mining districts? From 1s. to 2s. per ton. But what
is this coal sold at in the market? Why, not at 1s. or 2s.,
but at 8s. or 9s.; and, when you add to it the various
profits that are filched away, it is sold here in London,
apart from the cost of transport and the cost of transference
from the railway stations to your houses at a profit of
from 8s. to 10s. per ton in many instances and in others
4s. to 5s. I ask, therefore, what is the fact? Do the
workers gain any advantage out of these good times of
trade—the good times of trade which follow after these

bad times of which my opponent has spoken? No, they
do not. The amount of percentage which they gain in the
rise of their wages is comparatively small as against the
large benefit which goes to the capitalist class from the
work which they do. (Cheers.) Their wages rise 10 or
15 per cent, but profit rises 20 or 30 and even more per
cent, and at this present time out of the work of this
country how much do the workers themselves get if it
reduced itself even to this question of wages, which
I shall not long dwell upon? Out of the total produce
of this country, amounting to £1,300,000,000, some part of
which is doubtless counted more than once—the figures are
common—they have passed into a by-word since we have
sent them through the length and breadth of the land by
means of the Social Democratic Federation—the workers
receive in wages one-fourth or at the outside one-third.
I say, therefore, there is no difficulty whatsoever about
protecting your industries, if they are placed under
the control of those who have to work them, not for the
benefit of a small class, but for the benefit of the whole
community who do the work. My opponent says that he
is strongly in favor of a curtailment of the hours of labor,
and that capital is well able to take care of itself. But
the workers are not. ("Quite true.") That is why we call
upon the legislature to interfere upon their behalf. If the
workers were able to take very good care of themselves, it
would not be necessary for us to appeal to the legislature
to protect them in any shape or way. But how can they
obtain shorter hours of labor, if the capitalist will not
listen to their mild persuasion?—which I do not find by
experience that he does. They can only gain it by strikes.
Now what is the effect of strikes on the working classes?
What is the effect on the men? What is the effect on the
women and children? And how many of these strikes
succeed? Taking the United States, as to which my friend
Herbert Burrows has provided me with these figures: from
1881 to 1887 the employees striking and involved amounted
to 1,323,203. Of those 143,000 succeeded partially;
518,000 succeeded wholly; 660,000 failed. Of the strikes
for reduced hours; 25 per cent succeeded; 22 per cent
partly succeeded; 53 per cent failed. Then my opponent
quotes from an Anarchist organ that the eight hour movement has "fizzled out". He knows a great deal more

about it than he pretends to know. He knows that that organ from which he quoted has nothing whatever to do with the eight hour movement, but is entirely opposed to it in every shape or way. But at the present time he will be happy to hear that the eight hour movement is progressing in America, and with greater rapidity than ever before, and if he wants to know where to find proof of that, he will find it even in the organs of the capitalist press. (Loud cheers.) Here is a list of strikes in endeavoring to bring pressure to bear upon the capitalist, and is the endeavour peacefully and harmoniously to bring about some arrangement. There were 14,700,759 hours' work of unsuccessful strikers on this list, and 3,808,642 of successful. Look at the enormous waste that has been brought about in endeavoring to obtain shorter hours of labor. (Applause.) And further, what arises out of there strikes? Riot, as we know perfectly well. In Chicago, in Leeds, and elsewhere, strikes for the reduction of hours of labor, on the principle of some amicable settlement with employers, only produced that which he himself is most opposed to. Very well. My opponent says I have brought forward no argument, no figures. I say that the figures meet you at every point that you touch on the whole circle of production. I contend further that he has not touched in any shape or way or dealt in any form with my argument in relation to the Factory Acts, and how they acted on the industries of this country. The Factory Acts were applied to the very cotton industries which he has been speaking of, and applied to the coal industries, the very industry that he instanced. They were applied to almost every industry in this country; they were not applied rigorously enough. Not one word have we heard in answer to my challenge to show me that between the year 1847 and the year 1871, when the trade of this country was increasing at a greater degree than at any other time—not one word has he said to show that my contention in that respect is not perfectly just. Further than that, at this present moment the demand for the eight hour day is by no means confined to this country. The meeting at Berlin showed that, even although those sent there were representatives practically of the capitalist class; because at this present moment it is felt throughout Europe that the multiplying the power of man—and here again I will give one or two

figures: In the boot trade at the present time a man can
do twenty-seven times what he could fifty years ago; and
in the cotton trade one woman can do something like 100
times more than she could do 100 years ago.   At this
present time a woman working in a mill in Lancashire is
doing more in eight hours than she was doing in twelve
hours' work before the Factory Acts were introduced.   I
say therefore that it is an entire delusion on my opponent's
part to imagine that we are not perfectly acquainted with
the details of these various trades.   We understand them
perfectly well.   We know perfectly well for example that
in the railway service the imposition of eight hours a day
would cost the shareholders probably at first ½ per cent.
It is very probable it would.   But how much do the shareholders get at this minute out of the product of these
railways?   They get £33,000,000 sterling out of a total of
£70,000,000 of the gross earnings, and we can take the
Eight Hour Bill out of that.   (Cheers.)

Mr. BRADLAUGH: I invite my opponent when he rises
again, to quote precisely the words from the report of the
International Labor Conference at Berlin which he mis-
stated to you just now.   (Hear, hear.)   There are no such
words.   There is no such general statement, there is not
even sufficient of intermediate statement to justify the construction which he put upon the proceedings of the Berlin
Conference.   (Cheers.)   Possibly because I did not make
myself clear, although in the correction I tried to do it,
my opponent said that I quoted in the cotton industry a
period of depression.   I quoted the five years ending with
1889.   Does he mean to tell this audience that he suggests
that the years 1887-8-9 can by any stretch of imagination
be described as periods of depression.   He said he would
give the figures, but he did nothing of the kind.   He did
not touch a single textile industry.   He made some
general assertion about the amount on which income tax
was levied, and added some vague allegations as to the
proportion of wage to that, but the burden is upon him to
adduce precise facts.   With reference to the 800,000 odd
persons employed in the textile industries, and the more
than half a million employed in mines, the burden is upon
him to show that those figures have relation specifically to
those industries.   The amount of rent received by somebody else, the amount of interest received by some bank,

large or small, might not have, and I say has not, the
slightest bearing in enabling you to answer the questions
that I put. Then I did not say that the speaker had said
nothing about Government factories. (" Oh ! ") What I did
say was, and the report will show it when it is printed—
(hear, hear)—that his Bill and his proposition conflicted,
that the proposition only applied to adults, while the Bill
applied to everybody ; that his proposition only applied to
businesses conducted for profit, and therefore could not
apply to Government work which was dealt with by the
Bill. Of course that may be an incorrect view of mine, but
that was the view I took, and that was not the statement
which appeared in the caricature presented of my words.
(Laughter.) The speaker says if the workers wish to
limit the output "let them " and you cheered him—(hear,
hear)—but if the workers do not wish to limit the output
may you make them ? That is quite a different thing.
(Cheers.) Some worker may desire to see his children
better clad and better fed, with opportunities for more
enjoyment—(hear, hear)—and he may specially exert himself, while he thinks he is well and strong, to make provision for the future and to exercise that thrift which is
so much sneered at. (Cheers.) (A voice : " Thrift on 18
bob a week ? Bosh ! ") Yes, thrift is bosh in the words
of those who are opposing me, but it is the life and soul
of our country, it is that which made it what it is.
(Cheers and great uproar.) It is no business of mine to
argue in favor of strikes ; I have always tried to prevent
them, which is more than my opponent can say—(more
interruption)—I refuse to be drifted away from the subject
I have to deal with to discuss either strikes or the operation
of Acts of Parliament, which are not the same in any
respect as those which my opponent proposes to enact,
and I submit this as against the regulation of the hours
of labor by law that Parliament ought not to limit the freedom of the individual—(" Oh, oh ! ")—except in acts injurious to the life, health, or property of other individuals.
That the function of the legislature and of the executive
authorised by the legislature should be the protection
of each individual against the criminal acts of other
individuals and the protection of all citizens against
foreign enemies—(hear, hear)—and I say that whenever the legislature has tried, as it did three hundred

years ago, to interfere as to how men should work,
and when they should work, and as to the hours and
methods of their work, that equally the employers in
whose interest the Acts were then passed, and the
employed, helped to evade them. And I urge upon you
that it would be impossible to suppose that you can
interfere with the industries which the people exercise at
home. I will read you what has been said upon this
by working men themselves. My opponent talks of
mines as though the mining industry was the same in all
parts of England. It is nothing of the kind. In hard
veins and in soft veins, in deep pits with long workings
away from the shaft, and pits with workings near the
shaft, differences arise in which, if you made an eight
hours standard, you might very easily do the most fearful
injustice—(laughter and interruption)—as the worker is
paid by weight. In Durham at the present moment the
county average is about 4½ days a week, or about 27 hours,
giving 7 hours and a quarter work from surface to surface.
From the surface to the working place it takes an average
of about 25 minutes. The hours in Northumberland and
Durham are, I think, almost uniform. The fore-shift
men descend at a particular hour, and 6 hours and a half
afterwards the men, their partners of the next shift,
descend to relieve them; but I will give you one exceptional instance, and I want to know how an eight hour
law will work in a place like that. Take the Byron
Colliery in Northumberland. The workings in this
colliery extend three miles, and if you were to limit the
men and say they should not work except under some Act
of Parliament, which may suit some other colliery very
well, you may do in fact an injury to these men in limiting
their earnings which is fearful to contemplate—(cheers
and laughter)—and what do the Northumberland miners
themselves say? I understood my opponent to say that
he is not contending for one shift of eight hours a day;
then, if he is not, he has deceived you in quoting the
miners in his opening, because, except Northumberland
and Durham, they are all or nearly all agitating for it
on the one shift a day. There are some collieries
in Yorkshire I will exempt. What did the Northumberland
miners on the 28th of January of this year, by resolution
of their delegates, since confirmed by a vote of the whole

county, say? They say: "An absolute and uniform eight hours single shift for all classes of workmen was considered, and we found that it would be utterly impracticable for this county; it would necessarily mean an extension of hours to all the hewers, and it would certainly mean the discharge of some thousands of workmen." I let the workmen speak for themselves. (Cheers.) Mr. Hyndman says that the Social Democratic Federation—(a voice: "Good luck to them")—speaks for the industry of this country. If his statement is evidence of his allegation, I cannot do otherwise than say it is not so, and leave you to judge by the declarations of the working men themselves that I will read to you. Now what first do the workmen understand of this? Do they understand first there must be no freedom anywhere? ("Yes.") Do they understand that every man who works by piece will be paid so much less. (A voice: "We don't want it.") You say you do not want it; in many places you begged for it, and have gone back to it. Now what do the Trade Unions themselves say? I hold in my hand the returns to the Labor Statistic Department from 104 Trade Unions. It is not the return of one-third of the whole of them, but it is the return of the largest, and out of 104 how many do you think expressed any opinion about eight hours at all? Only four—(laughter)—and how many of these four do you think are in favor of it? None of them. (Cheers.) I will read to you from only one. I will read from the others when my opponent has answered that. It says: "The fixing of working hours by Act of Parliament is being forced to the front from different quarters with a persistency which speaks well for the courage of its advocates, but which will be certainly opposed by the majority of *bond fide* Trade Unionists". (A voice: "A lie.") You say a lie, but these Trade Unionists say it is true. (Cheers and uproar.) They point out in this, which is their language and not mine—("Paid agents".) If you talk about paid agents, what about the dock strike? (Cheers and uproar.) I am only dealing here with the matters alleged against me; there can be no personality when I am told that these honest men are paid agents in turning the tables on those who allege it. What do these men say: They say: "The time was when our forefathers toiled unlimited hours, but they did not appeal to the

D

State to reduce them ". (A voice : " They did ".) They did not; you probably never read as to what happened before you were born, but I have. They did not appeal to the State to reduce them, " they entered into combination with each other and paid liberal contributions out of their limited earnings, and then when the opportunity afforded itself they fought tenaciously for decreased hours "; and more has been got by voluntary and conciliatory combination than is got by any attempt at strike. Why the textile men of Oldham sent me this morning an agreement for holidays that they made with their employers by mutual consent, and they begged me to read it to this meeting to show how an Act of Parliament might prevent such an agreement as that. The Amalgamated Society of Engineers, with 53,740 men then returned (there are more now), declared against it. (" No.") No! but they say they do. (Cries of " Order " and interruption.) Mr. Chapman, Mr. Kelly, and Mr. Heasleden at the Bradford Conference (and if it be denied I will read it) pointed out that thousands of men in these trades worked in their own homes; and I ask you, are you going to allow the police spies to come into your home and say how long you shall work ? (" No, no.") Are you going to drive industries out of healthy factories, into which there is a tendency to take them in the boot trade at any rate, into homes where there will be unhealthy working? At the Dundee Congress a speech was made by Mr. Mosses which I wish my time permitted me to read to this meeting. Mr. Parkinson on behalf of the engineers, Mr. Knight on behalf of the boilermakers, all of them show how every attempt by legislation to interfere with their hours of working had been a failure in the past, and they protested against the demoralisation and destruction of their self-reliance which would come from any attempt in the present. I beg you in the last speech of my opponent not to let any expression of dissent interrupt him, for we are getting warm; at least let the half-hour pass, for to me it is a greater trial than I dreamed of when I commenced it, and I desire to deal with it as fairly as strength will permit. (Cheers.)

Mr. HYNDMAN : Mr. Chairman, it will be observed that my opponent has throughout spoken as if I were advocating a hard and fast line of an eight hour day. (" Oh ! ") What I have advocated, and what I advocate now, is, that no one should work more than an eight hour day. Does not my opponent know the meaning of the word "maximum"? Is he not perfectly well aware that anybody can work as much less as he can get? He must be perfectly well aware of it, and therefore I ask you not to allow yourselves to be influenced by the greater part of his last speech at all—(laughter)—because it was based upon a complete mis-statement from first to last. But now what has he been talking about? About the number of miners. The Northumberland and Durham miners constitute but 73,600 out of a total number of 603,000 miners working in this country, as my friend, Mr. Cuninghame Graham, has just informed me. I knew it before, but I am very much obliged to him for bringing me the figures. Again, he says, there are about four men who are in favor of this —(a voice: "Unions")—and he reads them to you. Now at the Congress of Dundee nineteen solid trades voted for the Eight Hour Bill—(cheers)—and at Jolimont, only a few weeks ago, the organised miners of this country and the continent, as miners, voted solid for an Eight Hour Bill, and Mr. Burt himself, who has delivered a speech against it, did not hold up his hand against the resolution. So that as far as regards these figures it is not the case, as has been alleged by my opponent, that the miners of Northumberland and Durham represent the miners of England in any shape or way, and even at Jolimont many of them voted, as I am informed, for a compulsory eight hour day. But now he has stated further that some workings are three miles underground. But remember a man is underground when he is going to and from his work, and we calculate it on that basis, that the man who is under ground is practically at work. (Hear.) But he says with that appeal to the instinct of the profit-monger, which is represented by thrift: "Look at the thriftiness of the English working man; look at what he ought to save and lay by; let him argue with his employer, let him save, and thus let him gain". But he goes further, and says, Parliament has only interfered to protect the property, life, and health of the individual. That is precisely what we are asking it to do here to-night. (Hear, hear.) But what is the sole property that a working man as a rule has? His labor; and it is that we are endeavoring to protect. Then he turns to the man

D 2

who has been out of work and says he is to work overtime,
perhaps half fed, in order to make up the period. For
whom? For the capitalist's benefit, not for his own.
(Hear, hear.) In the overtime and overwork, for every
stroke that he does it is three for the capitalist and one
for himself. We desire to limit seriously this power of
robbery; to interfere by the State on behalf of the labor
of the people, and the health of the people, and the life
of the people, by restricting those hours of labor. I say
that my opponent has in no wise shown that an eight
hour day in the Government establishments, in the railways, in the tramways and the omnibuses, or in the bake-
houses, which practically are non-competitive industries
with foreign countries—he has entirely failed to show that
an Eight Hour Law, as far as they are concerned, would not
be beneficial to every man and woman working in them.
(Applause.) He, has never touched in any shape or way
the unemployed difficulty. He has never touched it in
any manner at all. He has never dealt with this question
of industrial anarchy. And yet what do we find? At this
very time those who are watching the business of this
country can plainly see that we are approaching another
period of industrial distress and trouble. What shall we
see then? Hundreds and thousands of men out of work.
There are more than 20,000 persons, according to official
information, adult men, out of work in London to-day.
There were at the last period of depression 200,000.
Why? Because the capitalist class in this country
would not allow them to work except at a profit, and at
that very period when those men were out of work there
were others working thirteen, fourteen, fifteen, and sixteen
hours a day. How is it, Mr. Chairman, and how is it,
Friends and Fellow-Citizens, that my opponent, who
is ready to meet any clap-trap remark—or any other
remark that may be made from the audience—does not
deal with these facts which I allege here on this platform?
He said the engineers are not in favor of the eight-hour
day. Whether they are or not does not affect the facts or go
to the root of the argument we are putting on this platform;
but I contend they are in favor of the eight-hour day.
There are engineers in this hall who know that perfectly
well, and the next Trade Union Congress will show that it
is so. What we are arguing here is both matter of prin-

ciple and matter of detail. I wanted to separate the two. I wanted to argue the principle first and the detail afterwards, but it is my opponent's fault for trying to put a quart into a pint pot. But let us see the position as it stands to-day. We do not contend—those whom I represent here on this platform do not contend—that an Eight-Hour Bill is a solution of the social question. We say that it is merely a palliative of the evils of our present condition. We say that to put 200,000 or 300,000 more men into work at the present time would greatly enhance the well-being of, and give a greater outlet to the commodities produced by, the workers of this country. We contend that at the present time there are thousands of women, about whom my opponent has not said one single word, who are being over-worked, and have no chance of convincing their employers, either by combination or in any other way, for whom he seems not to have the slightest inclination to move hand or foot. (Cheers.) Those adults are worthy of consideration, but he does not pay any attention to them. I say, further, whatever he may state about the Berlin Conference, that the Berlin Conference was held altogether in consequence and because of the movement for an eight-hour day and of Socialism. There was but one Socialist there, but that man voiced the aspirations of multitudes of the people. I never claimed that the Social Democratic Federation represents the majority of the workers of this country. It does not to-day, but it will. But, again, I repeat we do not contend as Social Democrats that an Eight-Hour Bill, beneficial as it would be to men and women and to every worker in this country, would do all that was required. My arguments here have not been met in any shape or way. (Cheers and interruption.) These various statistics that my opponent has threatened to bring forth, these various ideas he has laid before you of thrift, and the benefit derived from our ancestors and what not, I say have nothing to do with the Bill he caused me to formulate, not one clause of which has he dealt with here to-night. Why did he call upon me to formulate an Eight Hours' Bill when he has never dealt with one single clause of it? Why is it he was so anxious for detail when he has not brought forward a single detail to deal with those principles I have laid before

you? ("Oh!") I say he has not. There is not one of
them that touches the bases of the principles I have laid
before you—not one—not one single one; and as he
refers to the *verbatim* report, so I refer you to the *verbatim*
report, to see how he will come out of this argument
on the Eight Hours' Bill. What we are working
for is for a reduction of the hours of labor in order for
what? Let us after all get away for a moment, if we
can, from the mere question of Bradlaugh and Hyndman,
or the mere question as to this Bill or that, and let us
consider for one moment what it is that we all—all here—
ought to endeavor to obtain. Surely it cannot but be
admitted that there are thousands and tens of thousands
and millions of people in this country who are working away their very life's blood to-day for the benefit
of a class. Surely my opponent cannot deny that at
this very hour there are people working 16 hours a
day—far more than it is well that any man should
do, no matter how profitable it may be to another.
Can he deny that one of the great difficulties in dealing
with the question at this moment is that the workers have
not time to consider the problems around them, and the
political disabilities under which they lie? Mr. Chairman,
I contend that throughout the arguments here I have gone
upon the basis of fact, and that my theories and principles
are sound; but assuming them not to be—let us assume
for the moment that he has gained here—which he has
not—(cries of "Yes," and "No,")—then I say still that
we are championing a cause which, though it be but a
palliative, still may accelerate the emancipation of the
workers. I say throughout this great England of ours,
which is a capitalist-ridden country to-day—the House of
Commons in which he sits is nothing but representative of
the landlord and capitalist class. (Cheers and interruption.)
I say, Mr. Chairman, that at any rate, as the representative
of the Revolutionary Social Democratic party on this
platform, not only of England, but of all the civilised
world, we are working for more than an Eight Hours' Bill.
We are working for a palliative to-day, but we are working for the complete ownership of the means and instruments of production, and we tell our opponent here that
our sole object in bringing forward this Eight Hours'
measure is to produce in a peaceful, organised and decent

manner that which otherwise cannot but come about with bloodshed and anarchy. (Loud applause.)

[Mr. Bradlaugh, on rising for the last time, was received with a storm of intermingled cheers and groans, two red flags being waved, and the Chairman had to intervene.]

The CHAIRMAN: We have so far, I am glad to state, been enabled to conduct our proceedings decently and in order, and I trust you will keep up the fair name of this meeting of working-men by helping order to the end.

Mr. BRADLAUGH: I will venture to recall to you the last words almost that were spoken by my opponent. He says that Parliament only represents the landlords—(a cry: "Thieves!")—capitalists, and persons of that kind, and yet it is to that Parliament that he is asking working-men to appeal to make laws regulating their labor. If Parliament be such a vile institution, then working men least of all should entrust to it the power of regulating the condition of labor, which, if it means anything at all, would mean equally lengthening the hours, and reducing the wage as well as shortening the hours. (Cheers.) The words my opponent professed to quote from the Berlin Conference have not yet been given.

Mr. HYNDMAN: I rise to order. I never professed to quote any words at all.

Mr. BRADLAUGH: The reference made by my opponent to the Berlin Conference as being in favor of the eight hours' movement has been in no shape vouched by evidence because it could not be.

Mr. HYNDMAN: I did not say so. (A voice: "Sit down".)

Mr. BRADLAUGH: I can quite understand that but little mercy will be given to me in this speech so far as my opponent and those who support him are concerned, but I shall talk to the end of my time at any rate. (Cheers.) He said, which was equally inaccurate, that the delegate, or some of the delegates, of the Northumberland and Durham miners at Jolimont voted for the compulsory Eight Hours' movement. That was spoken either upon misinformation—and my opponent ought not to have come here without being well-informed upon it—(hear, hear)—or his memory has betrayed him, or his sense of what is exact was not complete. There has been no attempt to deal with the particulars of production on reduced hours in textile fabrics, in proof of which I gave figures. (A Voice: "What about the railways?") I have always proposed that those who have monopolies of railways in this country, and who work their employees to an extent which is perilous to life and limb, shall be punishable by law for that. (Cheers.) The speaker was good enough to tell you that I never stirred hand or foot for women. ("Shame!") If it had been true, it would have been nothing in favor of his proposition. It would only have shown that I did not always keep my promises. (Mr. Cuninghame Graham, M.P.: "Hear, hear".) But, curiously, while the legislator who says "hear, hear", behind me has been perfectly silent on this in the House, on two occasions recently I have applied to the Government to employ women in Government departments for which they were fitted. I know I am subjected to considerable abuse, especially by those who know nothing whatever of what I do. (Hear, hear.) Then we are told that when men work one proportion is for themselves and three for the capitalist. (Hear, hear.) But bare assertion is no proof, and there has not been any attempt at proof. There was an opportunity of showing that in connexion with the eight and a half hours reduction in the textile trade. (Uproar.) Repeating nonsense of this kind until you induce working men to strike, is a criminal act. (Applause.) Saying it on a platform, where it can be contradicted at once, and where it will remain in print, is a foolish and absurd thing. My opponent says that I have said nothing about the unemployed. (Hear, hear.) That has not been my fault. It has been the fault of the minutes at my service. As he desires I will deal with that which I have repeatedly dealt with in the articles which I have written on the subject. Are your unemployed in the particular trades in which you are going to reduce the hours af labor? I agree that in large aggregations of population you get enormous numbers of people, some unthrifty— (laughter)—some, unfortunately, sick and unable, some only able to follow casual employments; but I deny that making men work shorter hours of labor in skilled industries would afford employment for these men. It would do nothing of the kind. (Hear, hear.) If you are going to shorten the hours of skilled artisan labor before you can put this mass of the unemployed into it, you must show that they are fit for the employment you choose to give them. (Hear, hear, and cheers.) Again, if it be true as my opponent said in his last speech, that hundreds and thousands of unemployed would find employment where they are now starving, it can only be by increasing the cost of production or by reducing the wage of those who are already employed. ("No, no.") One of two things it must be. You say "No", but one thing must be true: either you pay both and then it costs more —("No, no.")—Well, I can understand that with you two shillings is not twice one shilling: but then I am only addressing myself to working men who have brains, not to Revolutionary Social Democrats. ("What about 30 per cent?") I am told that an enormous number of men are out of work in London; and that is true, and it is one of the great evils of modern times—one which no legislation can cope with; that in this huge hive, part of industry and part of misery, and somewhat of crime, you get the extremes of poverty and the extremes of wealth so close to one another that when the storm-cloud passes the lightning flashes more here than elsewhere; but it is not fair to measure the industries of England by the casual population of London. It is not fair to measure our mines by Northumberland and Durham, and the speaker said that they only represented something over 70,000, and that the remainder, he said 600,000, were the other way; but he did not venture to answer my point that all these miners who are the other way were chiefly so for the one-shift system and the reduction of out-put. If he had ventured to answer it I would have read page after page which I have here. My difficulty is that with the burden of proof on him we have had nothing but the fizz of the champagne —(hear, hear, and interruption)—of what revolution is going to do. Instead of that there should have been an endeavor to prove that the legal enactment of eight hours per day for all adults in all industries would affect and improve the well-being of the people throughout the country. There is no shadow of attempt to prove it. He speaks loosely of the price of food, and all kind of vague things about the increase of the purchasing power of gold, but not one word of the application of it to any one of the great industries; large statements have been made about the unemployed, but there are less unemployed than there were. How do you make out your industrial anarchy? In the great centres where men strive for life with great desperation, and where they are pushed under over and over again in the struggle by their fellows, there is much misery and hunger; but do not believe that an Act of Parliament can make bread spring out of the ground into an empty cupboard—(cheers) —do not believe that it will clothe the ragged, or educate the ignorant, and still less believe in the men who appeal to revolution, and who instead of occupying their time with the dry proof of details which were needed for the proposition talk about the Social Democratic Federation. Does Europe go for the Eight Hours system? Why even the longer hours in France, as fixed by law, have been exceeded by the men themselves. In what country is there an eight hours law? In none in the world where it is obeyed. ("Oh!") You say "Oh", but I have the facts here, and your advocate has only been silent on these matters of fact because in each case I was prepared to prove them. I pray your pardon if, in an hasty response, I have been offensive to any, but my tongue is now getting too old to flatter, it never did so and it never shall. What I deem to be right, here, and in the House of Commons as long as my constituents trust me, I will affirm. (Cheers.)

Mr. HYNDMAN: I rise here, and have a very pleasing duty to perform which those who are making obstruction should be the first to listen to. I have to propose a vote of thanks to our chairman. I do not know whether our chairman agrees with me or with Mr. Bradlaugh. I do not know whether he will support our Eight Hours Bill when it is brought into the House of Commons, or whether he will not: but I will say this, that nothing can be fairer, nothing more truly courteous than our Chairman's conduct here to-night, and I have the greatest pleasure in moving a hearty vote of thanks to Mr. Sydney Buxton for his conduct in the chair.

Mr. BRADLAUGH: I beg to second that vote; you that are in favor of it hold up your hands. It is unanimously voted.

The CHAIRMAN: I thank you very heartily for the kind

way in which you have attended to your chairman this evening. There may have been a little natural excitement at some times, but I think on the whole we have had most satisfactory order.

APPENDIX.

A Bill

ENTITLED AN ACT TO LIMIT THE HOURS OF LABOR TO EIGHT HOURS A DAY.

1. This Act may be cited as the Eight Hours of Labor Act, 1890.

2. This Act shall come into operation on the first day of January, 1891.

3. In all contracts for the hire of labor or the employment of personal service in any capacity whatever, a day shall be deemed to mean a period not exceeding eight working hours, and a week shall be deemed to mean a maximum period of forty-eight working hours.

4. No person employed under the Crown in the United Kingdom, in any department of the public service, or in any Arsenal, Small Arms Factory, Dockyard, Clothing Establishment, or other industrial business, or by any County Council, Municipal Corporation, Vestry, Local Sanitary Authority, School Board, Guardians of the Poor, Dock or Harbor Trustees, District Council, Improvement Commissioners, Commissioners of Police, Commissioners of Sewers, of Public Libraries, or Baths and Washhouses, or by any other Public Administrative Authority, shall, except in case of special unforeseen emergency, be employed for a longer period than eight working hours in any one day, or for more than forty-eight working hours in any one week.

Any public officer or public functionary ordering or

requiring any person in public employment to remain at work for a period in excess of eight working hours in any one day, or forty-eight hours in any one week, except in case of special unforeseen emergency, shall be liable to a fine of not less than fifty pounds for each such contravention of the provisions of this section, on conviction thereof; and one half of all fines so imposed shall be paid over without any deduction whatsoever, to the person or persons directly or indirectly affected by such contravention, whose action and evidence shall be the means of bringing home such offence to the perpetrator.

5. No person shall be employed by any Railway Company for a longer period than eight working hours in any one day, or forty-eight working hours in any one week, except in case of special unforeseen emergency.

The general manager of any railway company employing, or permitting to be employed, any person in contravention of this section shall be liable on conviction thereof to a fine of not less than fifty pounds for each such contravention, and one half of all fines so imposed shall be paid over without any deduction whatsoever to the person or persons directly or indirectly affected whose action and evidence shall be the means of bringing home such offence to the perpetrator.

6. No person shall be employed on any line of tramways, omnibuses, cars, wagons, or vehicles used for the transportation of goods or persons, except in case of special unforeseen emergency, for a longer period than eight working hours in any one day, or forty-eight working hours in any one week.

The general manager or manager of any company or firm, or any firm, or any individual employed, employing, or permitting to be employed any person in contravention of this section shall be liable on conviction thereof to a fine of not less than fifty pounds for each such contravention and one half of all fines so imposed shall be paid over without any deduction whatsoever to the person or persons directly or indirectly affected whose action and evidence shall be the means of bringing home such offence to the perpetrator.

7. No person shall be employed underground for hire in any mine for a longer period than eight working hours in any one day or more than forty-eight working hours

in any one week except in case of special unforeseen emergency.

The period of employment under ground in a mine shall for the purpose of this section be deemed to be the whole period for the time of leaving the surface of the ground to descend the mine to the time of return to the surface of the ground after cessation of work.

The manager of any mine employing or permitting to be employed any person in contravention of this section shall be liable on conviction thereof to a fine of not less than one hundred pounds for each such contravention, and one-half of all fines so imposed shall be paid over without any deduction whatsoever to the person or persons directly or indirectly affected whose action and evidence shall be the means of bringing home the offence to the perpetrator.

8. No person shall be employed in any factories, workshops, laundries or other industrial businesses conducted for profit for a longer period than eight working hours in any one day or forty-eight working hours in any one week except in case of special unforeseen emergency.

Any employer or manager employing or permitting to be employed any person in contravention of this section shall on conviction be liable to a fine of not less than fifty pounds for each such contravention, and one-half of all fines so imposed shall be paid over without any deduction whatsoever to the person or persons directly or indirectly affected whose action and evidence shall be the means of bringing home such offence to the perpetrator.

9. No person shall be employed to serve behind the counter or elsewhere in shops, co-operative stores, or magazines, or warehouses for the sale of goods by retail or otherwise, or shall be employed to serve behind bars to sell intoxicating or other drinks or to purvey food or other refreshments for a longer period than eight working hours in any one day or forty-eight working hours in any one week, except in case of special unforeseen emergency.

Any employer or manager employing or permitting to be employed any person in contravention of this section shall on conviction thereof be liable to a fine of not less than fifty pounds for each such contravention, and one-half of all fines so imposed shall be paid over without any deduction whatsoever to the person or persons directly or indirectly affected, whose action and evidence shall be the means of bringing home such offence to the perpetrator.

10. No domestic servant shall be employed in any club or in any hotel, lodging house, house or flat let in apartments, or other place in which accommodation or food is provided for payment, for more than eight working hours in any one day or more than forty-eight working hours in any one week, except in case of special unforeseen emergency.

Any employer, steward, or manager employing and permitting to be employed any person in contravention of this section shall on conviction be liable to a fine of not less than fifty pounds for each such contravention, and one-half of all fines so imposed shall be paid without any deduction whatsoever to the person or persons directly or indirectly affected, whose action and evidence shall be the means of bringing home such offence to the perpetrator.

11. No person shall be employed in agricultural labor for hire for a longer period than eight working hours in any one day or more than forty-eight working hours in any one week, except in case of special unforeseen emergency.

Any farmer, fruit or flower grower, market gardener, or other agriculturist employing or causing to be employed any person in contravention of this section shall be liable on conviction to a fine of not less than fifty pounds for each such contravention, and one-half of all fines so imposed shall be paid over without any deduction whatsoever to the person or persons directly or indirectly affected, whose action and evidence shall be the means of bringing home such offence to the perpetrator.

12. In the cases of special unforeseen emergency referred to in the above sections arising, each person who shall by reason of such emergency work beyond the period of eight working hours a day or forty-eight working hours a week therein enacted shall be entitled to receive and shall receive from the individual, firm, or company employing him double the rate of wages per hour that has been paid during the normal working period for each hour of such overtime so worked, notwithstanding any stipulation or contract implied or expressed to the contrary.

EMPLOYERS' LIABILITY BILL.

LETTER TO

THOMAS BURT, M.P.,

BY

CHARLES BRADLAUGH.

LONDON

A. BONNER, 63 FLEET STREET, E.C.

1888.

PRINTED BY
A. BONNER, 34 BOUVERIE STREET,
& 68 FLEET STREET, E.C.

EMPLOYERS' LIABILITY BILL.

LETTER TO THOMAS BURT, M.P.

DEAR MR. BURT,

I desire to make a special and detailed statement as to my exact position in relation to the Employers' Liability Bill, and I have selected the form of an open letter to yourself because of your life-long devotion to the cause of the workers, of my sincere recognition of your absolute unselfishness, of my most complete reliance on your unswerving truthfulness, and last, but not least, because of our long and hitherto unbroken friendship, commencing with personal kindness from yourself fully a quarter of a century ago, and continued with like personal kindness in Parliament when few others showed me any. I address you in your capacity as a miner's representative, as one of the earliest labor members of the House, and as President of the Miners' National Union. I write to you because I wish my words to reach those amongst the workers who rightly respect you for your loyal service, and need scarcely say that any words you choose to send in reply shall have the same publicity. I see many papers declare that I ought not to speak or vote against the wishes of the workmen on a labor question, and I quite recognise that I take on myself grave responsibility if I controvert the well-informed opinions of workmen on any points materially affecting themselves. For that reason I proffered to Mr. Broadhurst to debate the whole matter in St. James' Hall before an audience of Trades Unionists, but I can hardly accept resolutions which seem to me to have been passed on an entire misapprehension consequent on partial and incomplete information, especially when, as in this case, I have earnestly striven to acquaint myself with the facts.

I commence by referring to the Session of 1886, at a time when the Conservatives were in Office, when " a Bill to amend the Employers Liability Act 1880 " was introduced by yourself and Mr. Broadhurst, supported by Mr. Joicey, Mr. Haldane, and Mr. Lockwood. This Bill was in every sense the Bill of the Trades Unions, supported by the Parliamentary Committee of those Unions, and may be fairly taken to be what the labor members—then stronger in the House than they are at present—thought that they might fairly ask from a House of Commons in which, though the Conservatives were in office, there was then a Liberal majority. I will therefore—in view of what is now being rather sharply said against myself, and of what the labor members generally have said against the Employers' Liability Bill of the present Session—point out what the Bill of 1886 proposed and what it did not propose.

(1) It re-enacted the Act of 1880, making it permament.

(2) It forbade future contracting out.

(3) It, in doing this, legalised all contracting out up to the time of passing the Act.

(4) It provided that in determining compensation to the workman the Court might amongst other things take into consideration payment made by the employer to any insurance fund, to the extent to which the workman had actually received compensation.

(5) It forbade removal to superior court unless amount claimed exceeded £100.

(6) It gave the court power to dispense with notice of injury in the event of (1) the employer having knowledge of the injury within six weeks, or (2) that there was reasonable excuse for the omission of notice.

a. The Bill of 1886 did not legislate against the London and North Western Railway scheme or any other arrangement for contracting out then existing.

b. It did not in any fashion, except as stated in 2, 3, 4, 5, and 6, extend or vary the Act of 1880.

c. That is, it was quite silent on the doctrine of common employment. It made no proposal to amend the definition of superintendence. It did not seek to make employers liable for sub-contractors. It did not try to enlarge the time for giving notice of injury; nor did it facilitate the service of such notice. It did not propose to increase the amount of damage receivable by the workman. On these last five points it was less favorable to the workman than the Bill of the present Session. It contained a recognition of contribution by the employer to an insurance fund to which I have to draw fuller attention later.

Resolutions in support of this Bill of 1886 were enthusiastically passed at many trades union meetings, and petitions from organised trades were presented to the House of Commons in its favor. I presume, therefore, that in 1886 that Bill was considered by the labor party as a good Bill, and one which in the interests of workmen ought to have been passed into law. This is material, because I think I shall show you clearly, and beyond the possibility of contradiction, that the Employers' Liability Bill, 1888, which has just been abandoned on the opposition of yourself and your fellow labor members, is in many material respects a better Bill than the labor party's own Bill of 1886, and that the matters alleged by labor members against the Bill of 1888 are (with two exceptions) all matters which might have been equally urged by them against their own Bill of 1886, which they then praised.

After the Bill of 1886 had been printed, but before the date of its second reading, the Conservative Government resigned and the Liberals came into office, and on the 11th March, 1886, the Bill of 1886 was referred to a Select Committee, together with another amending Bill, introduced by Mr. Arthur O'Connor. That Committee consisted first of 16, afterwards of 18 members, viz. 9 Liberals, 2 for the Irish party, 7 Conservatives The Liberals were in the usual way selected by the Government whips, Mr. Broadhurst being a member of the Government. No sort of objection was ever taken by the labor members in the House to the constitution of the Committee. I did not know of the proposed Committee until I was asked to join it, and though, believing it gave me opportunity for service to the people, I was very pleased to be one of those selected, I neither directly nor indirectly solicited the nomination, which to me involved an enormous addition to my already heavy parliamentary work. The Committee held eighteen sittings, seventeen of four hours each. I attended throughout every meeting. Mr. William Crawford of the Durham Miners was also a member, and was present at eleven sittings, his health preventing his more regular attendance. Sir Thomas Brassey (now Lord Brassey) was chairman, and attended fifteen out of the seventeen important sittings. The Committee found considerable difficulty in getting the necessary evidence for the case of the workmen, for while the employers of every section had arranged to present evidence before the Committee, no arrangements appeared to have been made by the Parliamentary Committee of the Trades Unions, and except Mr. George Shipton, who attended on my request, no single witness was ever presented on behalf of that Committee. I applied in writing to Mr. Broadhurst and Abraham, and verbally to you and to Messrs. Fenwick and Pickard to provide evidence to be given before the Committee. From yourself, Mr. Fenwick, and Mr. Pickard, I received the assistance of witnesses from the Northumberland and Yorkshire miners. Mr. Crawford, of course, arranged for the Durham miners. Mr. Abraham repeatedly promised, but his witnesses from Wales never came. Mr. Broadhurst furnished me with a list of trades unions, to all of which bodies I wrote, but none of the representatives ever gave evidence, though some of them attended as the public during the meetings of the Committee. I communicated this more than once to Mr. Broadhurst, and to Mr. Shipton, to whom he had referred me. Mr. Arthur O'Connor procured very valuable legal evidence from Scotland, and I was fortunate enough to obtain the evidence of Mr. Shaen and Mr. Woods. Mr. Murchie wrote, and afterwards came, from Manchester, saying that he did so in consequence of the complaints I had

made in the *National Reformer* of the difficulty in getting
evidence.

It is due to the Select Committee to say that they worked
earnestly to evolve the best possible Bill in view of the
maintenance of the great industries of the country. Mr.
Arthur O'Connor, whose proposals in his Bill were more
advanced than those contained in the Bill promoted by the
labor members, was never absent from a single sitting.
Sir Thomas Brassey was not only most assiduous, but
seemed ever ready to champion the interests of the employed.

The report of the Select Committee was presented to the
House and ordered to be printed on the 11th June, 1886,
and I am not aware that Mr. Broadhurst, or the labor
members, or any of the Trades Unions or the Trades
Congresses, ever made any unfavorable criticisms on that
report. Certainly no such communication ever reached
me. I regretted that the Conservative Government did
not, in 1887, introduce any Bill to amend and make permanent the Act of 1880, which, but for the Continuance
Bill, would have expired last year; and I repeatedly
pressed the Government with questions on this point. I
still more regret that the Government did not proceed at
once with the Bill introduced on the 27th February, 1888.
My greatest regret is that when the Bill was printed,
although it was then seen to be in most respects an
advance in the interests of the workman, not only on the
Act of 1880, but also on the Bill of 1886, it should have
provoked such strong denunciation. Mr. Benjamin Pickard
has, outside the House, described it as "the worst Bill ever
introduced by a Tory Government". Mr. Broadhurst
denounced it as "a sham, misleading, mischievous—the

worst Bill ever introduced to the House". What is really the character of the Bill of 1888 so denounced? Except in one or two respects, it is either the re-enactment of the Act of 1880, or it is the adoption of suggestions contained in the report of the Select Committee of 1886. Those suggestions were certainly intended in the interest of the workmen.

I have been much blamed in the press and by some speakers for the personal attack on Mr. Broadhurst which characterised my speech in the House; but I would dare appeal to you whether the provocation and justification for every word I used was not to be found in the reckless array of epithets with which Mr. Broadhurst's speech abounded against the Bill. He described it as a London and North Western Protection Bill; but while that was not true, it was true that his own Bill in 1886 did effectually protect the London and North Western Railway Company. He described it as an attempt by a Tory Government to introduce German Socialism into this country. I do not find the attempt in the Bill, but, presuming that he referred to Clause 3, then this was not the work of the Tory Government but was due to the unanimous report of a committee on which there were only seven Tories out of eighteen members. It is said that it was no part of my duty to defend the Government, but it was surely my duty to defend the work of a Select Committee of 1886, especially as the Chairman was no longer a member of the House.

In his speech, in the House of Commons, Mr. Broadhurst spoke of an amendment which he said he had tried to induce the Government to accept, which amendment he stated had been printed; and, if it had been accepted by the

Government, he said the Bill might have been allowed to pass this Session. This amendment was in the following words :

"Clause 3, page 3, leave out all after ('void ') in line 25, and insert—('Provided, that where, before the commencement of this Act, an employer has made with his workmen, or any of them, a contract whereby the workmen have for valuable consideration deprived themselves of any right under this Act, this section shall not apply to a workman working for that employer or his successors in business, and shall not prevent similar contracts being made by that employer or his successors in business with the workmen at any time hereafter employed by or working for him or them.')

"Leave out clause 4."

and further, the Act was to commence May 1st.

The effect of this amendment would have actually been to legalise, *inter alia*, the very arrangement of the London and North Western Railway Company, which has been so strongly denounced by several of your labor colleagues. It might have legalised for ever every contracting out already perfected, and it would have left the matter open for further contracting out up to May 1st. Under this amendment no employee of the London and North Western Railway Company, or of any other employer, would have had any appeal except as to whether he had received "valuable consideration", whatever that may mean, for signing away his rights under the Act. What was the case sought to be made out against the Bill and the Government by Mr. Broadhurst, and supported by the labor members? First, that the Home Secretary sat like "a stone wall " in the Grand Committee on Law, and would allow no amendments. As a mere matter of fact this is inaccurate. The Bill, as it went into

committee, occupied nine printed pages. As it came out;
of committee it occupied eleven and a quarter pages, and
in addition, the Home Secretary promised on report to
amend Clause 3, so as to prevent collusive contracts; and,
before report, in accordance with that promise, he had
placed on the paper an amendment to give effect to his
pledge.

The next objection urged by the Labor Members was that
the Bill did not get rid of the doctrine of common employment, *i.e.*, the rule of law that where an employee suffers
injury from the act of a fellow employee, the injured
workman cannot sue the common employer. To this
doctrine the Act of 1880 made some exceptions, but it
was found that the workman suffered in the courts because
sec. 1 of the Act 1880 said:

" The expression 'person who has superintendence entrusted
to him', means a person whose sole or principal duty is that of
superintendence, and who is not ordinarily engaged in manual
labor."

The evidence before the Select Committee shewed that
many persons having effective superintendence were often
engaged in manual labor, and that several workmen had
on this point failed in court in recovering damages.

The Labor Members' Bill of 1886 unfortunately left the
Act of 1880 untouched in this respect, and was silent on
the doctrine of common employment. The Bill of 1888
did do something to help the workman in this respect, for
by sec. 15 it proposed to enact:

" The expression 'superintendence' means such general
superintendence over workmen as is exercised by a foreman, or
person in a like position to a foreman, whether the person

exercising superintendence is, or is not, ordinarily engaged in manual labor."

I am not in favor of the doctrine of common employment; but the Liberal Government did not try to abolish it in 1880. The Trades Union Bill did not propose to abolish it, or even to diminish it, in 1886. The Bill of 1888 had the merit that it tried to lessen it.

Mr. Broadhurst strongly attacked the Bill on account of Clause 5, which requires notice of injury within three months; but he must have forgotten that the Bill he thought good enough in 1886 required the notice of injury to be given within six weeks. The Bill of this year was at least preferable in lengthening the time. It also gave facilities to the workman for serving and proving the notice which were not contained in the Bill of 1886. The present Bill, like that of 1886, had also a clause that want of notice should be no bar if the court was of opinion that there was reasonable excuse. It may be that no notice ought to be required, and I so argued in the Select Committee; but, as the labor party did not try to abolish notice in 1886, they ought hardly to denounce the Government for not doing it in 1888.

Another point strongly attacked by Mr. Broadhurst was the limit in Clause 9 of the compensation as not to

"exceed either such sum as may be found to be equivalent to the estimated earnings during the three years preceding the injury of a person in the same grade, employed during those years in the like employment, and within the district in which the workman is employed at the time of the injury, or two hundred and fifty pounds, whichever is the larger".

But Mr. Broadhurst, in the Bill of 1886, had proposed

to re-enact only the Act of 1880, sec. 3 of which, stopping at the word "injury", limited the compensation recoverable to the three years' estimated earnings. The evidence taken showed that in cases of apprentices and learners this operated harshly; and the Government, on the recommendation of the Committee, have actually increased the limit beyond what the labor members thought sufficient in 1886.

Clause 12 of the Bill, which was also attacked, gives an advantage to workmen in permitting them to join a common law claim in a county court plaint with a claim under the Act. It is objectionable in depriving the workman of his right to have a claim at common law decided by action brought in the superior court. I have proposed to omit the words "and shall not be brought otherwise". This would avoid the objection, and I have reason to believe that my amendment would now be accepted.

The great array of objections comes, however, to the third clause, which I therefore reprint:

"3.—(1) Any contract made after the commencement of this Act, whereby a workman deprives himself of any right under this Act, shall be void, unless made in pursuance of a request in writing from every such workman with whom the contract is to be made, and unless it is made in consideration of such undertaking by the employer as herein-after mentioned, and that undertaking is duly fulfilled.

"(2) The undertaking shall be to make, so long as the workman continues in his employment, an adequate contribution towards such insurance as herein-after mentioned of the workman or, in case of death, his representatives against every accident occurring in the course of his employment, and to make good to the workman, or, in case of death, his representatives, any sum which becomes payable in respect of the insurance, but which is not paid.

"(3) The insurance shall be to such amount and on such conditions as will insure to the workman, or in case of death, his representatives, a benefit equivalent to the compensation recoverable under this Act.

"(4) If any question arises whether an undertaking by an employer sufficiently complies with the requirements of this section, evidence that a similar undertaking has or has not been accepted as sufficient by persons employed under similar circumstances or in the same class of employment shall be admissible as evidence of the sufficiency or insufficiency of the undertaking.

"(5) On the application of a workman in any coal mine, metalliferous mine, factory, or workshop, or of his employer, one of her Majesty's Principal Secretaries of State, and on the application of a workman in any other employment, or of his employer, the Board of Trade, may (a) consider and decide whether a contract made or proposed to be made between the workman and his employer whereby the workman deprives himself of any right under this Act, is made, or proposed to be made, on such consideration as in this section mentioned, and if the Secretary of State or Board of Trade decide and certify that the contract is so made, or is proposed to be so made, then not only that contract, but contracts in similar terms with other workmen engaged under the same employer or his successor in business and in a similar employment under similar circumstances, shall, without further proof, be deemed to have been made on such consideration as in this section mentioned (b).

"(6) The compensation payable in pursuance of the insurance may be either a capital sum or an annual or other periodical payment to the person injured or his representatives."

(a). The Home Secretary proposed

"after 'may', to insert 'after such notice to other workmen engaged under the same employer as they think necessary'.

(b). "And after 'mentioned', to insert 'provided always, that the Secretary of State or Board of Trade may at any time, on the like application, review and reverse or confirm any decision previously given under this section; and such previous decision, if reversed, shall thereafter have no effect'."

Personally, I should prefer to omit the words "made after the commencement of this Act" from the first line of the clause, so as to make its provisions apply to all contracts, whether before or after; but the Government have dealt with existing contracts on the lines of the proposals of the Trades Union Bill of 1886. This clause, amended in Grand Committee, was an attempt by the Government draughtsman to embody the following recommendation of the Select Committee:

"No contract or agreement made or entered into with a workman shall be a bar or constitute any defence to an action for the recovery, under this Act, of compensation for any injury, unless on entering into or making such contract or agreement there was other consideration than that of such workman being taken into or continued in the employment of the defendant.

"Such other consideration shall be:

"(a). That the employer shall have contributed to an insurance fund for the benefit of such workman against every accident arising in such employment.

"(b). That it has been certified by a competent authority that the employer's contribution to such fund bears a full proportion to the contribution of such workman, and that the benefit to be received by such workman from such fund is fully adequate, having regard amongst other things to the amounts recoverable as compensation under the Act, provided always that if any amounts payable by such society or fund shall not be paid in accordance with the rules, the employer shall be liable to make good any deficiency so arising."

It appeared in evidence, and was practically undisputed before the Select Committee, that out of the total accidents occurring there are very few for which the injured person is entitled, either under the Act or at Common Law, to recover damages. Many accidents result from contributory negligence on the part of the person injured. Many accidents result from disputable causes, and as to which conclusive evidence is often wholly unobtainable. Many accidents result from causes as to which difference of opinion may honestly prevail. The Select Committee thought, therefore, that a mutual fund to which the employer adequately contributed, and which provided against every accident, would in all cases be desirable if it could be effected.

It is urged by the labor members that they desire in the Employers' Liability Bill to secure increased safety for life and limb amongst the workers rather than to obtain pecuniary recompense for injury. On this I would observe that where a statute is directed to attain such an object, then the breach by the employer must be followed by imprisonment or fine, or by civil remedy for damages. No one suggests that the employer should be criminally prosecuted except for criminal negligence, and with this the Employers' Liability Act has no concern whatever. Its enactments are not even needed for any case of personal negligence or misdoing by the employer. For such the remedy is complete at common law. It is, therefore only possible in an Employers' Liability Bill to provide a pecuniary remedy for injury suffered.

It is alleged that where employers have insured against their liability under the Act there has been greater carelessness and more accidents; and I understood Mr. Fenwick to try to prove this by figures, which he alleged showed that where employers had contracted out of the Act the loss of life was greater than where the Act was in force. This argument is, in any case, confusing. If employers have nakedly contracted out of the Act, then they do not need to insure, and in fact do not insure, themselves against liability under the Act, for they have no such liability. When employers insure themselves with a great company against damages possibly accruing from liability under the Act, it is when they have not contracted themselves out. It was contended at the Bradford Congress, and also in the House of Commons, that insurance by an employer against his liabilities under the Act ought not to be allowed, but no attempt to prevent insurance of this kind was ever proposed by the Trades Union Bill of 1886.

The cases of mutual funds contributed to in agreed proportions by both employers and employed, to provide for specified payments against every kind of accident, stand on quite a different footing from mere insurances against liability under the Act. But even here it is urged that "an employer who contributes by regular instalments to an accident or death fund has no inducement to take extra care to ensure the safety of his workmen. Whether there be few accidents or many his outlay is the same." On this, Mr. A. M. Chance, who was examined before the Select Committee, writes to the *Times*, under date December 8th:

"One strong argument against sanctioning such contracts seems to be that masters will be less careful, and that accidents will be more frequent at works where such friendly arrangements are in force. In my evidence before the Select Committee in 1886, see pages 350 to 359 of the report, I endeavored to combat this view, and the figures which I now submit, for a still longer period, tend to still further strengthen my opinion as to the advantages thus accruing to the workpeople themselves by diminishing the number of serious accidents. At these works, where some 650 men find regular employment, during the nine years 1872 to 1880 inclusive seven deaths occurred from accidents.

"On the 1st of January, 1881, the provident accident scheme which I framed came into operation, and during the eight years commencing 1881 I rejoice to say that we have not had one single fatal accident. This immunity from serious accidents I largely attribute to the greater care and vigilance exercised by the men themselves, in consequence of the interest which our scheme throws upon them."

The reasons which moved the Select Committee of 1886 to make the reccommendation on which this clause was based were as follows; that contracting out of the Act had been very common, and in some cases had been forced upon the men without any advantage accruing to the men for the loss of the statutory rights. This the Select Committee desired to prevent. On the other hand, there was evidence of contracts in which the men did obtain sensible advantage; contracts which the men themselves desired to preserve, and which they in very large numbers asked the Committee and Parliament not to annul. Such contracts, where clearly advantageous to the men, the Committee desired to do nothing to destroy.

Mr. Ruegg, a counsel of great experience in cases under the Act of 1880, and who was called by Mr. A. O'Connor, said: "I think that any good insurance scheme contributed to by the employers and workmen is far better for the workmen than their chance of recovering damages under the Employers' Liability Act".

Your eloquent colleague in the representation of the Northumberland Miners quoted a number of figures to the House, which, he contended, made out that where the men had contracted out of the Act, there had been increased insecurity to life and limb. I was unable by the rules of debate to then offer any reply to Mr. Fenwick, whose conclusions I dispute, and whose method of stating figures I venture to challenge. First, I object that to take the four years which Mr. Fenwick alone quoted is insufficient, and that to confine the figures to one industry would not be conclusive. That in order to ascertain how far the Employers' Liability Act of 1880 really affected this question of improved safety to life and limb, comparison should, if possible, be made in all industries in specified districts prior to 1880, and in those districts after its passing, distinguishing where the Act was in operation and where there had been contracting out. Comparisons between different mining districts may be wholly misleading in consequence of the difference in the dangerous character of the seams and methods of working. A practical and most intelligent miner has furnished me with a tabulated statement compiled from the yearly official reports of the Inspectors of Mines, which are published as Parliamentary papers, and showing the percentage of loss of life in the very districts referred to by Mr. Fenwick for the seven years immediately preceding the operation of the Act, and for the seven years since it has been in operation, and also showing the figures for the four years named by Mr. Fenwick; and so far from proving Mr. Fenwick's contention, it is shown in both cases that there has been a greater improvement in the districts where the men contracted out of the Act, than where the Act was allowed to remain in full force. That is, I contend that the figures taken with reasonable fairness, show exactly the opposite of Mr. Fenwick's contention, and read by the light of the evidence taken before the Select Committee, shew that

the mutual funds have been accompanied with increased
safety to the men. Nos. 1 and 2 of the following tables
are for the districts in which the Act is in full operation.
Nos. 3 and 4 are for districts where contracting out of the
Act has prevailed.

NUMBER OF PERSONS EMPLOYED PER LIFE LOST.

No. 1.—Northumberland, Cumberland, and North Durham :

1874	 722		1881	 740
1875	 686		1882	 672
1876	 696		1883	 691
1877	 727		1884	 793
1878	 890		1885	 582
1879	 716		1886	 938
1880	 834		1887	 769

Average—753   Average—740·71

1·6 more lives lost than before the introduction of the Act.

No. 2.—South Durham, Westmoreland, and North Riding
of Yorkshire :

1874	 710		1881	 605
1875	 709		1882	 305
1876	 728		1883	 801
1877	 570		1884	 744
1878	 610		1885	 708
1879	 823		1886	 622
1880	 236		1887	 758

Average—626·57   Average—649

3·5 fewer lives lost than before the Act came into operation.

No. 3.—West Lancashire and North Wales :

1874	 380		1878	 128
1875	 349		1879	 407
1876	 348		1880	 443
1877	 318		1881	 262
1882	 426		1885	 428
1883	 502		1886	 449
1884	 460		1887	 485

Average—339·28   Average—430·28

26·8 fewer lives lost during the last seven years than in the previous seven years.

No. 4.—South Wales:

1874 384	1881 402
1875 404	1882 379
1876 396	1883 325
1877 .. . 367	1884 349
1878 357	1885 275
1879 346	1886 391
1880 208	1887 319
Average—351·71	Average—348·57

0·9 more lives lost than in the seven years previous to the introduction of the Act.

The result for the four years selected by Mr. Fenwick, that is, comparing four years before the passing of the Act, with the last four years under the Act, is as follows:

	Percentage reduction in loss of life.	Increase in loss of life.
No. 1 District, where Act is in operation.	—	2·7%
No. 2 District, where Act is in operation.	26%	
No. 3 District, where men contracted out of the Act. ..	40·5%	
No. 4 District, where men contracted out of the Act. ..	5·2%	

Mr. George Lamb Campbell, secretary to the Central Association for dealing with distress caused by mining accidents, gave most important evidence before the Select Committee of 1886 on this point. He presented tables (pp. 529-30, 31 of Report) showing deaths by fatal accident, disablement cases, and the number of miners' permanent societies who in 1886 had, and the number who then had not, contracted out of the Act; and in answer to questions 3496-7 he stated that the North Wales district, in which the whole of the miners were contracted out of the Act by an arrangement of a permanent fund, "shows the lowest rate of disablement accidents in the kingdom, and that this rate has been steadily decreasing since the Employers' Liability Act came into operation". This evidence gains in importance when taken in connexion with the quotation from the letter of Mr. Chance.

Strong objection has been taken to the opportunity given by the Bill for employers and workmen to submit the fairness of the mutual insurance contract to the decision of a Government official; but to whom would you propose to submit such contract for decision? If you say that it must be left in each case to a judge and jury, then you are confronted by the workmen's just complaint that even where they recover damages large extra costs go to the attorney, and are also met by the declaration of the employer that even where he is held to be right he is, from the poverty of the workman, unable to recover.

I believe that you have always recognised that the subject is one of great delicacy and difficulty in its treatment, and I venture to express my deepest regret that the extraordinary and unwarranted language of denunciation applied by Mr. Broadhurst to the motives which prompted the present shape of the Bill, and which denunciation, if just, fell on the Select Committee of 1886, compelled me to speak with distinctness and severity in reply. I defended my own work as one of that Committee. I do not pretend that there is infallibility or perfection in the suggestions embodied in the Committee's Report, but I do assert that we all did our best, in view of conflicting interests and opinions, to pass a Bill which on the one hand should be clearly more beneficial to the workman than the law as it stands at present, and on the other hand should be as little injurious as possible to the interests of employers. It is to me sore proof that we failed lamentably, if you even acquiesce by silence in the astounding declaration of Mr. Broadhurst, that the Bill is the worst ever introduced into the House of Commons.

WORKMEN AND THEIR WAGES.

THE TRUCK LAW,

AND HOW TO ENFORCE IT.

BY

CHARLES BRADLAUGH.

Price 8d.; Post free, 8½d.

A. BONNER, 63 FLEET STREET, LONDON, E.C.

CAPITAL AND LABOR.

BY

CHARLES BRADLAUGH.

[SECOND EDITION.]

LONDON:

FREETHOUGHT PUBLISHING COMPANY,

63 FLEET STREET, E.C.

1888.

—

PRICE TWOPENCE.

LONDON :

PRINTED BY ANNIE BESANT AND CHARLES BRADLAUGH,

63 FLEET STREET, E.C.

CAPITAL AND LABOR.

On 7th January, 1886, Mr. Charles Bradlaugh, M.P., delivered a lecture on "Capital and Labor," under the auspices of the Northampton branch of the National Union of Operative Boot and Shoe Rivetters and Finishers. A verbatim report of the lecture appeared in the *Northampton Guardian* and has since been reprinted in pamphlet form. The edition having been exhausted and a new edition called for, it is now carefully revised.

Mr. Bradlaugh: There is probably no subject on which any man could be invited to speak more serious—not only in its actual influence, but in what must come from it during the next few years—than that of Capital and Labor. In old times the laborer was not reckoned at all, except perhaps as a superior sort of animal—a kind of conscious machine. He was never treated as a human being to be reasoned with. If any of you take up any of the old Roman books you find work and slavery not simply immediately connected, but both having nearly the same signification—in fact in your language there is even yet preserved the evidence of that old slave notion. In connexion with all kinds of labor, the man who directed the labor was called master, the man who performed the labor was called servant; and the servant, or serf, or slave, or bond-man, was owned by his lord and master, owned as to life, as to liberty—as to brain it was seldom considered. During late years there has been a vast change, but Professor Thorold Rogers, in a volume or rather two volumes recently issued, entitled, *Six Centuries af Work and Wages*, says that "the pauperism and degradation of the English laborer were the result of a series of Acts of Parliament and acts of government which were designed or adopted with the express purpose of compelling the laborer to work at the lowest rate of wages possible, and which succeeded at last in affecting that purpose ". And if you look back to our old legislation you would be astounded : there were statutes directing that wage should not exceed this amount or that amount ; there were statutes making it crime to claim higher wages ; there were statutes against combinations of workers ; and the people were treated as dangerous, not as men, not as women, but as the lower classes—the dangerous classes, and the treatment sometimes made them so. Men who were not reckoned with as thinking human beings, sometimes, in times of despair, times of political excitement, times of starvation, times of anger, acted as though they were unthinking, wild, ferocious beasts. If you use the whip, the whipped one turns sometimes ; if you use the fetter, when the fetter breaks there is no restraining influence on the hand ; if you constantly drive by fear, if there is no outlet of hope, if there is no opportunity, no sort of break in the dark life, then when the day of mischief comes it is fearful. And in every country it has been so. In the past times the uprisings of the poor, the revolts of the slaves, the wars of the peasants, the revolution of the starved of France—coming to more modern times, the riots of the Blanketteers in Lancashire, the riots in various trades—these all were when men had no right of meeting, when such a meeting as this could not have been held, when the fact that a trades organisation convened a meeting for a man to address it on the relations between Capital and Labor would have been considered such an element of danger that the magistrates would have prevented it, the military would have been called in to disperse it, and the people who took part in planning it would have been prosecuted. It was perfectly true as Professor Thorold Rogers points out, that there have been great changes ; laws have been repealed :—"The despotic law," he says, "of parochial settlement has been materially modified, working-men are no longer liable to imprisonment and penal servitude, for trying to sell their labor at the best advantage ; and the wages of labor are no longer mulcted by Corn Laws and other restraints of trade ". But, although that is true, many of the effects of old bad laws still remain.

Trades Unions, which have only had legal protection the last few years comparatively, have not yet been able to grow into the exercise of the full moral control I trust they will exercise by-and-by. Take for example one of the latest classes of labor in which organisation has been attempted—I mean the agricultural laborer. If it had not been for the work of men like Joseph Arch and a number of others who have been associated with him, especially for the last fifteen or twenty years, the Franchise, just acquired, would have been simply a weapon for injury rather than a tool for utility, simply a sword for mischief, rather than a shield for defence; it would not have been, as it is in the hands of educated persons, the opportunity of delivering a verdict, the opportunity of exercising a judgment; it would only have been an opportunity for mischief, because the class had ever been oppressed and there did not seem a possibility of their redemption. But Mr. Arch has taught that class the advantages of organisation, he has taught them the advantages of education, he has taught them the advantages of sober, steady work for the deliverance of their fellows, and he has enabled them to play a part in the election which has just taken place which has won the admiration even of the foes of them in the judgment they have exercised.

In dealing with the relations of Labor and Capital, I occupy an exceedingly difficult position: I have no capital, and I have hardly the right save that of sympathy, to speak for those who are ordinarily called those who live by labor—not that my life is ever free from labor, or that my day is ever an idle one—I have the difficulty in trying to treat the subject impartially, as I hope I shall; fairly, as I trust I may; but with my sympathy with those of whom I was born, and to whom I belong—the poor of this land. I feel that I render myself open to criticism, open perhaps to reproach, from both sides; those who own capital may fear my counsels as extravagant, and those who plead for labor may think me diffident and hesitating in the remedies I recommend; and yet I trust that all will do me this justice: that I shall not speak simply to please, that I shall not counsel simply to gain favor, and that the language I use is the language I have used for more than a quarter of a century of my life to those who have permitted me from time to time to address them on subjects of this character. I take it then that by all reasonable men, the laborer is to-day reckoned with not as a servant, not as a mere serf, or slave, but he is reckoned with as a person, who has his labor to sell, and who is entitled to make a fair bargain for that labor before the world; and there is neither inferiority nor superiority between the buyer of labor and the seller, so long as they are both honest; that the inferiority comes in when either tries to cheat. If trade being good, if profit being large, the owner of capital conceals the fact of his large profit and the goodness of his trade, in order to extort from the hungry seller of labor a hard bargain and a harsh contract, then that employer is lower than the laborer whom he cheats. If the laborer having agreed to labor, having contracted to perform a duty, is idle, lazy, dishonest, fraudulent, then he is the lower, and he deserves the contempt and scorn of those whose labor he ruins by his dishonesty. Unfortunately, the purchaser of labor and the seller of labor do not meet on equal conditions. The laborer must sell his labor at a fair price or starve; the capitalist who does not buy his labor may live, sometimes comfortably, till better times come. Hunger cannot wait; if the man would, his wife cannot; if his wife would, the children cannot; there must be breakfast, there must be food, and hunger frightens often a weak man into having day by day less than he should have in his struggle of life. I propose to enquire what are the rights of Labor, what its duties : what the rights and privileges of Capital; what the duties of those who possess it. I affirm that every laborer willing to work has the right to life; and by life I do not mean merely existence from day to day, I do not mean merely continuing on sufferance from to-day till to-morrow, I do not mean one constant round of toil that makes all life a gloomy cloud, and has no gleam of sunshine in it— I mean life, reasonable life, life with leisure in it, life with hope in it, life with relaxation in it, life with fair reasonable shelter, food, clothing, won by the wage-earner for himself, and for those of his family who are yet unable to win it— short enough hours of toil to give possibility of enjoyment for all, education for all, hope for all; time sometimes for music, if music may be; time for looking at sculpture, if sculpture be near; time for pictures, if pictures be gathered in your public galleries; and if you tell me that music, poetry, sculpture and painting are luxuries, I say they may be luxuries for the rich but they should be necessaries for the poor, the gleams of sunshine softening life and making it worth living. How can you wonder at men being rough and brutal, whose life has nothing soft, cheering or humanising in it; how can you wonder at men using rough words and coarse epithets, if no harmony comes into their daily life; how can you wonder at the surroundings of men being brutal, if you never show them the beautiful, or give them the opportunity of imparting their knowledge of it to those whom they rear around them?

In the report issued in 1875 by the Labor Bureau of Massachusetts, the Chief Commissioner, Mr. Carroll D. Wright, a gentleman to whom labor is much indebted, says, in a report made by him under the Legislature to the Senate of Massachusetts:—" It seems natural and just that a man's labor should be worth, and that his wages should be, as much as, with economy and prudence, will comfortably maintain himself and family, enable him to educate his children, and also to lay by enough for his decent support when his laboring powers have failed ". If you tell me that in any country, a laborer cannot win that much, then I say that must be a pitiful country, a country that ought not to be able to afford any Rothschilds, that ought not to be able to indulge in any wars, that ought not to be able to afford any costly generals, that ought not to waste any of its money in cannon, that ought to be economical in Royal grants, and sparing in the matter of pensions. I can understand that there may be countries, where trade is so bad, where commerce is slack, where enterprise has been so crushed, that no kind of effort can bring anything in surplus over subsistence, but England, at any rate, is not one of those countries yet. And such an unhappy land should be the country where there are no great landlords; that should be the country where there are no enormous rent-rolls; that should be the country where no man could take huge royalties from mines and minerals, and being worth himself hundreds of thousands, say that Labor has too much, and is driving the trade away.

What are the rights of Capital? For Capital has rights. There are people who talk absolute nonsense and say that Capital should be given without interest and used without profit to the capitalist, and who talk of forcible revolution against the capitalist class. Those men are either enemies of the people, or they are idiots; they are either traitors to the people, or they are madmen. If you want to dig a

field and you have no spade, if you can earn something by
digging and some other one has that spade, you must pay
for the loan and user of that spade. It is impossible that
Capital will enterprise itself to make you live more easily
unless Capital has some inducement.

What is Capital? Sir Thomas Brassey, speaking at the
Industrial Remuneration Conference, and I think that was
a good sign—rich men and poor men, men with millions and
men with nothing, met together in Piccadilly, London, in
1885, to discuss if it were possible to improve the relations
between Capital and Labor. It is the first time that that
ever was so done in England. It should be done again and
again until working men and the people owning capital
understand one another, so that lock-outs and strikes will
be regarded as insanities of the past, and not weapons
with which either should meet the other. Sir Thomas
Brassey, speaking at the Industrial Remuneration Conference, speaking as a representative of Capital, used these
three phrases. He said: "(1) Abstinence from enjoyment
is the only source of Capital: (2) it is upon the increase
of Capital that advances of wages depend; (3) while
Labor is the vivifying principle which preserves Capital
from decay". Permit me to make one or two comments on
the first and second parts of this proposition. While it is
true that all Capital arises from abstinence from enjoyment,
is it not true that Capital is to be found always, or mostly,
in the hands of those who abstain. The enormous accumulations of Capital, in the hands of an Overstone, a Baring,
a Rothschild or Vanderbilt—these did not come by
any stroke of wit: there is no fashion of striking one
blow upon the rock and a stream of Capital pouring
out. This Capital represented pence there, shillings
here, pounds there, which were the surplus which men
created by their labor beyond what those men had to live
upon.

If men could save amongst themselves, if men would
knit their savings together amongst themselves for trade
enterprises which they all understood, the Capital and profit
would pass into their hands. That will not come to-day nor
to-morrow, and I will tell you why: you are not educated
enough for that ; you mistrust one another too much.
Until men trust one another more, and that means until
you are truer to one another, for you would not mis-

trust one another so much if you were all true to one another; it is because so many of you know that in the struggle of life, sometimes driven by hardship, I admit, you have pushed others out of your way, that you do not trust your fellows as much as you should. The accumulations of the produce of labor are Capital. Those accumulations come into the hands of the crafty sometimes, the clever sometimes. Sometimes the crafty and the clever leave them to fools after them. But whoever may have the accumulated wealth, you cannot expect, if you have nothing but your labor, nothing but your muscle and sinew—that Capital shall clothe you, feed you, while you are working, unless you pay Capital something for it. Capital is entitled to fair profit and reasonable insurance against loss, and there must be hope for some prize for the Capitalist in the struggle of life or he would not make the endeavor. Men will not risk thousands in hazardous speculations say of mining or manufacture, hundreds of thousands in enterprises which may fail, unless they have some hope that they will gain some possible prizes.

The mistake that Capital has made, and the mistake that Labor has made too, but that Capital made with its eyes open, and Labor never having been permitted to see, was that they believed that the interests of Capital and Labor were hostile to one another, and the man who bought Labor bought it as they buy pigs, except that he bought it to starve instead of to fatten. Wiser counsels are prevailing, wiser thoughts are growing; it is beginning to be admitted that hostility between Capital and Labor is injurious to both, and it is beginning to be urged that the best method for men to grow rich is to give the opportunity to those who make their riches of sharing some of the enjoyments that are accompanying the work they conduct. Unfortunately many employers of Labor have deemed, and some still deem, that is good policy to get Labor too cheap. It is not, not even for them, for if you buy Labor too cheap, that is, if you buy it so that it leaves the laborer no margin, if you buy so that the purchase involves poverty and hunger, what happens? That poverty you have to feed; you have unwholesome and dangerous employment; you have unhealthy and immoral dwellings; you have disease; and you have crime. Poverty, disease, and crime, cost more when they break out into mischief both to rich and poor than any possible advantage in the temporary bargain.

I copied to-day from the report of the Agricultural Commission of 1867 some words written by the then Rev. John Fraser, whom many of you have since known as the Bishop of Manchester, whose death all regret, whether they are friend or foe to him, for he was a man, who, although very ardent in his faith, although very bitter against those he disagreed with, was a good, earnest, true man, endeavoring to make life better for all, and devoting himself, according to his light, to the task of so making it. Now, he, dealing with the Agricultural laborer, said, speaking of some dwellings he visited:—"Modesty must be an unknown virtue, decency an unimaginable thing, where in one small chamber with the beds lying as thickly as they can be packed, father, mother, young men, lads, grown and growing up girls— two and sometimes three generations—are herded promiscuously; where every operation of the toilette and of nature—dressings, undressings, births, deaths—is performed by each within the sight or hearing of all; where children of both sexes to as high an age as twelve or fourteen, or even more, occupy the same bed; where the whole atmosphere is sensual, and human nature is degraded into something below the level of the swine. It is a hideous picture; and the picture is drawn from life." That is what the Bishop of Manchester said in 1867. You may tell me: "That is eighteen years ago". But there was a Commission on the Housing of the Poor, which reported during last year, and they said, not of agricultural districts, not of country places, but of great cities like Liverpool, like Manchester, like London itself, almost under the very shelter of palaces, close to warehouses where millions of pounds worth of goods were stored, they said that in little rooms, in filthy alleys, that even now in London itself, you could sometimes find more than one family in one room, several families in one house. There it is where typhoid comes, there it is where small-pox touches, there it is where fever rages. It is on the hungry, on the poor, on the miserable, that squalor and disease lay their foul touch; and the men who bought labor too cheap, the men who exacted the sale in despair, pay in crime—these make the burglars, these the robbers in the streets; and the gaol and the poorhouse stand as monuments to mark the crimes of the nefarious transaction.

I am encouraged to hope because there has been a vast change in the last few years. Sir Thomas Brassey said : "It is in the highest degree desirable, as far as possible, to liberate industry from the deadening influence caused by the antagonism between Capital and Labor ". Sir Thomas Brassey said that which Trades Union leaders had been assailed for saying. It was once thought that there could be no hostility, that Capital was so strong that it could ride over all ; and in some countries it has. It has done it in Russia, it has done it in parts of Austria, it has done it in parts of Italy, and you have Socialism, Internationalism, Anarchism—the revolt of hunger, and the stiletto, dynamite and other explosive. These are the results of ignorance, misery, poverty, and despair, breaking out of all control. The question is how can Capital and Labor be reconciled, how far is the reconcilement possible ?

Once the capitalist foolishly thought that an Act of Parliament would do his work, and enacted that a man should not have more than so much. You have only to read the story of it all in your own country in Thorold Rogers' *Six Centuries of Work and Wages.* You read stories of battles—battles where generals lead, battles where men draw the sword, but any real history of the struggle of work for wages contains the narratives of battles more severe, more enduring, more full of pain, more full of heroism too ; battles where the men are working that men may live, not die ; battles for their wives' lives, battles for their children's lives, battling with pick and bar, battling in the mine against fire-damp, gas, and water—the one blows them limb from limb, another stifles them, another drowns them. And the workers go with the courage of despair day by day down in the cage again, always facing death in this never ceasing struggle for life ; and these make the heroes out of whom the country grows. I say that Capital and Labor may be reconciled by treating men fairly and reasonably on one side, and by the laborers knitting themselves together in the effort to try and treat others fairly and reasonably too. I will not disguise the difficulties; I know there are many; I know when disputes arise that on the one side the employer thinks you are doing something unfair if you ask him how much profit he makes, and that on the other you are not sufficiently careful sometimes when you think how little profit he may make.

Sir Thomas Brassey—and you will pardon me quoting him so often, but it was a speech he made at the Industrial Conference, which has not been enough commented upon —said, " The rate of profit in business is a subject of great importance to the laborer ". That was perhaps the first time that that was so plainly admitted by a great employer of labor. The employers of labor have said, " You have no right to know our profits ". The truth is that you have a right to know and the duty to submit. And what you have the right to say is, " But you have never told us your profits. We have seen some growing rich, and we thought all could ; we have seen some have costly mansions, and we knew sometimes we had no carpet to our floors, and we cannot help noticing it." Sir Thomas Brassey says, " More or less, wages must follow the fluctuations in profits ". Men say, " Yes, we are content with that, if they shall follow them upwards as well as downwards ". "In many cases and in many trades", Sir Thomas Brassey says, " the want of correct information as to the profits realised by their employers constitutes a great difficulty as to workmen. They do not know when to press their demand, nor when to acquiesce in reduction in the rate of remuneration for their labor."

Mr. Giffen, in an essay on the progress of the working classes during fifty years prior to 1883, points out that by the end of 1883 there had been a general improvement in the wage of the classes he deals with ; but Professor Thorold Rogers makes a comment upon that which ought to have special interest for you. He says : " It is noteworthy that the kinds of labor for which Mr. Giffen has adduced evidence have all been aided and protected by Trades Unions ". That is, in England, where men have stood alone, the stronger have pushed them down, and it is only where they have been organised, well organised, carefully led, thoroughly trusting, that they have been able to realise the improvement in their wage, which should go with the improvement of profits made. This shows the clear advantage of association. It is the old fable of the bundle of sticks ; the one broken by itself with ease—to break the bundle impossible for the strongest man on his knee; he can but hurt his own knee in the endeavor. Now men of capital have long recognised the advantages of association. The great bankers, the great railways, the great canal companies, the tramways, the insurance companies, all these are associations of people of capital, and do together what one or two cannot do by themselves. And you ought to learn the lesson, too. Why it is that there is much of the capital that the bankers use from your shillings and from your sixpences which you put into the savings bank, and which they are able to use better than you? Why better than you? If you put them together under special control in your own hands, why should not you use them as well? It is not because you cannot. The Co-operative stores in the country have shown what you can do if you try to do it. Although only on a small scale, your own Sick and Trade Societies are showing what you can do if you will. I say only on a small scale, for although it amounts to many hundreds of thousands of pounds, it is small compared with the millions you put into the hands of others to use. And what you do in the Co-operative system, what you have done in Industrial Insurance, with sick and benefit societies in connexion with your trades, what you have done with your trades' associations, you ought to be constantly doing. If you say you cannot, you deserve to be serfs, slaves, animals to be whipped, imposed upon, and you have no right to claim for yourselves the rights of human beings. I urge that there is a duty of association, as well as a right that all workers should unite together. Every man who does not unite in an association with which his trade is connected, is failing in duty to himself and them, failing in duty to them if he is strong, failing in duty if he is wise, for it is his duty to give them the benefit of his strength and wisdom; failing in duty to them if he is weak and ignorant, because his weakness and ignorance make them weaker in the struggle in which he gives way. Now there are two great trade societies in this country which for many years have permitted me to talk to them. I mean the Northumberland Miners and the Durham Miners. When they had no Unions their homes—why what the Bishop said about the agricultural laborer's home was true of almost every miner's home. It was not his

fault he could not get any other home. They were the
pit cottages built by the pit owners. The kennels for the
owner's dogs were better than the miner's dwelling, and
yet good folk grumbled that these men went to the public-
house. Why when these men came out of the pit, the coal
dust caked upon them through the sweat, dirty to a dirty
house, they washed in it as best they could. They worked
nearly naked in the pit; they had to strip naked to wash—
wives, growing girls, and lodgers round them. Can you
wonder at immorality? The wonder is that our people
have been so moral and so good, and have improved so
much as they have done. During the last fifteen years
and during the last ten years especially, there have been
literally thousands of new houses built in Northumberland
and Durham. The pitmen have got votes, and they have
elected the Local Boards of Health, and they have made
proper drainage, and they have done this under the
guidance of wise leaders.

It is only right I should say, because the Northumberland and Durham pitmen, if they were here, would say it,
that for many years they have found the employers of
labor ready to meet them in this new work. There are
some exceptions, I am sorry to say; still the best of the
men and the best of the employers are making the worst
of the men and the worst of the employers better than
they were. And the tendency is to do everything by arbitration and conciliation. There have been some failures;
I will try to show the remedies. The dwellings have
improved, the wages have improved, and at the present
moment the Trades' Unions of Northumberland and
Durham set an example to the whole nation by having
returned their own representatives of their own class into
Parliament, whose election expenses they have paid,
and whose salaries they pay while they are there.
The Society under whose auspices I speak here to-night—
I mean the National Union of Operative Boot and Shoe
Rivetters and Finishers—is not so large as the Northumberland Miners', it is not so big as the Durham Miners',
it is not so large as it ought to be; but it is large enough
to be useful. I would like to see it much more extensive,
much more efficient, much more wealthy; and one of my
objects here to-night is, if I can, to induce men who do not
belong to that Union to join it. I especially address my

remarks to those who do not approve of it amongst the workmen. I say that it is necessary that there should be a Union in the trade, and if this one is not as good as they think it could be, let them join it and make it better. Standing outside, they weaken it and themselves. And I say to the employers, it is to your interest that this Society should be made so powerful, that it shall do for you what the coal owners of Durham and the coal owners of Northumberland admit that the Trades Unions of Northumberland and Durham have done for them—avoid disputes, and enable enterprises to be conducted with more profit to the owners of capital, as well as with more advantage to the men who worked in them. Although I do not call yours a big society, it is not a little one. I understand that you have something like 11,000 members; that since 1874 you have paid some £20,234 in connexion with trade conflicts; and that since 1875 you have paid £19,450 in sick relief and in funeral grants to those who are your members and have been your members. Workmen, to provide against distress, should rely upon themselves, and not on the parish. If you say, "My trade society won't give me medicine for my children", I reply that it will if you make your Society effective enough to extort from the buyers of labor a full price for your labor. It would be no dearer for the employers of labor to pay a full price, and it is less dishonorable than paying it in the Poor Rate. Unfairly low wage is dishonoring to payer and receiver. Labor does not want charity, it wants justice; it wants life, and that when it is struck in battle by sickness, by disease, or when the wage-earner is struck by death, there shall be some protecting hand other than the Board of Guardians, other than the Union Workhouse. I understand that you have a balance in hand of some £8,447, of which £4,215 is in the hand of your Central Union, and the other £4,232 in the hand of your branches. You ought to have ten times as much as that in hand. You ought to be in a position to do this: Suppose you said to a great shoe manufacturer, "I know you are making an enormous fortune"; suppose he answered, "I am making a loss"; you ought to be in a position to start a factory of your own, where you could make the same things and know then your own profit and loss, and then when you understood whether it were true that profit

could be realised, you would be able to enforce the claim
if it were true, and not be foolish enough to persist in
it if it were a mad declaration.   Number 15 of your
rules desires to promote conciliation and arbitration.
Every sane man must agree that a strike is an evil.   It is
an evil even when it is successful; it is a horrible evil, if
not a crime, when it is a failure.   It is an evil because you
do not fight on like bases. A day's labor once lost you can
never get back; it is gone, it is so much of the capital of
your life gone.   Enforced idleness from a strike is bad,
existence on charity has a demoralising influence, the
influence on the home is degrading.   Strikes are always
bad.   I admit that if a man has only the choice between
starving and striking, it is very hard to counsel him against
a strike.   I don't blame every man who has advised a
strike, or every man who has taken part in one; but I do
say that the experience of England, of America, of every
country in the world, has shown that the horrible evils that
come out of great strikes are such as to outweigh any
advantages gained from them.   Why is there not more
arbitration and conciliation?   An answer was given at the
Industrial Conference.   Mr. Lloyd Jones complained that
arbitration had failed in the opinion of the men, because,
he said amongst other things, there were not sufficient and
not correct enough data to base any decision upon.   In
America they have tried to cure this by having special
statistics collected without reference to disputes; when
disputes arise both of you are interested in making out the
worst case.   Americans have these statistics collected not
simply in one establishment where they may be misleading,
nor in one town where they may not speak the whole truth,
but right through the whole of the country.   In 1860 the
Labor Bureau of Statistics in Boston, Massachusetts, was
established, and each year the Bureau publishes a report.
At first everybody cried out against it, the workmen said
it was inquisitorial, the employers said it was abominable.
But by-and-by both found it admirable.   Two other States
took it up, and then four others, till at last more than
twenty States of the Union, and the Province of Ontario in
Canada, have Labor Bureaus, all of which are issuing
statistics showing the cost of living, the rate of wages, the
number of hours worked, the number of people—men,
women and children—and ages, the rate of wage each

class earns, how long they work in the year, how much capital is used in each kind of enterprise, how much raw material is required for it, what rate of profit is made, and what the proportion it bears towards wage. Well, I hope within four weeks to propose in the House of Commons that there be established an office or Bureau of Labor Statistics to chronicle the following things :—

1.—Character, and number of each character, of the various industries of the United Kingdom, number of persons and amount of capital employed in each, specifying when any of these industries are increasing or diminishing, and why, and whether any special industry is limited to any particular locality, and the reasons, if known, for such local limitation.

2.—The hazardous nature or otherwise of each class of industry with the results to life, limb, and general health and habits of life in each industry, giving also particulars as to laborers' dwellings, and whether held from employers, and on what conditions.

—I may say that some of the revelations in America have shown that the different kind of trades not only lead to different kinds of diseases—that has been known for a long time, but also to special habits, either morality or immorality as the case may be.

3.—Showing how many cases of exploitation in each industry by limited liability companies or other corporations with their subscribed and actually paid-up capital, and profit, and loss, distinguishing cases where workers to any extent share profits.

4.—The minimum, maximum, and average amounts of capital embarked in each industry, distinguishing fixed and floating capital, the raw material used, the gross wages paid, the value of manufactures produced, and the gross and net profit.

5.—The individual wages paid in each industry, distinguishing men, women, boys, and girls, and specifying highest, lowest, and average wage; also showing whether wage paid weekly or at long periods, and in latter case, whether companies' shop exist.

—Because I find that in several parts of the United Kingdom the misery and demoralisation arising from a long wage-period and advances have never been properly estimated or dealt with.[1]

---

[1] I have endeavored to diminish this evil by the 3rd section of the Truck Act compelling advances without interest or discount.

Also showing the longest, shortest, and average number
of hours worked per day, and the industries in which
there is both night and day work; and showing the
average duration of employment in each industry
during each year, and showing the cost of, and nature
of living, including rent, food, clothing, necessaries,
and luxuries; specifying the cases: (1) in which the
earnings of individuals and of families, where more
than one individual was wage-earner in a family, were
large enough to leave a surplus beyond fair subsistence; (2) in which the family has subsisted without
incurring debt or receiving poor-law relief; (3) in
which the earnings did not equal the cost of subsistence. Showing what trades and Friendly Societies
exist in connexion with various industries, with the
amount of subscriptions and accumulated capital of
each, with annual amounts spent in strikes, sick and
other relief, etc., and whether such societies are registered under the Friendly Societies Acts; number of
Unionists and non-Unionists in each trade; compara-
tive states of trades in which Unions exist extensively
as against those having no Unions; amount of Savings
Banks deposits, and occupation of depositors.

6.—Specifying the other countries where any, and which,
similar industries are carried on, with similar details
where ascertainable.

—All these statistics can be procured with comparatively
little cost. A number of them already exist, but separated
in books so as to be utterly inaccessible. Those relating to
foreign countries are, many of them, contained in our Con-
sular reports. They want systematising and gathering together, and then people would be in a better position to
win their fair rights in any wage contest.

I am pleased in Rule 34 to see that you give bonds on behalf of your members as sureties for honesty. While
workmen are sureties for one another the practise of honesty is made more thorough amongst them. Poverty has
often compelled dishonesty, despair has often made men
drink, the wretched home has driven men away, and what
was not intended for dishonesty became it. But the
knowledge that your fellows are responsible for you will
make you truer to one another, braver and more loyal.
I am glad to see you are willing to take women among
your members. The only unions that can well exist are

unions in which the whole family have an interest, in which the wife feels that the man does not go away from her once a week to simply drink. Connected with your unions you can establish, and you ought to, places of meeting in each town, where you have your little reading-room and library, and place of entertainment. You can do it without trenching upon your means, and thus help yourselves step by step. I am glad to see that you have means for helping your sick, that you have duly registered yourselves under the law. The great struggles of the future will be not between Republicans and kings, not between heretics and churches, but between laborers and employers of labor. Those struggles may be beneficial to both, if they are struggles of reason—if they are conducted considerately, usefully, thoughtfully; but they will be struggles ruinous to both if they are conducted with the notion that either has the right or the duty to destroy the other. The progress of both can go together—one may grow richer as the other grows happier; it is only wanted that there should be fairness, openness. There is no secret in this; the man's muscle and the man's profit, the man's hammer, his chisel, and his plough—all these are things that can be seen; and—by those who know—the other man's profit is seen just as clearly. Fiction, fraud, are dishonorable to all, and I plead here to laborers to meet Capital not with the notion of vengeance for the past, but for good living in the future. And I plead to owners of Capital if I may; I plead to them that the others are the strongest. Money is not the strongest, all they own of it only makes two or three years' earnings. You can earn it—the Rothschild's wealth, the Overstone's wealth, the Baring's wealth; you, the millions, if you are only loyal to yourselves and to one another, may put all this into your own Savings Banks, and your own friendly societies, and your own trades unions, within a dozen years. You accumulate it for others; you can do it for yourselves. And I plead to you that your wives may be happier, that your children may be more moral, that your homes may be more pure, more clean, more wholesome; I plead that your whole lives may be better worth living.

I was successful, in 1886, in the House of Commons in securing the establishment of a Labor Statistic Department under the Board of Trade, and several valuable Parliamentary papers have been already issued by Mr. Giffen, the Assistant Secretary of the Board, and by Mr. Burnett, the Labor Correspondent. At present neither employers nor employed facilitate the collection of current labor statistics, but I venture to hope that, as in the United States, the great advantage of accurate statistics will become so evident that all classes will aid the Department.

In 1887 I also succeeded, with the willing aid of the Conservatives, in carrying a Truck Law Amendment Act to prevent frauds on the wage receivers ; and I was fortunate enough to obtain the appointment of a Royal Commission on Market Rights and Tolls, the evidence before which, I trust, may lay the foundation for legislation which will materially cheapen food supplies. These are all small points, but they are each intended to lessen, and I believe in the aggregate will materially lessen, the difficulties with which the poorest wage earners have to contend.

It ought perhaps to be noted that with the depression of the coal industry in the deep pits of Northumberland a divided feeling has arisen amongst the men as to the continuance of the payment to their Parliamentary representatives. A hostile vote was carried, and though on a second appeal to the collieries throughout the county this has been rescinded, even the latter and more considered voting has shown such a large minority opposed to the continuance of the payment by the men that it is more than possible Mr. Burt—who is a man of the very highest honor—may feel called on to terminate the present arrangement. I have personally always supported the payment from the Consolidated Fund of all members of the House of Commons.

Parliament and the Poor:

WHAT THE LEGISLATURE CAN DO;
WHAT IT OUGHT TO DO.

BY

CHARLES BRADLAUGH.

LONDON:
FREETHOUGHT PUBLISHING COMPANY,
63 FLEET STREET, E.C.
1889.

PRICE TWOPENCE.

LONDON:
PRINTED BY ANNIE BESANT AND CHARLES BRADLAUGH,
63 FLEET STREET, E.C.

Parliament and the Poor:

WHAT THE LEGISLATURE CAN DO; WHAT IT OUGHT TO DO.

————•————

By "poor" I mean the mass of the wage-earners: those whose only property is their labor, the sale of which labor in good times leaves them but narrow margin for thrift, or luxury, or waste, and who in bad times, as of slack employment, strike, lock-out, or ill-health, are poor indeed —so that the question might fairly be written: "What can and ought Parliament to do for the wage-earners of this country"? Excepting physical and economic limitations, Parliament is competent for any and every statute it chooses to enact. Constitutionally there is no limit whatever to the power of Parliament. In this country the legislature is supreme. We have no written constitution, such as exists in the United States of America, limiting the authority and jurisdiction of the legislature. We have no tribunal with the right—possessed by the Supreme Court of the United States—to declare that any statute is null and void because unconstitutional. The constitution of Great Britain and Ireland for the time being is the totality of the common law and statute law of the Kingdom. A new Act conflicting with part, or contrary to the whole, of the hitherto existing law, is not unconstitutional. It simply amends, modifies, abrogates, or enlarges what was theretofore the constitution.

Some of us who look with hope to a possible federation of the whole of the dominions now nominally or really subject to British rule, recognise that we shall then have to face the huge difficulty of constitution-making, and sometimes wonder how much of king, lords, and commons, would emerge from the crucible.

All progressive legislation in this country is necessarily compromise. It is not possible to legislate on hard and fast lines of principle alone. A state of things has grown up through generations which can only be gradually changed. The expedient has to be considered in all law-making. Legal interpretations of right have received judicial sanction, which have become so much part of our general political and social system that sudden reversal would be attended often with the gravest mischief. Temporary concessions have usually to be made on the one side to win consent from the other to a sure step in advance; but no compromise is final. Parliament does not bind its successor, and the new step won in one crisis serves as foothold for reaching further concession at a later date.

With the enormous increase of the suffrage of 1884, and the fuller though yet incomplete redistribution of political power in 1885, the Constitution of the House of Commons rests entirely in the hands of the male section of the wage earners. It is true that these have not yet learned to permanently act together for political objects, even in any one department of industry. Many of the great trades organisations and friendly societies have until recently

prided themselves on being non-political. Some of the
trade societies and nearly all the friendly societies still
so pride themselves. This has been a serious blunder,
especially in a country where much legislation has been
the work of a very limited class for the conservation of
their own privileges. A reading of the old Commons
journals for the three hundred years they cover prior to the
present reign would demonstrate how the governing classes
made the mistake of supposing that it is possible for mere
statutory enactments to affect values of labor or produce.
To-day advocates of labor seem making the like blunder,
and, in view of vastly increased knowledge, with less excuse.
And to-day, in one Chamber at any rate, it is impossible
for the legislature to ignore the voice of labor if spoken
with well-informed moderation. In the House of Commons
a large and growing proportion of the members are now
compelled to consider in giving each vote not only, and
indeed not so much, the desires of the party leaders or the
party whips, as the manner in which the vote will be
regarded by the bulk of their constituents. And almost
everywhere this bulk is of wage-earners—not united, not
watchful, or they would be nearly omnipotent.

A good working doctrine for legislatures should be to
mould conduct rather by the development of sound public
opinion than by the operation of penal laws. Especially
should the legislature be careful not to profess to do that
for the worker which it is reasonably possible for him to
do for himself without the aid of the law. A duty enforced
by others is seldom as well performed as a duty affirmed
by the doer. The results are better from the willing
hammerman's work than from the slave at the anvil fearing the overlooker's lash. In self-regarding matters, social

reforms, and domestic concerns, the motto should be "the most self-reliant liberty, the least statutory restriction or compulsion".

There is a disposition on the part of so-called, and of some real, philanthropists to legislate for the guidance and government of the masses in their amusements, their opinions, their literature; and, on the other hand, there are some who by the aid of the law desire to enforce their own view of what bargains should be possible between adults in matters relating to labor. I hold that both are utterly wrong.

A tendency, which, to me, is very dangerous, seems largely developing in Europe, and somewhat distinctly here, *i.e.*, the tendency for the workmen to look to "the Government" or to "the State" or to Parliament for the general redress of all grievances, for the cure of all ills, for remedies against poverty, lack of employment, poor wage, or long hours.

Parliament cannot fix the hours of adult labor, or the rate of wage which shall be paid by the employer. If it ventures, as it often has done, to enact as to rate of wage, history shows clearly that the very employers who sought the law as means of pressure have to evade or disobey the very statutes of which they have obtained the passage. These matters of wage and hours are points which should be mutually determined between employer and employed, and as the individual laborer is generally in the weaker position of the two contractants, he should strengthen himself by the aid of his co-workers, and act in union and organisation with his fellows. Organised labor has advantages of information and of associated resource during temporary individual adversity. Parliament might and ought to help employers and employed to make fair bargains by collecting labor statistics for workmen, as it has collected agricultural statistics for landowners and farmers, trade statistics for merchants, and financial statistics for capitalists. It was to do something in this direction that I in 1886 moved and carried the resolution for the establishment of a labor statistical department under the Board of Trade.

Parliament may enact to punish frauds on the part of any employers who try to cheat their workmen out of any portion of the agreed wage; but enactment will do little in this respect unless those employed are fairly self-reliant. If working folk are really self-reliant, then aid of the law will hardly be needed : men in union can protect one another. The history of the various Truck Acts is worth study on this head. "Truck" is the legal word for payment of wage partly in kind in lieu of in coin; or the payment under conditions which prevent the full amount agreed to be paid from actually reaching the workman. The word "truck" means exchange or barter; and in Scotland there are unfortunately still some few occupations in which the result of the industry is bartered. Legislation against truck evils can be traced back certainly as far as the reign of Edward IV. With the growth of education the improvement has been enormous; it is doubtful if the law has effected much. Despite the amendment of the law and the increased facilities for its enforcement, truck still prevails amongst the less educated; and it so prevails because of the persistent complicity of the cheated with the cheaters. Except so far as the statute I procured in 1887 may prove educational, I fear that it will do very little to put an end to truck. Where the workmen are well educated and fairly organised, truck practices rapidly break down; but amongst the Rhymney iron workers, the Middlesex brick makers, the London fruit porters, and the Scotch knitters, the whole machinery of the law has been arrested, the victims lacking either the courage or the desire to help, though the only help required from them was to state the facts in the witness box.

Working men are now asking that Parliament shall limit the working day of adults to eight hours. And I note that some members of the House of Commons give hesitating and evasive replies to questions addressed to them. It is not quite clear what is meant by the eight hours proposal, or whether all workmen mean the same thing. Mr. W. Abraham, M.P. for the Rhondda miners, speaks of it as if there should be no more than eight hours' work in any one day in any mine, foundry, mill, or manufactory. If this is seriously meant, then it would involve the most shocking mischief to the workmen themselves; for it would mean at once the closing of many collieries and great works which are now only carried on profitably because with more than one shift. If it means that where men are now working nine or nine and a-half hours per day they shall work only eight hours and nevertheless receive the same total amount for the eight hours labor that they now receive for the nine or nine and a-half hours, this in many industries may render the continuance of the industry in this country impossible. The manufacturer would transfer his capital to countries where profitable enterprise was permissible. If it means that the laborer is to be paid only by the actual hours worked—and is therefore to receive either $\frac{1}{8}$ or $\frac{3}{18}$ less wage—I would ask sober and thrifty artizans whether they really mean that if their wage has been 27s. per week

they will be content in future with 24s. or 22s. 6d., or that
if the wage has been 18s. they will be content with
16s. or 15s. Even if the artizans would be content
with the reduced pay, it may be physically impossible in many industries for the manufacturer to make
profit with the lessened production. And if the workmen contend that Parliament may fix the hours of
labor, do they mean that Parliament may increase as well
as reduce? I am in favor of short hours of labor—the
shorter, consistent with practicability, the better; but such
hours ought to be, and indeed must be, the subject of
mutual arrangement, under differing conditions of differing
employments, between employer and employed. In some
industries it may be unavoidably necessary, from the costly
nature of the plant or the great capital required for the
exploitation, that by the practice of double or treble shifts
very long hours of constant production should be maintained. The requirements of various manufactures differ
very considerably. Workmen ought to be able by co-operative production to know exactly the least time per day
required for the profitable conduct of each class of enterprise. Until they are so able, it is at least rash to seek to
fix hard and fast lines of hours of labor. With the great
trades organisations now existing, they should be able,
either with their own savings or those of their fellows, to
conduct for themselves any works in which they could
earn more or work less time than is now the case. Do the
men propose that any adult who desires to work more than
eight hours per day shall be punished? or do they only
propose to punish the employers?

Parliament may really increase wage by augmenting its
purchasing power. That is, it may abolish artificial hin-

drances to the cultivation of foods, and thus facilitate the
increase of the food supply. It may annul all privileges
given to individuals relating to the sale of foods, placing
all market rights in the hands of local authorities, and
forbidding the imposition of tolls which are prohibitive of
small farming. It was in the hope of doing effective work
on this head that I in 1887 moved and carried the appointment of a Royal Commission to enquire fully into the facts,
and when the Commission reports I shall press for legislation. Parliament may prevent railways, to which it has
granted monopolies of carriage, from imposing unduly
heavy rates for carriage of small quantities of home-grown
produce.

In recent meetings of the unemployed, and in speeches
by Mr. Cunninghame Graham, M.P., demands have been
made that Parliament, or the State, or Government, should
provide employment for the destitute. First, it is clearly
impossible for the State to compete in this country in
ordinary trades and manufactures, without serious injury
to the individual enterprise which has developed our
national industries. In any case the State can only act
in relation to some monopolies, and then only if such a
monopoly is co-extensive with its dominion. Local works
should be solely controlled by the local authorities. Parliament can, it is true, vote money for public works, as
harbors, forts, etc.; but these are exceedingly costly, and
have to be paid for out of the earnings of those who are
in work, and can hardly ever provide the kind of employment required by those who are out of work. By
"Government" can only be meant the executive, which
has no means save what it raises by taxation. If the
unemployed are taught that the Government must always

find employment for those who need it, great disasters may be provoked without any real advantage to those who are in want. Roads and harbors afford rough employment, which, in most cases, would totally unfit skilled artisans for readily resuming their ordinary avocations. If the work enterprised by the Government is of unproductive character, the payment of the cost must be an actual reduction of earnings of those in employment.

Parliament can effectively increase the purchasing power of wage, by diminishing all unproductive national expenditure. It is upon the wage-earners ultimately that the great burden of taxation falls; and all excessive naval and military expenditure is therefore equivalent to so much reduction of the actual wage. A lesson to British workers may be unfortunately too easily read at the present moment in almost every European country. For the past twenty-five or thirty years each of the Great Powers has year by year increased its peace establishments of army and navy. For the past ten years the war cloud has always been gathering, and has often seemed near bursting, and even the avoidance of general war, if armaments are increased, is likely to involve the possibility of the revolution earthquake as the result of unbearable misery. Italy is despairingly hungry; France is overtaxed, dissatisfied and uneasy; Germany's ill-fed people may at any moment use against its rulers the weapons it has been trained to wear. England's Parliament ought to restrain England's Ministers from joining in any engagements with foreign powers which may involve this country in war or warlike enterprises. Parliament can slightly increase wage by checking and reducing the ever-swelling non-effective vote which

alone is now larger in amount than was the total expenditure of Great Britain and Ireland two centuries
ago. It can increase it a little more by reducing some
of the higher paid superabundant officers in public departments.

Parliament can increase wage by abolishing any artificial hindrances to home employment. It might place a
penalty tax on all uncultivated lands, as has been done
by the present Conservative Government in Cyprus, or,
failing this, it might enact the confiscation of such lands
for the benefit of the local authority, as has also been done
in Cyprus. It might—if this be thought too drastic—
authorise the local authorities to facilitate the reclamation
of uncultivated lands and the creation of small farms.
That the poor may be fairly heard in Parliament, opportunities should be increased for them to choose their own
mouthpiece; and the cost of elections should be reduced to
as low a sum as practicable, and should be borne by the
county rates. The members elected should be paid from
the consolidated fund. If this sum were fixed, say at
£300 a year for all members not holding official position,
the cost, £195,000, of about 650 members could easily be
made up by reasonable economy in various higher branches
of the army, navy, and civil service.

In the matter of local government, wage may be considerably affected by the increase or decrease of local
burdens. This really rests with the electors themselves.
The total of local debt up to 1888 is over two hundred
millions sterling, and the pressure of this debt varies
considerably. In Bradford it is as high as £22 16s. per
head; in Manchester nearly £19 per head; and in Birmingham very little less. These debts are mortgages on all

the earnings of living workers; they are mortgages on the earnings of children yet unborn. The local taxation is growing with astounding rapidity. I. do not mean that all local expenditure is necessarily unduly costly to the one who pays it; because it may be that in improved sanitation and in other fashions the health of the wage earner is secured and his comfort increased by the local authority, so that the labor he has to sell is of a higher value, and brings a higher return than without that expenditure. But in the matter of debt men are too apt to spend a large sum because credit is good, without reckoning that the times may come when credit is bad, and when the pressure comes most hardly upon those who can bear it the least.

In the question of the collection of labor statistics, the working men of this country, whether union or non-union, have as yet taken comparatively little interest; and on the inquiry into the operations of market tolls and regulations as affecting the price of food, they have up to the present been almost utterly indifferent. Yet in both cases the willing assistance of the people most affected would have facilitated the collection of evidence material in the highest degree to their welfare.

Subject to what is urged at the commencement of this paper, I put it as a principle governing what Parliament ought to do with reference to adults—that it ought not to legislate on any matters on which the people are, or reasonably ought to be, able to protect themselves; that it ought not to enact what people shall do or shall not do in respect. to self-regarding matters on which the people can fairly decide for themselves; that in respect to social reforms and domestic concerns the duty of Parliament is to interfere as little as possible, and only for the purpose of preventing those frauds which are in the nature of crimes; that in fact Parliament should do nothing which robs men of that self-reliance, which on the whole makes society progressive wherever it obtains with the individual.

POLITICAL WORKS by C. BRADLAUGH.

THE TRUCK LAW AND HOW TO ENFORCE IT.

Price Threepence.

THE EMPLOYERS' LIABILITY BILL

An Open Letter to Mr. Thomas Burt, M.P.

Price Threepence.

TAXATION:

How it originated, how it is spent, and who bears it.

Second edition.   Completely revised to date.   Price 6d.

THE RADICAL PROGRAMME.

New edition.   Price Twopence.

MR. GLADSTONE OR LORD SALISBURY: WHICH?

An Appeal to the Electors.   12 pages, One Penny.

CROMWELL AND WASHINGTON: A CONTRAST.

Price Sixpence.

London: Freethought Publishing Company, 63 Fleet Street, E.O.

POLITICAL WORKS by C. BRADLAUGH.

CIVIL LISTS AND GRANTS TO THE ROYAL FAMILY.

New edition.   One Penny.

WILL SOCIALISM BENEFIT THE ENGLISH PEOPLE?

One night's debate with H. M. HYNDMAN.   Price Threepence.

WILL SOCIALISM BENEFIT THE ENGLISH PEOPLE?

Written debate with E. BELFORT BAX.   Price Sixpence.

SOCIALISM: FOR AND AGAINST.

Written debate with ANNIE BESANT.   Price Fourpence.

CAPITAL AND LABOR.

New edition.   Price Twopence.

THE CHANNEL TUNNEL:

Ought the Democracy to Support or Oppose it?

Price Twopence.

THE PARLIAMENTARY STRUGGLE.

Containing the whole of the Documents.   Cloth, One Shilling.

London: FREETHOUGHT PUBLISHING COMPANY, 63 Fleet Street, E.C.

LABOR'S PRAYER.

BY CHARLES BRADLAUGH.

———◆———

"Give us this day our daily bread" is the entreaty addressed by the tiller of the soil to the "Our Father" who has promised to answer prayer. And what answer cometh from heaven to this the bread-winner's petition? Walk amongst the cotton workers of Lancashire, the clothweavers of Yorkshire, the Durham pitmen, the Staffordshire puddlers, the Cornish miners, the London dock laborers, go anywhere where hands are roughened with toil, where foreheads are bedewed with sweat of work, and see the Lord's response to the prayer, the father's answer to his children! The only bread they get is the bread they take; in their hard struggle for life-sustenance, the loaves come but slowly, and heaven adds not a crust, even though the worker be hungry when he rises from his toil-won meal. Not even the sight of pale-faced wife and thin forms of half-starved infants can move to generosity the Ruler of the world. The laborer may pray, but, if work be scant and wages low, he pines to death while praying. His prayer gives no relief, and misery's answer is the mocking echo to his demand.

It is said by many a pious tongue that God helps the poor; the wretchedness of some of their hovel houses—found, alas! too often in the suburbs of our wealthiest cities—grimy, black, squalid, and miserable; the threadbare raggedness of their garments; the unwholesomeness of the food they eat; the poisoned air they breathe in their narrow wynds and filthy alleys—all these tell how much God helps the poor. Do you want to see how God helps the poor? go into any police court when some little child-thief is brought up for hearing; see him shoeless, with ragged trousers, threadbare, grimy vest hardly hanging to his poor body, shirt that seems as though it never could have been white, skin dull-brown with dirt, hair innocent of comb or brush, eye ignorantly, sullenly defiant, yet downcast; born poor, born wretched, born in ignorance, educated amongst criminals, crime the atmosphere in which he moved; and society, his nurse and creator, is now virtuously aghast at the depravity of this its own neglected nursling, and a poor creature whom God alone hath helped. Go where the weakly wife in a narrow room huddles herself and little children day after day, and where the husband crowds in to lie down at night; they are poor and honest, but their honesty bars not the approach of disease, fever, sorrow, death—God helps not the line of health to their poor wan cheeks. Go to the country workhouse in which is temporarily housed the worn-out farm laborer, who, while strength enough remained, starved through weary years with wife and several children on eight shillings per week—it is thus God helps the poor. And the poor are taught to pray for a continuance of this help, and to be thankful and content to pray that to-morrow may be like to-day, thankful that yesterday was no worse than it was, and content that to-day is as good as it is.

Are there many repining at their miseries? The preacher, with gracious intonation, answers rebukingly that God, in his wisdom, has sent these troubles upon them as chastisement for their sins. So, says the Church, all are sinners, rich as well as poor, but rich sinners feel that the chastising rod is laid more lightly on their backs than it is upon those of their meaner brethren. Week-day and Sunday, it is the same contrast: one wears fustian, the other broadcloth; one prepares for heaven in the velvet cushioned pew, the other on the wooden benches of the free seats. In heaven it will be different—there above all are to wear crowns of gold and fine linen; and, therefore, here below the poor man is to be satisfied with the state of life into which it has pleased God to call him. The pastor who tells him this looks upon the laborer as an inferior animal, and the laborer by force of habit regards the great landowner and peer, who patronises his endeavors, as a being of a superior order.

Is there no new form of prayer that labor might be taught

to utter, no other power to which his petition might be addressed? Prayer to the Unknown for aid gives no strength to the prayer. In each beseeching he loses dignity and self-reliance: he trusts to he knows not what for an answer which cometh he knows not when, and mayhap may never come at all. Let labor pray in the future in another fashion and at another altar. Let laborer pray to laborer that each may know labor's rights, and be able to fulfil labor's duties. The size of the loaf of daily bread must depend on the amount of the daily wages, and the laborer must pray for better wages. But his prayer must take the form of earnest, educated endeavor to obtain the result desired. Let workmen, instead of praying to God in their distress, ask one another why are wages low? how can wages be raised? can we raise our own wages? having raised them, can we keep them fixed at the sum desired? what causes produce a rise and fall in wages? are high wages beneficial to the laborer? These are questions the pulpit has no concern with. The reverend pastor will tell you that the "wages of sin is death", and will rail against "filthy lucre"; but he has no inclination for answering the queries here propounded.

Why are wages low? Wages are low because the wage-winners crowd too closely. Wages are low because too many seek to share one fund. Wages are lower still because the laborer fights against unfair odds; the laws of the country, over-riding the laws of humanity, have been enacted without the laborer's consent, although his obedience to them is enforced. The fund is unfairly distributed as well as too widely divided. Statutes are gradually being modified, and the working man may hope for ampler justice from the employer in the immediate future than was possible in the past, but high and healthy wages depend on the working man himself. Wages can be raised by the working classes exercising a moderate degree of caution in increasing their numbers. Wages must increase when capital increases more rapidly than population, and it is the duty of the working man, therefore, to take every reasonable precaution to check the increase of population, and to accelerate the augmentation of capital.

Can working men, by combination, permanently raise the

rate of wages? One gentleman presiding at a meeting of the National Association for the Promotion of Social Science for the discussion of the labor question, very fairly said, "It is not in the power of the men alone, or of the masters alone, or of both combined, to say what shall be the amount of wages at any particular time in any trade or country. The men and the masters are, at most, competitors for the division at a certain rate of a certain fund, provided by [themselves and] others—that is, by the consumers. If that fund is small, no device can make the rate of profit or rate of wages higher." This is in theory quite correct, if it means that no device can make the total divisible greater than it is, but not if it refers to the increase of profit or wages by partial distribution. In practice, although it is true that if the fund be small and the seekers to share it be many, the quotient to each must be necessarily very small, yet it is also true that a few of the competitors—*i.e.*, the capitalists—may and do absorb for their portions of profits an improper and unfairly large amount, thus still further reducing the wretchedly small pittance in any case receivable by the mass of laborers.

It is warmly contended that the capitalist and laborer contend for division of the fund appropriable in fair and open field; that the capitalist has his money to employ, the man his labor to sell; that if workmen are in excess of the capitalist's requirements, so that the laborer has to supplicate for employment, wages cannot rise, and will probably fall; but that if, on the contrary, capital has need to invite additional laborers, then wages must rise. That is the law of supply and demand brought prominently forward. In great part this is true, but it is not true that capital and labor compete in fair and open field, any more than it is true that an iron-clad war vessel, with heavy ordnance, would compete in fair field with a wooden frigate, equipped with the *matériel* in use thirty years ago. Capital is gold-plated, and carries too many guns for unprotected labor. The intelligent capitalist makes the laws affecting master and servant, which the uneducated laborer must obey, but has no effective voice to alter. The capitalist forms the Government of the country, which in turn protects capital against labor; this Government the laborer must sustain, and dares not modify. The capitalist does combine, and has combined, and the result of this combination has been an unfair appropriation of the divisible fund.

Why should not the laborer combine also? The answer is truly that no combination of workmen can increase the rate of wages, if at the same time the number of laborers increases more rapidly than the capital out of which their wages must be paid. But the men may combine to instruct one another in the laws of political economy; they may combine to apply their knowledge of those laws to the contracts between employer and employed. They may combine to compel the repeal of unjust enactments under which an unfair distribution of the labor fund is not only possible, but certain. Organisations of laborers are, therefore, wise and necessary: the object of such organisations should be the permanent elevation and enfranchisement of the members. No combination of workmen which merely dictates a temporary cessation from labor can ultimately and permanently benefit the laborer, while it certainly immediately injures him and deteriorates his condition, making his home wretched, his family paupers. Nor can even co-operative combination, praiseworthy as it certainly is to procure for the laborer a larger share of the profits of his labor, permanently benefit him, except in so far that, temporarily alleviating his condition and giving him leisure for study, it enables him to educate himself: unless, at the same time, the co-operator is conscious that the increase or reduction in the amount of wages depends entirely on the ratio of relation preserved between population and its means of subsistence, the former always having a tendency to increase more rapidly than the latter.

It is with the problem of too many mouths for too little bread that the laborer has really to deal: if he must pray, it should be for more bread and for fewer mouths. The answer often given by the workman himself to the advocate of Malthusian views is, that the world is wide enough for all, that there are fields yet unploughed broad enough to bear more corn than man at present could eat, and that there is neither too little food nor are there too many mouths; that there is, in fact, none of that over-population with which it is sought to affright the working-man. Over-population in the sense that the whole world is too full to contain its inhabitants, or that it will ever become too full to contain them, is certainly a fallacy, but over-population is a lamentable truth in its relative sense. We find evidences of over-population in every old country in the world. The test of over-population is the existence of poverty, squalor, wretchedness, disease, ignorance, misery, and crime. Low rates of wages, and food dear: here you have two certain indices of relative over-population. Wages depending on the demand for and supply of laborers, wherever wages are low it is a certain sign that there are too many candidates for employment in that phase of the labor market. The increased cost of production of food, and its consequent higher price, also mark that the cultivation has been forced by the numbers of the people to descend to less productive soils. Poverty is the test and result of over-population.

It is not against some possible increase of their numbers, which may produce possibly greater affliction, that the working men are entreated to agitate. It is against the existing evils which afflict their ranks, evils alleged by sound students of political economy to have already resulted from inattention to the population question, that the energies of the people are sought to be directed. The operation of the law of population has been for centuries entirely ignored by those who have felt its adverse influence most severely. It is only during the last thirty years that any of the working classes have turned their attention to the question; and only during the last few years that it has been to any extent discussed amongst them. Yet all the prayers that labor ever uttered since the first breath of human life have not availed so much for human happiness as will the earnest examination by one generation of this, the greatest of all social questions, the root of all political problems, the foundation of all civil progress. Poor—man must be wretched. Poor—he must be ignorant. Poor—he must be criminal; and poor he must be till the cause of poverty has been ascertained by the poor man himself, and its cure planned by the poor man's brain and effected by the poor man's hand.

Outside his own rank none can save the poor. Others

may show him the abyss, but he must avoid its dangerous brink himself. Others may point out to him the chasm, but he must build his own bridge over. Labor's prayer must be to labor's head for help from labor's hand to strike the blow that severs labor's chain, and terminates the too long era of labor's suffering.

During the last few years our daily papers and various periodicals, magazines, and reviews have been more frequently, and much less partially, devoted than of old to the discussion of questions relating to the laborer's condition and the means of ameliorating it. In the Legislative Assembly debates have taken place which would have been impossible fifty years since. Works on political economy are now more easily within the reach of the working man than they were some few years ago. People's editions are now published of treatises on political economy which half a century back people were unable to read. It is now possible for the laborer, and it is the laborer's duty, to make himself master of the laws which govern the production and distribution of wealth. Undoubtedly there is much grievous wrong in the mode of distribution of wealth, by which the evils that afflict the poorest strugglers are often specially and tenfold aggravated. The monopoly of land, the serf state of the laborer, are points requiring energetic agitation.

The grave and real question is, however, that which lies at the root of all, the increase of wealth as against the increase of those whom it subsists. The leaders of the great trades' unions of the country, if they really desire to permanently increase the happiness of the classes amongst whom they exercise influence, can speedily promote this object by encouraging their members to discuss freely the relations of labor to capital; not moving in one groove, as if labor and capital were necessarily antagonistic, and that therefore labor must always have rough-armed hand to protect itself from the attacks of capital; but, taking new ground, to inquire if labor and capital are bound to each other by any and what ties, ascertaining if the share of the laborer in the capital fund depends, except so far as affected by inequality in distribution, on the proportion between the number of laborers and the amount of the fund. The discussing, examining, and dealing generally with these topics, would necessarily compel the working man to a more correct appreciation of his position.

Any such doctrine as that "the poor shall never cease out of the land", or that we are to be content with the station of life into which it has pleased God to call us, or that we are to ask and we shall receive, must no longer avail. Schiller most effectively answers the advocates of prayer : ·

> "Help, Lord, help! Look with pity down!
> A paternoster pray ;
> What God does, that is justly done,
> His grace endures for aye.

> "Oh, mother! empty mockery,
> God hath not justly dealt by me :
> Have I not begged and prayed in vain ;
> What boots it now to pray again ? "

Labor's only and effective prayer must be in life action for its own redemption ; action founded on thought, crude thought, and sometimes erring at first, but ultimately developed into useful thinking, by much patient experimenting for the right and true.

PRICE ONE PENNY.
(6s. per 100 for distribution.)

Reprinted and Published by A. & H. B. BONNER, 63 Fleet St., E.C.
1895.

The Atheistic Platform.

VII.

SOME

OBJECTIONS

TO SOCIALISM.

BY

CHARLES BRADLAUGH.

LONDON:
FREETHOUGHT PUBLISHING COMPANY,
63 FLEET STREET, E.C.
1884

—

PRICE ONE PENNY

THE ATHEISTIC PLATFORM.

Under this title is being issued a fortnightly publication, each number of which consists of a lecture delivered by a well-known Freethought advocate. Any question may be selected, provided that it has formed the subject of a lecture delivered from the platform by an Atheist. It is desired to show that the Atheistic platform is used for the service of humanity, and that Atheists war against tyranny of every kind, tyranny of king and god, political, social, and theological.

Each issue consists of sixteen pages, and is published at one penny. Each writer is responsible only for his or her own views.

I. "What is the use of Prayer?" Second Edition. By ANNIE BESANT.

II. "Mind Considered as a Bodily Function." By ALICE BRADLAUGH.

III. "The Gospel of Evolution." By EDWARD AVELING, D.Sc.

IV. "England's Balance Sheet." By CHARLES BRADLAUGH.

V. "The Story of the Soudan." By ANNIE BESANT.

VI. "Nature and the Gods." By A. B. MOSS.

These six in wrapper, sixpence. Post free, sevenpence.

SOME OBJECTIONS TO SOCIALISM.

BY CHARLES BRADLAUGH.

THE great evils connected with and resulting from poverty—evils which are so prominent and so terrible in old countries, and especially in populous cities—have, in our own land compelled the attention, and excited the sympathy, of persons in every rank of society. Many remedies have been suggested and attempted, and from time to time, during the present century, there have been men who, believing that the abolition of individual private property would cure the misery abounding, have advocated Socialism. Some pure-hearted and well-meaning men and women, as Robert Owen, Abram Combe, and Frances Wright, have spent large fortunes, and devoted much of their lives in the essay to test their theories by experiments. As communities, none of these attempts have been permanently successful, though they have doubtless, by encouraging and suggesting co-operative effort in England, done something to modify the fierceness of the life struggle, in which too often the strongest and most unscrupulous succeeded by destroying his weaker brother. Some Socialistic associations in the United States,[1] as the Shakers and the Oneida community, have been held together in limited numbers as religious societies, but only even apparently successful, while the numbers of each community remained comparatively few. Some communities have for many years bravely endured the burden of debt, penury, and discomfort, to be loyal to the memory of their founder, as in the case at Icaria of the followers of Cabet. But

---

[1] Particulars of all existing Socialistic communities in the United States are given in the works of Mr. Hinds and Mr. Nordhoff.

in none of these was the sense óf private property
entirely lost; the numbers were relatively so small that
all increase of comfort was appreciable, and in nearly
all the communities there was option of the withdrawal
of the individual, and with him of a proportion of the
property he had helped to create or increase.

During the past generation, Socialistic theory has
been specially urged in Germany, and the Socialist
leaders there have acquired greater influence because
of the poverty of the people, and because too of the
cruel persecution to which Social Reformers, as well
as Socialists, have been subjected by Prince Bismarck's
despotic government.

A difficulty arising from the repressive measures
resorted to in Germany has been that German emigrants to the United States and to Great Britain, speak
and write as if precisely the same wrongs had to be
assailed in the lands of their adoption as in the land of
their birth.

Very recently in England—and largely at the instance of foreigners—there has been a revival of
Socialist propaganda, though only on a small scale
compared with fifty years ago, by persons claiming
to be "Scientific Socialists," who declare that such
Socialists as Robert Owen and his friends were utopian
in thinking that any communities could be successfully
founded while ordinary society exists. These Scientific
Socialists—mostly middle-class men—declare their intense hatred of the *bourgeoisie,* and affirm that the
Social State they desire to create can only be established
on the ruins of the present society, by a revolution
which they say must come in any event, but which
they strive to accelerate. These Scientific Socialists
deny that they ought to be required to propound any
social scheme, and they contemptuously refuse to discuss
any of the details connected with the future of the
new Social State, to make way for which the present is
to be cleared away. Most of the points touched on in
this lecture were raised in the discussion on Socialism
between myself and Mr. Hyndman recently held in
St. James's Hall. Others of the questions have been
raised in my articles in *Our Corner,* and in the reply
there by Mr. Joynes.

The Socialists of the Democratic Federation say that "Socialism is an endeavor to substitute an organised co-operation for existence" for the present strife, but they refuse to be precise as to the method or character of the organisation, or the lines upon which it is to be carried out. Their reason is, probably, that they have not even made the slightest effort to frame any plan, but would be content to try first to destroy all existing government. I suggest that this want and avoidance of foresight is, in the honest, folly, and in the wise, criminality. They mix up some desirable objects which are not all Socialistic with others that are not necessarily Socialistic, and add to these declarations which are either so vague as to be meaningless, or else in the highest degree Socialistic and revolutionary.

Whilst Mr. Hyndman, one of the prominent members of the Democratic Federation, thus speaks of Socialism as endeavoring "to substitute an organised co-operation," Mr. E. Belfort Bax, another prominent member and co-signatory of the manifesto, emphatically says, "no 'scientific' socialist pretends to have any 'scheme' or detailed plan of organisation." When organisation can be spoken of as possible without any scheme or detailed plan, it shows that words are used without regard to serious meaning.

These Socialists declare that there must be "organisation of agricultural and industrial armies under State control," and that the exchange of all production must be controlled by the workers; but they decline to explain how this control is to be exercised, and on what principles. We agree that there are often too many concerned in the distribution of the necessaries of life, and that the cost to the consumer is often outrageously augmented; but we suggest that this may be reformed gradually and in detail by individual effort through local societies, and that it ought not to be any part of the work of the State. We point to the fact that there are now in Great Britain—all established during the present reign—nearly one thousand distributive co-operative societies, with more than half a million members, with over seventeen and three-quarter millions of pounds of yearly sales, with two and a half millions of stock-in-trade, with five and a quarter millions of working capital, and dividing one and a half millions of annual profit ; and that these societies, each keeping its own property, still further co-operate with one another to reduce loss in exchange by having a wholesale co-operative society in England, with sales in 1882 exceeding three and a half millions sterling, and another similar wholesale society in Scotland, with transactions in the same year to nearly one million sterling. We say the way to render the cost of exchange of products less onerous to the laborer is by the extension and perfection of this organisation of co-operative distribution, and that this may be and is being done successfully and usefully, ameliorating gradually the condition and developing the self-reliance of the individual workers who take part in such co-operative stores, and thus inciting and inducing other individuals to join the societies already founded, or to establish others, and so educating individual after individual to better habits of exchange. We say that this is more useful than to denounce as idlers and robbers "the shopkeepers and their hangers on," as is done by the present teachers of Socialism. We object that the organisation of all industry under State control must paralyse industrial energy and discourage and neutralise individual effort.

The Socialists claim that there shall be "collective ownership of land, capital, machinery and credit by the complete ownership of the people," and yet they object that they are misrepresented when told that they want to take the private economies of millions of industrious wage-earners in this kingdom for the benefit of those who may have neither been thrifty nor industrious. The truth is that, if language is to have any meaning, the definitions must stand given by me and unchallenged by my opponent in the St. James's Hall debate, viz. : (1) " Socialism denies all individual private property, and affirms that society, organised as the state, should own all wealth, direct all labor, and compel the equal distribution of all produce." (2) "A Socialistic State would be a State in which everything would be held in common, in which the labor of each individual would be directed and controlled by the

State, to which would belong all results of __
labor." The realisation of a Socialistic State in this
country would, as I then urged, require (1) a physical
force revolution, in which all the present property
owners unwilling to surrender their private properties
to the common fund would be forcibly dispossessed.
This revolution would be in the highest degree difficult,
if not impossible, for property holders are the enormous
majority.

Mr. Joynes, in an article published in *Our Corner*, does
challenge my definition, and says that the immediate
aim of Socialism "is not the abolition of private property, but its establishment by means of the emancipation of labor on the only sound basis. It is private
capital we attack, the power to hire laborers at starvation wages, and not the independent enjoyment of the
fruits of labor by the individual who produces them."
And he refers me to a paragraph previously dealt with
by me as an illustration of contradictory statement, in
which he and his cosignatories write : "Do any say
we attack private property? We deny it. We only
attack that private property for a few thousand loiterers
and slave-drivers, which renders all property in the
fruits of their own labor impossible for millions. We
challenge that private property which renders poverty
at once a necessity and a crime." But surely this flatly
contradicts the declaration by Mr. Hyndman in the
debate, of "the collective ownership of land, capital,
machinery, and credit." I am afraid that Mr. Joynes
has in his mind some other unexplained meaning for
the words "capital" and "property." To me it seems
impossible that if everything be owned collectively,
anything can be owned individually, separately, and
privately.

Mr. Joynes, however, apparently concedes that it is
true that the private property of "a few thousand
loiterers and slave-drivers" is attacked. Though he
does not in his reply explain who these "few
thousand" are, I find in "The Summary of the Principles of Socialism," signed by Mr. Joynes, that they
are "the capitalist class, the factory owners, the
farmers, the bankers, the brokers, the shopkeepers, and
their hangers-on, the landlords." But these make much

more than a "few thousand." The census returns for England and Wales alone show under the headings professional classes, 647,075 ; commercial classes, 980,128 (and these do not include the ordinary shop-keepers) ; farmers and graziers, 249,907 ; and unoccupied males over twenty, 182,282. Add to these proportional figures for Scotland and Ireland, and it is at once seen how misleading it is to speak of these as a "few thousand." Mr. Joynes disapproves of my "small army of statistics." I object that he and his friends never examine or verify the figures on which they found their allegations. Mr. Joynes says that it is not private property, the fruits of labor, that is attacked by the Socialists, but "private capital, the power to hire laborers." Does that mean that £30 saved by an artisan would not be attacked so long as he kept it useless, but that if he deposited it with a banker who used it in industrial enterprise, or if he invested it in railway shares, it would be forfeited ? If an artisan may, out of the fruits of his labor, buy for £3 and keep as his own a silver watch, why is the £3 to be confiscated when it gets into the hands of the Cheapside or Cornhill watch dealer ?

A property owner is not only a Rothschild, a Baring, or an Overstone, he is that person who has anything whatever beyond that which is necessary for actual existence at the moment. Thus, all savings however moderate ; all household furniture, books, indeed everything but the simplest clothing are property, and the property owners belong to all classes. The wage-earning classes, being largely property owners, viz., not only by their household goods, but by their investments, building societies, their small deposits in savings banks, their periodical payments to their trade societies and friendly societies, they would naturally and wisely defend these against confiscation. If the physical force revolution were possible, because of the desperate energy of those owning nothing, its success would be achieved with serious immediate crime, and would be attended with consequent social mischief and terrible demoralisation extending over a long period.

Mr. Hyndman has written that "force, or fear of force, is, unfortunately, the only reasoning which can

appeal to a dominant estate, or will ever induce them
to surrender any portion of their property." I read
these words to him in the debate, and he made no reply
to them. I object that a Socialistic State to be realised
by force can only be so realised after a period of civil
war shocking to contemplate, and one in which the
wisest would go near madness.

But a Socialistic State, even if achieved, could not be
maintained without a second (mental) revolution, in
which the present ideas and forms of expression concerning property would have to be effaced, and the
habit of life (resulting from long-continued teachings
and long-enduring traditions) would have to be broken.
The words " my house," " my coat," " my horse," " my
watch," " my book," are all affirmations of private property which would have to be unlearned. The whole
current of human thought would have to be changed.

In a Socialistic State there would be no inducement
to thrift, no encouragement to individual saving,
no protection for individual accumulation, no check
upon, no discouragement to waste.

Nor, if such a Socialistic State be established, is it
easy to conceive how free expression of individual
opinion, either by press or platform, can be preserved
and maintained. All means of publicity will belong
to, and be controlled by, the State. But what will this
mean? Will a Socialistic government furnish halls to
its adversaries, print books for its opponents, organise
costly journals for those who are hostile to it? If not,
there must come utter stagnation of opinion.

And what could the organisation and controlling of
all labor by the State mean? In what could it end?
By whom, and in what manner, would the selection of
each individual for the pursuit, profession, or handicraft for which he was fittest be determined?

I object that the Socialistic advocates exaggerate and
distort real evils, and thus do mischief to those who
are seeking to effect social reforms. For example, they
declare that the whole of the land of the country is
held by " a handful of marauders," who ought to be
dispossessed, and when told that there are 852,438
persons owning on an average less than one fifth of an
acre each, holding probably in the neighborhood of

towns, and that more than half a million of these persons are members of building societies, paying for their small properties out of their wage-earnings, they only say : "Do you suppose those who hold building allotments will be dispossessed ?" But if they are not dispossessed, if their private property is left to them, then "collective ownership" must have a new meaning. Pressed with the fact that there are 205,358 owning on an average fifteen acres each, they make no other answer. Yet this 1,037,896, representing with their families more than four millions of human beings, are clearly not a "handful," nor is there any evidence offered that they are "marauders." My complaint is that the possibility of early Land Law Reform is injured and retarded by such rashness. It is an undoubted evil that in this crowded kingdom so few as 2,238 persons should own 39,924,232 acres of land, and that the enormous holdings should be inadequately taxed, but we need the influence of the one million small landowners to enable us legally to reform and modify those obnoxious land laws which have facilitated the accumulation of such vast estates in so few hands. In the debate with myself, Mr. Hyndman spoke very contemptuously of the "small ownerships" and "paltry building allotments," yet he ought to know that the holders of these houses are law-abiding, peace-promoting citizens, who are encouraged by these slight possessions, which give promise of comfort in life, to strive so that the comfort shall be extended and secured.

A sample of the wild and extraordinary exaggeration indulged in by the Democratic Federation may be. found on p. 48 of the "Summary of the Principles of Socialism," where it is gravely declared that the "idlers who eat enormously and produce not at all form the majority of the population," and this may be fairly contrasted with another statement by the same persons that the present conditions of labor have "brought luxury for the few, misery and degradation for the many." If the latter be accurate, the former must be a perversion.

The Socialists say that there are a few thousand persons who own the National Debt, and they recommend its extinction ; usually leaving it in doubt as to whether this is to be by wholesale or by partial repudiation. When reminded that there are an enormous number of small depositors (at least 4,500,000 accounts in one year) owning through the ordinary savings banks £45,403,569, and through the Post Office Savings Bank, £36,194,495, they neither explain the allegation as to the few thousands, nor do they condescend to offer the slightest explanation as to how any savings have been possible if all the wealth created by labor has been " devoured only by the rich and their hangers-on." Repudiation of the National Debt would ruin the whole of these. The Socialist leader says that the small ownership of land and these small savings do not really benefit the working classes, for that in times of depression the savings are soon used up. That may often be true, but if there were no savings, then it must be starvation, pauperism, or crime ; at least the saving mitigates the suffering. When told that there are 2,300,000 members of friendly societies, who must represent at least 9,000,000 of the inhabitants of this country, and that these, amongst other investments, have £1,397,730 in the National Debt, we are answered that these are mere details. On this point I think Mr. Joynes a little fails in candor. He takes one set of my figures, and says " the share of each individual is on the average a little more than £3 3s., and the dividend which annually accrues to each of these propertied persons is slightly over 2s. It does not require a very high standard of intelligence to enable a man to perceive that Socialists who intend to deprive him of these 2s., and at the same time to secure him the full value of his work, are proposing not to diminish his income, but to raise it in a very high degree." Let me first say that the friendly society represents to each artisan investor, not the 2s. per year, but his possible sick money, gratuity on disablement, allowance whilst unemployed, etc. ; next, that here Mr. Joynes does in this actually admit an attack on the private property of the laborer, and does propose to take away the accumulated " fruits of labor " from the independent enjoyment of the individual who earned it. And the working-man's house ? and his savings in the savings-bank, or in the co-operative store? Are these to be taken too? If not, why not? and if yes, of how much of the fruits of his labor is the laborer to be left by the Socialists in "independent enjoyment"? When pressed that the confiscation of the railways "without compensation," would bankrupt every life assurance company, and thus destroy the provision made for hundreds of thousands of families, because in addition to about £5,262,000 in the Funds, and about £75,000,000 invested on mortgages of houses and land, the life insurance companies are extensive holders of railway securities—the advocates of Socialism only condescend to say: "Who are the shareholders in the railways? Do they ever do any good in the world? They are simply using the labor of the dead in order to get the labor of the living." But is this true? The shareholders originally found the means to plan, legalise, and construct the railway, to buy the land, to pay the laborer day by day his wage, whilst yet the railway could bring no profit, to buy the materials for the permanent way, to purchase and maintain the rolling stock. Many hundreds of shareholders in unsuccessful lines have never received back one farthing of what they paid to the laborer. No laborer worked on those unsuccessful lines without wage. Some railway shareholders have got too much, but there are thousands of comparatively poor shareholders who are to be ruined by the seizure of their shares without compensation. It is not at all true that railway shareholders use "the labor of the dead in order to get the labor of the living." On the contrary, during the last few years the tendency on lines like the Midland, has been to afford the widest facilities, and the greatest possible comfort consistent with cheapness, to working-folk travelling for need or pleasure. That all railway managers are not equally far-seeing is true, that much more might be done in this direction is certain, that some managing directors are over-greedy is clear, but that the change has been for the better during the past twenty years none would deny who had any regard for truth. That railway porters, pointsmen, guards, firemen, and drivers are, as Mr. Joynes well urges, often badly paid, and nearly always overworked, is true, but

making the railways State property would not necessarily improve this. The Post Office is controlled by
the State for the State, and the letter-carriers and
sorters are as a body disgracefully remunerated.

Mr. Joynes complains that I have not met the question of the "surplus value" of labor, which he says "is
the keystone of the Socialistic argument." He does
not explain upon what basis the alleged surplus value
is calculated, but shelters himself behind a vague,
and I submit incorrect, reference to a declaration
by Mr. Hoyle, the well-known earnest temperance advocate. Mr. Joynes says that in one and a-half hours
the laborer earns enough for subsistence. Mr. Hoyle's
often-repeated declaration is in substance to the effect,
that if the whole drink traffic of the country were
abolished, and neither wines, beers, nor spirits drunk
by any of the industrial classes, then that the working
men could earn enough for comfort in very much less
time than they now do. Mr. Joynes here entirely
overlooks the substance of Mr. Hoyle's declaration,
which is, in effect, that the working men do now receive, and then spend wastefully, what would keep
them. I have always contended that in nearly every
department of industry labor has been insufficiently paid,
in some cases horribly paid, and I have claimed for
the laborer higher wages, and tried to help to teach
him, through trades' unions and otherwise, how to get
these higher wages ; but if Mr. Joynes and his friends
mean anything, wages are to disappear altogether, and
the State is to apportion to each a sort of equal subsistence, without regard to the skill or industry of the
individual laborer, so that the skilled engineer, the unskilled hod-carrier, the street sweeper, the ploughman,
and the physician, would each, in the Socialistic State,
have neither less nor more than the other.

The Socialists say "the laborers on the average replace the value of their wages for the capitalist class
in the first few hours of their day's work ; the exchange value of the goods produced in the remaining
hours of the day's work constitutes so much embodied
labor which is unpaid ; and this unpaid labor so embodied in articles of utility, the capitalist class, the
factory owners, the farmers, the bankers, the brokers,

the shopkeepers, and their hangers-on, the landlords, divide amongst themselves in the shape of profits, interests, discounts, commissions, rent, etc." But without the capitalist where would be the workshop, the plant, or the raw material? It would be better if in co-operative production workmen would be their own capitalists, but surely the owner of capital is entitled to some reward? If not how is he to be persuaded to put it into fixed capital as factory and plant? Why should he beforehand purchase raw material on which labor may be employed, subsist labor while so employed, and take the risk of loss as well as profit in exchanging the article produced? And why is not the farmer to be sustained by the laborers if that farmer grows the food the laborer requires? Why should not the shopkeeper be rewarded for bringing ready to the laborer articles which would be otherwise in the highest degree difficult to procure? If the laborer procured his own raw material, fashioned it into an exchangeable commodity, and then went and exchanged it, there are many to whom the raw material would be inaccessible, and more who would lose much of the profits of their labor in fruitless efforts to exchange. The vague declarations by the Socialist that production and exchange are to be organised are delusive without clear statement of the methods and principles of the organisation. Robert Owen is called "Utopian" by these Democratic Federation Socialists, but at least he did try to reduce to practice his theories of production and exchange. The Democratic Federation say that "surplus value" is produced by "labor applied to natural objects under the control of the capitalist class." I object that but for capital, fixed and circulating, there are many natural objects which would be utterly inaccessible to labor; many more which could only be reached and dealt with on a very limited scale. That but for capital the laborer would often be unable to exist until the object had exchangeable value, or until some one was found with an equivalent article ready to exchange, and I submit that the banker, the shopkeeper, the broker may and do facilitate the progress of labor, and would and could not do so without the incentive of profit.

We agree that "wage" is often much too low, and we urge the workers in each trade to join the unions already existing, and to form new unions, so that the combined knowledge and protection of the general body of workers as to the demand for, and value of, the labor, may be at the service of the weakest and most ignorant. We would advocate the establishment of labor bureaux, as in Massachusetts, so that careful and reliable statistics of the value of labor and cost of life may be easily accessible. We would urge the more thorough experiment on, and establishment of, co-operative productive societies in every branch of manufacture, so that the laborers furnishing their own capital and their own industry, may not only increase the profit result of labor to the laborer, but also afford at least a reasonable indication as to the possible profit realised by capitalists engaged in the same industries. We would increase wage (if not in amount, at any rate in its purchasing power), by diminishing the national and local expenditure, and thus also decreasing the cost of the necessaries of life. We would try to shift the pressing burden of taxation more on to land, and to the very large accumulation of wealth.

We contend that he or she who lives by the sale of labor should, with the purchase money, be able to buy life, not only for the worker, but for those for whom that worker is fairly bread-winner. And life means not only healthy food, reasonable clothing, cleanly, healthy shelter, education for the children until they are so sufficiently grown that labor shall not mean the crippling of after life—but also leisure. Leisure for some enjoyment, leisure for some stroll in the green fields, leisure for some look into the galleries of paintings and sculpture, leisure for some listening to the singer, the actor, the teacher; leisure that the sunshine of beauty may now and then gild the dull round of work-a-day life; and we assert that in any country where the price of honest earnest industry will not buy this, then that if there are any in that country who are very wealthy, there is social wrong to be reformed. But this is the distinction between those with whom I stand and the Socialists.

We want reform, gradual, sure, and helpful. They ask for revolution, and know not its morrow.

Revolution may be the only remedy in a country where there is no free press, no free speech, no asso-- ciation of workers, no representative institutions, and where the limits of despotic outrage are only marked by the personal fear of the despot. But in a country like our own, where the political power is gradually passing into the hands of the whole people, where, if the press is not entirely free it is in advance of almost every European country, and every shade of opinion may find its exponent, here revolution which required physical force to effect it would be a blunder as well as a crime. Here, where our workmen can organise and meet, we can claim reforms and win them. The wage-winners of Durham and Northumberland, under the guidance of able and earnest leaders, have won many ameliorations during the past twenty years. Each year the workers' Parliament meets in Trades Union Congress, to discuss and plan more complete success, and to note the gains of the year. Every twelve months, in the Co-operative Congresses, working men and women delegates gather together to consult and advise. Each annual period shows some progress, some advantage secured, and though there is much sore evil yet, much misery yet, much crime yet, much—far too much—poverty yet, to-day's progress from yesterday shows day-gleam for the people's morrow.

Printed by ANNIE BESANT and CHARLES BRADLAUGH, at 63, Fleet Street, London, E.C.—1884.

SOCIALISM:

ITS FALLACIES AND DANGERS.

BY

CHARLES BRADLAUGH.

[Reprinted from the "North American Review", January, 1887.]

LONDON:
FREETHOUGHT PUBLISHING COMPANY,
63, FLEET STREET, E.C.
1887.
—
PRICE TWOPENCE.

LONDON:

PRINTED BY ANNIE BESANT AND CHARLES BRADLAUGH,
63, FLEET STREET, E.C.

SOCIALISM:

ITS FALLACIES AND DANGERS.

THERE are so many grades and shades of diverse opinion loosely included in and attacked or defended as Socialism, that it is necessary to briefly make clear what it is that I attack in this paper. I understand and define Socialism as denying all individual private property, and as affirming that society, organised as the State, should own all wealth, direct all labor, and compel the equal distribution of all produce. I understand a Socialistic State to be that State in which everything would be common as to its user, and in which all labor would be controlled by the State, which, from the common stock, would maintain the laborer and would take all the produce of the labor. That is, I identify Socialism with Communism.

In England this definition, though admitted by some Socialist writers and speakers, is challenged by many honest, earnest Socialists, whose objections are entitled to respect; but, the more carefully I examine their several positions, the more thoroughly I am disposed to adhere to the above definition. Many who describe themselves as Socialists I should describe as social reformers, and with them I have little or no quarrel. There are some who attempt to explain Socialism so as to distinguish it from Communism. "Socialism", says Mrs. Besant, "merely implies that the raw material of the soil and the means of production shall not be the private property of individuals, but shall be under the control of the community; it leaves intact a man's control over himself and over the value of his work—subject to such general laws as are necessary in any community—but, by socialising land and capital, it deprives each of the power of enslaving his fellows and of living in idleness on the results of their labor instead of on the result of his own" ("Modern Socialism", p. 10). A great deal in this sentence turns on what is meant by "means of production". Does it, at the same time, include the rudest implement, the huge iron works and plant, and the most minute, delicate, and costly tools? Does it mean that in every-day life each citizen has equal right to require the State to place at her or his sole disposal, uncontrolled, and for such period as the worker may please, such "raw material" and "means of production" as the worker is of opinion are necessary to enable him to get the best value for his labor? If yes, where is the control of the means of production by the community? If no, how can the scheme leave intact a man's control over himself, and over the value of his work? How is the wilful damage or the deterioration of the means of production, by an incapable worker, to be guarded against? How is the abandonment of a difficult industry to be prevented? How are the instruments of production to be obtained by the laborer, and on what conditions, and under what security that they will be surrendered to, and kept in good condition for, the State? and if three laborers

require instruments of production of a kind of which there
only exists sufficient for two laborers, what is to happen?
How is the State, in furnishing the raw material and
means of production, to determine between a man who
thinks he can manufacture a medicine; one who believes
that he can make a watch; one who hopes that he can
execute a marble statue; one who is confident that he can
make a microscope; one who is sure that he can build an
aërial ship; one who guesses that he can find coal in an
untried district; and one who thinks that he can fill a tub
of coal or wagon of ironstone by means of a shaft
already sunken? Is the determination to be made by
authorities locally chosen to act in such localities or
nationally chosen to act for the whole country? and how
will it be possible to avoid favoritism between hard and
easy fashions of labor? If the State leaves intact a man's
control over himself, this determination is impossible.

Whoever, on behalf of the State, is guardian of the raw
material and means of production, must either in each case
determine the kind of labor for which the man or woman
is best fitted, or he must allot, first come first served, without reference to fitness. If all raw material is to be the
property of the State, may the person who has, in the process of manufacture, added value to some portion, take the
whole of that portion away to a foreign market where he
believes the highest value will be obtainable for it and for
his work upon it? If yes, how is the State to be sure that
the value of its raw material will ever come back? If the
State is to control the sale of the finished article, where is
the worker's intact control of the value of his work? Mr.
Hyndman says: "Socialism is an endeavor to substitute for
the anarchical struggle or fight for existence an organised

co-operation for existence ".[1] I note on this that while
the struggle for existence has been clearly far too bitter,
not only as between employer and employed, but also as
between the workers themselves, and has certainly been
most oppressive on the poorest and weakest, " anarchical "
is an absurd word of description, and that the vitality of
the whole definition depends on the translation of the
words " organised co-operation ". Voluntary co-operation
is organised co-operation determinable by the will of each
co-operator, as far as he or she is concerned, and subject
to the conditions agreed to as to such withdrawal, but this
clearly is not what is meant by Mr. Hyndman. When in
debate I pressed for an explanation, it was refused, and
Mr. J. L. Joynes, a prominent Socialist and one of the best
educated among them, wrote in rebuke of my demand that
" no ' scientific ' Socialist pretends to have any scheme or
detailed plan of organisation ". They only pretend to
desire to destroy existing society because of its evils ; to-
morrow may grow, if and how it can, without the slightest
precaution against the development of a worse state.
What Mr. Hyndman meant by anarchy he thus explained :
" There is many a man who works as a skilled laborer
to-day who, if a machine is invented whereby man may
benefit, will be turned out to compete against his fellows
on the streets to-morrow. That is what I say is anarchy."
And as the cure for this he asked for " the collective
ownership of land, capital, machinery, and credit by the
complete ownership of the people ". As to labor-saving
machinery, or cost-reducing machinery, or produce-in-

---

[1] All the quotations from Mr. Hyndman are from the debate with
myself : " Will Socialism benefit the English People ? "

creasing machinery, it is true that as each new invention
is introduced, the introduction very often renders it necessary that persons who have pursued one method of earning
their livelihood shall adopt new methods, and there is often
difficulty in finding new employment. If the worker is
advanced in life, it is very difficult for him to adapt himself to other labor.   But it is not true that the introduction
has permanently reduced the number of workers in the
country where most machinery is used, nor is it true that
the rate of pauperism has, on the whole, increased in the
countries where the most machinery has been introduced.
Mr. Hyndman's definition means Communism, or it means
nothing. If the collective ownership of everything by
everybody is not the total negation of private property,
then words have no value.

Many so-called socialistic experiments have been tried
in various parts of the world, but none of these have yet
been permanently successful. Such as have seemed temporarily to achieve a certain measure of success have been
held together : (1) By some religious or quasi-religious
tie, and those have in turn broken up when the effect of
the tie has weakened ; or (2) by personal devotion to
some one man, and these have broken up when the man
has died or grown weary ; or (3) while directed by some
strong chief or chiefs, and holding together only so long
as the direction endured. And even the temporary success
has only been maintained whilst the community were few
in number. Whenever an apparent success tempted many
recruits, then the experiment collapsed, and this because,
whilst the members in the community were limited, the
individual members of the community did not lose sight
of the personal advantages accruing from their individual

exertions. Each small community held its own property hostile to, or, at least, clearly distinguishable from, the property of other individuals, or communities, dwelling near. Every individual of the so-called socialistic community could estimate the addition to the common stock, the owners of which were so limited in number that he could calculate his share of the increased wealth. The incentive to increased exertion was constant in the hope of increased well-being, and in some of the communities the individual members had and often exercised an option of withdrawal, taking away with them on leaving a proportion of the property created or increased. But none of the communistic experiments, either in the United States or in this country, have been more than large co-operative enterprises, the property of the adventurers belonging to the corporate body. And there is little doubt that these experiments have done something to produce— as in the case of the Familistère of M. Godin—some modifications of the more unpleasant side of the fiercely competitive struggle for existence, and that they did pave the way, at any rate in England, for the co-operative institutions, which for exchange and distribution have already been eminently successful. And though co-operative enterprises for production have yet done comparatively little, it is in this direction that I look for the utilisation of the best in modern socialistic energy.

Modern Socialism is more ambitious of exercising State authority, and is therefore more dangerous than was the Socialism of fifty years ago. The Socialism of Owen, Cabet, and Frances Wright, was the experiment, in each case of a few, in their own persons, at their own risk and cost, patiently conducted, and, even in failure, giving

example of great devotion and much self-reliant effort.
Modern Socialists claim to experiment with the State as
a whole, and without waiting even to convert the majority.
Modern Socialism appeals to the poorest and most hungry
to break up all accumulated wealth. It works chiefly by
denunciations of the rich and well-fed. It has no patience
to gradually build up a new system. It regards reform
as its enemy. It proposes to begin by destroying the
existing state of things. Unfortunately, the social evils
in all old countries are great and sore, but if they are to
be diminished they must be reformed in detail: there is
no magic four-leaved shamrock at the disposal of the
reformer. The worst and most mischievous advocates of
Socialism are those who justify and encourage the unemployed in the use of force—and especially of the terrible
phase of force revealed by modern chemistry, as an agent
in changing the present state of society. In some countries
Socialists call themselves "Anarchists", repudiating alike
all law, rejecting all directing government; in other countries
they call themselves "Social Democrats", and call upon
the State to feed, clothe, and employ those who are ill fed,
badly clothed, or lack employment. These Socialists are
the real enemies of progress, they afford excuse to those
who desire reaction. The State can give the people neither
food, nor clothing, nor work, save to the extent that, and as,
the citizens themselves provide the State with the means
to do these things. If the State is to do for each individual that which the individual is unable to do for himself,
then if it be done at all it can only be done by a despotism.
State Socialism is utterly at variance with individual
liberty; it is totally hostile to the institutions of a free
democracy.

Great publicity has been recently obtained in England, and chiefly in London, for a comparatively small knot of men, styling themselves "Social Democrats", and also describing themselves as "Scientific Socialists", some of whom give us ill-digested versions of German Socialism. They have, like the Salvation Army, been chiefly prominent in holding meetings, to the detriment of traffic, in inconvenient places, whilst convenient places were disregarded by them. By these means they have brought on their heads several police prosecutions, which prosecutions had the color of unfairness, as being directed against hysteric Socialism, while hysteric Salvation-Armyism escaped scot free. They have also succeeded in provoking a criminal prosecution by the use of language which, if it had any meaning, was in the highest degree inflammatory and exciting, but which language was held not to be connected with or intended to provoke the riotous results which which followed its use. These men have, however, neither the influence nor the devotedness of the men who preached and practised experimental Socialism under Robert Owen from 1817, and who, fifty years ago, were stirring the whole of the midland and northern counties of England, holding great meetings and establishing scores of halls and institutions in the northern towns. The new Social Democrats, while calling loudly for the dissolution of the present social state, deny that they ought to be called upon to produce or formulate any scheme for the government of the society which is to follow the revolution they acclaim, and they refuse to discuss any of the details of life in the proposed new social state; though they profess at once to be ready by force, argument failing, to destroy what exists in order to make way for what they desire. Mr.

Hyndman, professing to be a leader of the Social Democrats, declares that "force, or fear of force, is unfortunately
the only reasoning which can appeal to a dominant estate,
or which will even induce them to surrender any portion
of their property". A Socialist State, if it could be
realised by force, which I do not believe, could only so be
realised after a shocking and murderous civil war; a war
which, however it ended, would leave, for more than one
generation, legacies of bitter hate and of demoralising
desire for revenge.

The Social Democrats mix up in their programme some
desirable objects which are not at all Socialistic with others
that are not necessarily Socialistic. They then add declarations conflicting in character, which are either so vague
as to be meaningless, or are else in the highest degree
communistic and revolutionary. They call for the "organisation of agricultural and industrial armies under State
control", and claim "that the exchange of all production
should be controlled by the workers"; but they decline to
explain how this is to be done, or to meet detail objections
urged against the feasibility of the proposals. All labor
under State control means the utter stagnation of special
industrial effort; the neutralisation of almost all industrial
enterprise; the stoppage of the most efficient incentive to
inventive initiative. What can the organisation and control of all labor by the State mean? In what would it
end? By whom and in what manner would the selection
of each individual be determined for the pursuit, profession, or handicraft, for which he was deemed fittest?
Would resistance or refusal on the part of any individual
to perform the labor for which he had been selected be
treated as crime? Would preference for any other kind

of labor than that allotted be allowed? I am told that thus I am raising undue difficulties, but I want at least to know how the new State machine will work before I consent to suddenly break up the old one. That there are many evils in connexion with exchange and distribution is true. In many departments there are too many concerned in the distribution of the necessaries of life, as brokers, merchants, and retailers, and the cost to the consumer is thus unnecessarily and outrageously augmented. But this can be cured by the gradual extension of the co-operative distributive institutions and stores which have already proved so useful. These co-operative societies, whilst rendering the cost of exchange less onerous and otherwise improving its character, also encourage habits of thrift and self-reliant effort on the part of the individual members. In a Socialistic State there would be no inducement to thrift; no encouragement to, no reward for, individual saving; no protection for individual accumulation; no check upon, no discouragement to, individual waste. If the establishment of a Socialistic State be conceived possible, it is certainly not possible to imagine such a State co-existing with free expression of individual opinion, either on platform or through the press. All means of publicity in a Socialistic State will belong to and will be controlled by the State. It is not conceivable that a Socialistic government would provide halls for its adversaries to agitate for its overthrow, print books and pamphlets for its opponents to show that its methods and actions were mischievous; organise costly journals and give the conduct to hostile men to excite public feeling—and yet, if all this were not done, utter stagnation of opinion is the only possible result. The "Social Democrats"

urge that the "surplus value" of labor is "the keystone of
the Socialistic argument". They say: "The laborers, on
the average, replace the value of their wages for the
capitalist class in the first few hours of their day's work;
the exchange value of the goods produced in the remaining
hours of the day's work constitutes so much embodied
labor which is unpaid; and this unpaid labor, so embodied
in articles of utility, the capitalist class, the factory owners,
the farmers, the bankers, the brokers, the shopkeepers and
their hangers-on, the landlords, divide amongst themselves
in the shape of profits, interests, discounts, commissions,
rent, etc." Is it at all true that wages and other outlay by
the capitalist are replaced in the first few hours? Are not
the large fortunes more usually the result of exploitation on
a very large scale, a small daily profit being secured on
each workman? And, without the capitalist, where would
be the workshop, the plant, or the raw material? It would
be far better if, in co-operative production, workmen would
be their own capitalists; but surely the owner of the
capital, without which the exploitation cannot take place,
is entitled to some reward. If not, what becomes of the first
inducement to economy and enterprise? How is the
capitalist to be persuaded to put his savings into fixed
capital as factory and plant? Why should he, beforehand,
purchase raw material on which labor may be employed,
and the value of which raw material may diminish? Why
should he subsist labor while so employed, and take the
risk of loss in exchanging the article produced, unless he
is to have some profit? And why should not the farmer
be sustained by the laborer, if that farmer grows the food
on which he subsists while working? Why should not the
shopkeeper be rewarded for bringing ready to the laborer

articles which would be otherwise difficult in the highest degree for the laborer to procure? If the laborer was obliged to procure his own raw material, to fashion it into an exchangeable commodity, and then had to find the person with whom he might exchange it, there are many to whom the raw material would be inaccessible, and more would lose much of the profits of their labor in fruitless efforts to exchange. But for capital, fixed and circulating, there are many natural objects which would be utterly inaccessible to labor; many more which could only be reached and dealt with on a very limited scale. But for capital, the laborer would be often unable to exist until the object had an exchangeable value, or until someone was found ready with an equivalent article and desiring to exchange, and the banker, the broker, the shopkeeper, though they are, unfortunately, sometimes too greedy for gain, may and do facilitate the progress of labor, and would not and could not do so without the incentive of profit.

It is too true that "wage" is often much too low, and that the conditions of labor are often oppressive, and to meet this I urge the workers in each trade to join the unions already existing and to form new unions, so that the combined knowledge and protection of the general body of workers may be at the service of the weakest and most ignorant. It is for this that I obtained from the House of Commons last February the establishment of a labor statistical department under the Board of Trade, so that careful and reliable statistics of the value of labor and cost of living may be easily accessible to the poorest laborers. I would further urge the more thorough experiment in, and establishment of, co-operative productive societies in every branch of manufacture, so that the laborers, directly furnishing their own capital, as well as their own industry, may not only increase the profit result of labor to the laborer, but may also afford at least a reasonable indication of the possible profit realised by capitalists engaged in the same kind of industries. I would also increase wage (if not in amount, at any rate in its purchasing power) by diminishing the national and local expenditure, especially the national expenditure for warlike purposes, thus decreasing the cost of the necessaries of life. I would, so far as Great Britain is concerned, try to shift the pressing burden of taxation from labor more on to land, and on to the very large inherited accumulations of wealth.

Socialism is dangerous in England, because it claims to be revolutionary in an age and in a country where the most extensive reforms have been peacefully effected during the past fifty years, and where the enormously wide extension of political power gives opportunity for the acceleration of the many reforms yet required. Socialism is dangerous here, for its present advocacy is hysterical not practical. While I do not believe that Socialism can make the revolution its advocates menace, I do believe it may make disorder, turmoil, riot, and disturbance. Socialism, as advocated by the Social Democrats, is especially dangerous because it furnishes excuse to reaction, and gives occasion for the possible restriction of the right of public meeting; a right which has so much aided political progress in this country during the present century. I may, perhaps, be permitted to terminate this article by repeating, with very slight variation, the words I used on April 17th, 1884, at the close of my debate with Mr. H. M. Hyndman, the elected representative of the Social Democratic Federation, at which debate fully 5,000 persons were present.

You say you desire revolution—you say you are clamoring for it. These are the words you use. You say: "We are urging it on"; and I say it is the duty of every honest man to delay and prevent revolution. Revolution, if it must come, is terrible; if it must come, it is horrible. Revolution means ruined homes; it leaves behind the memory of bloody deeds. I speak for the English people, who through generations of pain and toil gradually have climbed towards liberty, the liberty of which they have won some glimpses, and towards which they are climbing still. I speak for the people—who are ready to suffer much if they may redeem somewhat; who know that the errors of yesterday cannot be sponged away in a moment to-day; and who would try slowly, gradually, to mould, to modify, to build, but who refuse to destroy, and who declare that those who preach international Socialism, and talk vaguely about explosives, are playing into the hands of our enemies, and giving our enemies an excuse to coerce us.

Socialism:

FOR AND AGAINST.

BY

CHARLES BRADLAUGH AND ANNIE BESANT.

LONDON

FREETHOUGHT PUBLISHING COMPANY,

63, FLEET STREET, E.C.

1887.

PRICE FOURPENCE.

LONDON:
PRINTED BY ANNIE BESANT AND CHARLES BRADLAUGH,
63, FLEET STREET, E.C.

SOCIALISM: FOR AND AGAINST.

◆

SOCIALISM: ITS FALLACIES AND DANGERS.

My greatest difficulty in treating this subject is in discovering any general agreement as to what is now meant in England by the word "Socialism". There are so many grades and shades of diverse opinion loosely included in, and attacked, or defended, as Socialism, that—in default of any authoritative, or official, or even generally accepted definition—I will at any rate make clear what it is that I attack as Socialism, and will endeavor at least to show that even if I am in error, I have been misled by Socialist writers, and have not invented the definition, or arbitrarily framed a formula, or built up a man of straw, for the mere purpose of attack. I understand and define Socialism as (1) denying, or destroying, all individual private property; and (2) as affirming that Society organised as the State should own all wealth, direct all labor, and compel the equal distribution of all produce. I understand a Socialistic State to be (3) that State in which everything would be common as to its user, and in which all labor would be controlled by the State, which from the common stock would maintain the laborer, and would take all the produce of the labor. That is (4), I identify Socialism with Communism.

This was substantially the definition of Socialism put forward by me in the debate with Mr. Hyndman[1] (pp. 14, 15), and as I then reminded him (p. 37) my definition was

---

[1] "Will Socialism Benefit the English People?"

never denied, and though language sometimes inconsistent with it was used, no other definition was put in its place. The point that Socialism "denies all individual private property" was referred to in that debate by Mr. Hyndman (p. 23), but so far from repudiating the doctrine, he justified it as to the moneys in savings banks and "paltry building allotments" (p. 24). Mr. J. L. Joynes clearly includes in his view of Socialism the cancelment of all private interest in the National Debt, for, having calculated the average share therein of the 2,309,225 members of Friendly Societies, at 2s. per head, he justifies the confiscation of this private property on the ground that "It does not require a very high standard of intelligence to enable a man to perceive that Socialists, who intend to deprive him of these 2s., and at the same time to secure to him the full value of his work, are proposing, not to diminish his income, but, on the contrary, to raise it in a very high degree" (*Our Corner*, 1884, vol. iii., p. 335). Believing Mr. Joynes to be an earnest, truthful man, it is difficult to quite understand how he confined himself to this illustration of confiscation out of the many similar ones presented to his notice, and which I propose to carefully re-state in the course of this paper. Messrs. William Morris and E. Belfort Bax say: "The land, the capital, the machinery, factories, workshops, stores, means of transit, mines, banking, all means of production and distribution of wealth, must be declared and treated as the common property of all" ("Manifesto of the Socialist League", p. 6); and that there may be no misapprehension as to what this means Mr. Bax writes: "That for which the working classes have to strive is nothing less than for Communism or a collectivist Socialism, understanding by this the assumption by the people, in other words the concentration in the hands of a democratic State, of land, raw material, instruments of production, funded capital, etc." ("Religion of Socialism", p. 78); and, again, the same writer says: "Socialism has been well described as a new conception of the world presenting itself in industry as co-operative Communism" (p. 81). It is true that Messrs. Hyndman, Morris, and Joynes say, denying that they are rightfully charged with attacking private property, "We only attack that private property for a few thousand loiterers and slave drivers, which renders all property in the fruit of their own labor impossible for millions" ("Socialism Made Plain", p. 7); but it is also true that Messrs. Hyndman, Morris, Bax, and Joynes declare that "idlers who eat enormously and produce not at all form the majority of the population" ("Principles of Socialism", p. 48), so that it would be at any rate the private property of the majority they attack. Prince Kropotkin, who is advertised in England as a Socialist publicist, puts the case in its harshest form: "A feeble minority lays claim to the bulk of the national wealth, has town and country houses built for itself, and accumulates in banks the coin, notes, and documents of all sorts which represent the wealth produced by labor. All this we must seize, and by one and the same blow we shall set free the unhappy peasant whose plot of ground is burdened by a mortgage, the small shopkeeper who lives in constant dread of bankruptcy, and a wretched crowd of persons who have not bread enough for the morrow" ("Expropriation", p. 5). "We must clearly see that private property is a conscious or an unconscious theft of that which belongs to all, and we must be prepared to seize all with alacrity for the common use and benefit" (p. 7). Mr. H. H. Sparling, a prominent writer in the *Commonweal*—which journal is described as "the official organ of the Socialist League"—says in the number for January, 1887:

"Under Socialism all things necessary to the production of wealth will be held and possessed in common; there will be no special prerogative to one or to the other whereby he may take or claim for himself the benefit accruing from any work done for the community; private property will have perished, and with it the power of extorting a revenue from those desiring access to any of the means of life."

And again, in the same article,

"Under Socialism, where each would produce as well as consume, the accumulation would be enormously magnified, but the resultant mass of wealth would be held socially for common objects, and no longer individually for personal profit."

Some of the English Socialists claim to base their theories more or less directly upon the doctrines of Karl Marx, yet the manifesto which he issued conjointly with Engels in 1847 was expressly Communistic. There is one passage of it which has been often quoted: "The Communists scorn to conceal their views and purposes. They declare openly that their aims can be attained only by a violent overthrow of the existing social order. Let the ruling classes tremble before a Communistic Revolution."

And the use of force is contemplated by an editorial writer in *Justice*, No. 157, who says:

" It is for us then to compel the Government by every means in our power—using the argument of words or the argument of force, just as it suits our purpose—to carry into effect these proposals of ours which will necessarily lead to the complete emancipation of the workers."

Whilst my identification of Socialism with Communism is admitted by some Socialist writers and speakers, it is as distinctly and even vehemently repudiated by others, and is clearly challenged by many whose views are entitled to respectful and thorough examination. A careful examination of the various utterances compels me, for reasons I shall set out, to adhere to my own definition. Many who describe themselves as Socialists I should describe as social reformers, and with these I am mostly in sympathy as to the evils they seek to redress, although I cannot accept the methods of remedy they propose. Mrs. Besant —of whose earnest devotion to the movement for alleviating human suffering it is impossible to speak too highly— thinks that she so defines Socialism as to clearly distinguish it from Communism. In her pamphlet " Modern Socialism " she says:

"Communism implies the complete abolition of private property and the supply of the wants of each individual from a common store, without regard to the contributions to that common store which may, or may not, have been made by the individual. Socialism merely implies that the raw material of the soil and the means of production shall not be the private property of individuals, but shall be under the control of the community; it leaves intact a man's control over himself and over the value of his work—subject to such general laws as are necessary in any community — but by socialising land and capital it deprives each of the power of enslaving his fellows and of living in idleness on the results of their labor instead of on the results of his own."

It is right to add that Mrs. Besant says most distinctly that "for man as he is Communism would mean the living of the idle on the toil of the laborious ". It is unfortunate that on her own definition Socialism must—as I think can be made clear—if attempted in practice be Communism, or nothing but conflict and incoherence. It is clear, according to Mrs. Besant, that Socialism denies private property in land and capital. She defines capital as the accumulated unconsumed result of labor applied to raw material if devoted to purposes of profit. She endeavors to separate and distinguish capital from wealth. Wealth with her is the accumulated unconsumed result of labor applied to raw material, so long as it is not attempted to utilise such result for profit. Mrs. Besant would preserve private property in " wealth " in the hands of the laborer who created it. I do not think continuance of such private property possible under the terms of her own definition. There are many conceivable cases in which the surplus result of labor may fairly be reckoned as "means of production ", and would then forthwith cease to be the private property of the laborer. It is clear that the " wealth " admitted to be private property would often be susceptible of user as " capital ", and would then only remain private property while not utilised for increase.

The " wealth " which continued private property, whilst unproductive to anyone, would if converted, say, into the plant of a newspaper printing office, cease to be private property. There are some so-called Socialists, though I am not sure if Mrs. Besant would include herself with these, who would permit the ownership, as private property, of such wealth as would not enable the owner to avoid personal labor. In this description would come books, pictures, statuary, ornaments, household furniture, etc., though there is difference of opinion as to whether these descriptions of wealth may pass to others as private property by gift, inheritance, or bequest. It would be certainly in conflict with the definition that such chattels could be sold ; as this must open the door to trading for profit, and it is difficult to imagine how any new articles of this kind are ever to be acquired by individuals if trade for profit is forbidden, as it would be when the thing if used for profit reverted to the State. Of course a great deal turns on what is meant by the "means of production " being "under the control of the community ". At present machinery, plant, tools of the roughest and most minute

and delicate character are manufactured, and stored to
await purchasers, at the risk of those who, for possible
profit, wait the convenience of the customer needing each
article; but how is all this to be regulated when the means
of production are under the control of the community?
Under what conditions is the manufacture of means of
production otherwise than for possible profit to be arranged;
and how are such "means of production" to be placed at
the service of the individual worker? Mrs. Besant complains that in our present complex system, a would-be-
laborer "cannot get an instrument of production, and if
he could he would have nothing to use it on; he has
nothing but his labor-force, and he must either sell that
to some one who wants it or he must die". This is not
quite accurate. The laborer, if he would unite in co-operative
combination with other laborers, could now in many departments of industry obtain instruments of production and
many kinds of raw material. It is true that in all kinds of
mining industry the landowner has over-weighted industry
in very many instances with oppressive and almost prohibitive royalties. It is also true that the landlord has
crippled agriculture, and often paralysed manufacture by
rents and restrictive covenants. This may, and I hope
will, be remedied by the legislature. The landowners' so-
called rights are in these cases purely artificial creations.
They are the result of law made by a class legislature, in
which the landed interest was then all-powerful and labor
was then unrepresented. But how under Socialism is the
individual to obtain for his individual use and his individual advantage the means of production and raw
material, both of which are the property of the State?
Does Mrs. Besant mean that in every-day life each citizen
should have equal right to require the local representative
of the State to place at her or his sole and uncontrolled
disposition, and for such period as the worker may please,
such raw material and means of production as the worker
is of opinion may be necessary to enable him to get the
best value for his work? If yes, where is the control of
the means of production by the State? If no, how can
the scheme leave "intact a man's control over himself and
over the value of his work"? Some Socialists certainly
do not intend to "leave intact a man's control over himself", for in the pamphlet entitled "Socialism Made

Plain", signed by Herbert Burrows, H. H. Champion, H. M. Hyndman, and W. Morris, the "organisation of agricultural and industrial armies under State control" is advocated. Either this means that each individual must perform the labor task fixed for him by some State official or officials—much as in the army the soldier obeys his commanding officer—or it means nothing. Returning to Mrs. Besant's definition: How are the several officials having charge of raw material and of means of production to determine each individual's ability to utilise the special means or material demanded? Is the determination to be made by officials locally chosen to act in each locality or nationally chosen to act for the whole country? And how will it be possible to avoid favoritism and injustice in apportioning pleasant and easy employment as against unpleasant and difficult kinds of labor? May a man who thinks that he can make a watch or a delicate and costly machine insist on being furnished with the necessary means and material? How is the wilful damage or deterioration by an incapable worker of the material or means of production entrusted to him to be guarded against? How is the abandonment, involving perhaps enormous loss, of a difficult or unpleasant industry to be prevented? On what conditions, if any, are instruments of production to be furnished to the laborer? If more laborers demand at one time a kind of "means of production" than the State has at its immediate command, how is a selection to be made, and how are the laborers to be maintained who cannot work at the labor they have selected, and who will not work at any other? May the guardian of the means, or of the instruments, select which he shall furnish, or must they go "first come first served", without reference to fitness? In a word, can you have State control of industry and yet leave intact the freedom of the worker? When all raw material is the property of the State, and the added value of labor is the private property of the laborer, may the person who by his labor has added value to some portion take that portion away to a foreign market where he believes the highest value will be obtainable for the manufactured article? If yes, where is the guarantee that the sale value of the raw material will ever come back into this country? If the State is to control the sale of the finished article where is the worker's intact control of the value of his work? It is true that Messrs. Hyndman and Morris say "that exchange of produce should be social too and removed from the control of individual greed and individual profit". But exchange (that is, trade) has to be conducted with many foreign countries, from which we get raw material not producible here, and necessaries of food and medicine not grown within the limits of our own land. How is the great carrying trade of the country to be enterprised when the incitement of possible profit to the trader is erased?

"Socialism," says Mr. Hyndman ("Debate", p. 5), "is an endeavor to substitute for the anarchical struggle or fight for existence an organised co-operation for existence". While it is true that the struggle for existence has been far too bitter not only between employer and employed but also between the workers themselves, the brunt of the struggle being most severe on the poorest and weakest, the word "anarchical" is hardly explanatory as a word of description. The meaning of the definition depends on the translation of the words "organised co-operation". Voluntary co-operation is organised co-operation determinable—subject to the co-operative agreement—at the will of each co-operator, so far as he or she is concerned, but as each co-operator receives profit on his investment as well as his labor, and can withdraw his capital if he be not satisfied, this clearly is not what Mr. Hyndman meant, and when in debate he was pressed for explanation none was given. Mr. Joynes, commenting on this, rebuked the demand on the ground that "no scientific Socialist pretends to have any scheme or detailed plan of organisation". Surely to talk of organisation and yet to have no scheme is to waste words in the air. Mr. Hyndman did explain what he meant by anarchy. "There is, he said, "many a man who works as a skilled laborer to-day who if a machine is invented whereby man may benefit, will be turned out to compete against his fellows on the streets to-morrow. That is what I say is anarchy" ("Debate", p. 7); and he recommended as the cure for this "the collective ownership of land, capital, machinery, and credit by the complete ownership of the people". It is true that the introduction of each new labor-saving invention in machinery does deprive persons of methods of livelihood to which they have become accustomed. It is true that if the individual worker is advanced in life he will have great difficulty in adapting himself to new kinds of skilled employment. But it is not true that the introduction of machinery has permanently reduced the aggregate number of workers in the country where most machinery is used, nor is it true that the ratio of pauperism to population has, on the whole, increased in the countries where most machinery has been introduced. Mr. Hyndman's definition in the end means Communism or it means nothing. If the collective ownership of everything except labor, and the collective control of all the produce of labor for exchange, is not the total negation of private property, then words have no meaning.

Mrs. Besant says that "capital under our present industrial system is the result of unpaid labor". Most certainly this is not true of all capital: such capital as is now in the hands of the wage-paid laborer himself, or has been handed by him to others, can hardly come under this category. The illustrations may be given, say, in the 583,830 members of building societies, owning £52,611,198; 284,976 members of registered trade unions, owning £538,542; 572,610 members of co-operative societies, owning £8,209,722; 46,710 members of registered loan societies, owning £324,281; 1,582,474 savings bank depositors, owning £45,847,887 4s. 3d., this not including the 7,288 depositors in railway savings banks, owning £586,260; [1]2,300,000 members of friendly societies, owning £   ; members of industrial assurance societies registered as limited companies, owning £3,834,709. In the enormous number of small shareholders in home and foreign railways, in banks, in manufacturing concerns, small holders of consolidated stock, owners of small houses or plots of land not included in the building society statistics, small shopkeepers and the like, there must be an addition of capital which has been accumulated by the laborer out of payment received by him for his labor. Nor does the challenge to definition even stop at this point. The tailor sells to the laborer clothing cheaper than the laborer could make it; the clothing is necessary for the laborer; on each article of clothing a small profit is made by the tailor, and on the balance of

---

[1] The last returns are not made up; but the membership is now, I believe, over 2,500,000.

many such transactions, and after deducting the expenses of his business, there is a surplus "capital"; but it might well be that none of this "capital" was the result of unpaid labor. So of the baker, the butcher, the grocer, similar illustrations may be given. Even the capital of the great manufacturer who, employing hundreds or thousands of hands, grows rich in a brief space of years, is not always, or wholly, "the result of unpaid labor". A keen judgment which first utilises a new material as alpaca or alfa, or which initiates a fresh method of dealing with old material, or which discovers a market or employment of produce hitherto overlooked by others, may be rewarded by accumulated capital, which it is scarcely fair to describe as "the result of unpaid labor". Of course, all "wealth" originates with labor on raw material, but all capital is not the value of labor which has never been paid to the laborer.

Mrs. Besant—moved, and very properly moved intensely, by the suffering around her—is a little one-sided even in her coldest presentments. Take as illustration the following, vouched by her as "a statement of the facts as they are": "The worker produces a mass of commodities; the capitalist sells these commodities for what they will fetch in the market; . . . . the capitalist gives over to the producer sufficient of the results of the sale to enable the producer to exist, and pockets the remainder." Now this is not "the facts as they are" at all. The following corrected presentment would, I think, better represent the facts as they are: The worker, aided by the capitalist who furnishes raw material and means of production, produces a mass of commodities, and is paid by the capitalist a sum for his labor which seldom leaves a large margin over subsistence; the capitalist then sells these commodities for what they will fetch, recoups himself thereout for disbursements for raw material, working expenditure, and wages, pockets the remainder, if any, and bears the whole loss if the transaction should be unprofitable.

It is not that Mrs. Besant had herself overlooked the facts here restated; she gives them fairly enough at the top of the previous page of her own pamphlet ("Modern Socialism", p. 15).

CHARLES BRADLAUGH.

SOCIALISM: ITS TRUTHS AND ITS HOPES.

A REPLY.

KNOWING, as I do, that the one aim of my friend and colleague, Charles Bradlaugh, in dealing with the social problem, is to seek the best possible solution of a vexed and difficult question, and knowing also that my own aim is identical with his, I accept the challenge to criticise his paper as frankly as it was given, trusting that the honest speech of two honest thinkers may be useful to the students of Sociology.

The difficulty felt by Mr. Bradlaugh "in discovering any general agreement as to what is now meant in England by 'Socialism'" is a difficulty felt by all who endeavor to define with scientific accuracy a rough-and-ready popular name. The suggested alternative, "Social Reformers", would be even less definitive than the name "Socialists", for I am not aware of a single principle on which all Social Reformers are agreed; and it would, for instance, classify me with men like Lord Brabazon and Mr. Arnold White, to whose proposals and methods I am vehemently opposed. Every name which is borne by a political party covers a wide variety of opinions, and is exclusive rather than inclusive; it suggests what is rejected rather than what is accepted. The Radical may be taken as a denier of the divine right of kings, but his party name does not tell if he be constitutional Monarchist or Republican. In every advanced party "there are so many grades and shades of diverse opinion"; this variety is the condition of progress. Only in parties which exist by repeating shibboleths of the past can uniformity of opinion be looked for. No political party includes more grades of diverse opinion than does the best of them all, the Radical, and this diversity is a proof of its vitality. The name Radical is worn by Land Nationalisers and by promoters of peasant proprietorship; by Local Optionists and by the supporters of free trade in drink; by advocates and opponents of compulsory vaccination; by Home Rulers and anti-Home Rulers; by men who would increase, and by men who would decrease, the sphere of the State. If a party is to be attacked *as a party*, it must be attacked on some principle on which it is agreed, and not on the principles on which its sections differ. While it is fair to attack any individual Radical writer for opinions put forward by him, it would not be fair to father all his individual eccentricities on Radicalism; and while it is just to attack any individual Socialist writer for the opinions he advances, it is not just to foist all his personal views on Socialism.

Mr. Bradlaugh, however, wisely defines Socialism before he assails it, and thus enables his readers to grasp the views he is attacking. He writes:

"I understand and define Socialism as (1) denying, or destroying, all individual private property; and (2) as affirming that society organised as the State should own all wealth, direct all labor, and compel the equal distribution of all produce. I understand a Socialistic State to be (3) that State in which everything would be common as to its user, and in which all labor would be controlled by the State, which from the common stock would maintain the laborer, and would take all the produce of the labor. That is (4), I identify Socialism with Communism."

My first objection to this definition is that it excludes the vast majority of Socialists, if indeed it includes any, and it will be easy for me to show that the quotations by which Mr. Bradlaugh seeks to support it are insufficient for the task. (1) might possibly be accepted by the small group of Anarchists of whom, in England, Peter Kropotkin may be taken as a representative, but it is not accepted by the Collectivist school, which forms the great majority of the Socialist party in every civilised country. It is not accepted by Marx, Engels, Bebel, in Germany; by Schäffle, in Austria; by Colins, Agathon de Potter, in Belgium; by Gronlund in America; by the leading English Socialist writers. Marx and Engels say, in their famous "Manifesto to the Communists" of 1847: "When capital is converted into common property belonging to all members of society, personal property is not thereby changed into social property. . . . By no means do we want to abolish this personal appropriation of labor products for the support of life, an appropriation which leaves no surplus proceeds, no profit, and which can gain no control over other people's labor. . . . Communism deprives no one of the power to appropriate social products for his own use; it only deprives him of the power to subject others' labor by such appropriation" (pp. 14, 15). Bebel describes the worker as receiving "any kind of certificate, a printed piece of paper, gold, or brass", as a token of the time spent in labor, and this he can exchange for what he requires. "If he finds that his requirements are less than those covered by that which he receives for his work, he can work a correspondingly shorter time. If he prefers to give away his superfluity, no one can prevent him. . . . But no one can compel him to work for another, and no one can deprive him of a part of his claims for the work done" (Woman in the Past, Present, and Future," pp. 193, 194). Schäffle says that workmen are to be paid according to the quantity and the quality of the work they do (see *Fortnightly Review*, April, 1883, p. 556). Colins absolutely leaves untouched hereditary succession to property in the direct line, while vesting land and capital in the State (see *Ibid*, p. 555). Gronlund writes : "Instead of taking property away from everyone, it will enable everyone to acquire property. It will confirm the institution of individual ownership by placing property on an unimpeachable basis: that of being the result of the owner's exertions" ("Co-operative Commonwealth," p. 81). H. M. Hyndman, W. Morris, and J. L. Joynes, as Mr. Bradlaugh admits, deny that they attack private property, save that form of it which renders it impossible for millions, *i.e.*, as we shall see later, private property in the material of wealth-production. I submit, then, that these representative writers disprove that Socialism is that which it is affirmed to be in (1). (2) falls with (1), and it may be added that the "equal distribution of all produce " is no essential part of Socialism, as may be seen from the above citations. (3) appears to me to put forward a view impossible of realisation; how can "everything be common as to its user" when the necessity for individual use must imply individual possession? A pair of boots cannot be common as to the user, since the use of them by one person renders impossible their use by another. How would it be possible for the State—if by State is meant any central authority—to control and direct all labor, since for effective direction of labor the directors must be on the spot with the labor? How can' there be a "common stock" for a whole nation? In what Socialist work can these, or similar proposals, be found? None of the quotations given by Mr. Bradlaugh justify such assumptions. In (4) we read: "I identify Socialism with Communism". But if discussion of controverted questions is to be instructive, of what use is it to identify arbitrarily two schools which claim to be distinct, and which are recognised as distinct by all Socialists and by most Individualists? There is a sense in which the word "Communism" is used by Collectivist writers such as Marx, to which I shall presently refer, but the Communism which is sketched in Mr. Bradlaugh's four propositions is not the Communism of Marx. Surely nothing would be gained if in arguing against Radicalism I used the word Liberalism to include the most stationary of old Whigs and the most progressive of modern Radicals, and then, stating that I identified Whiggism and Radicalism, went on to quote some of the most fossil utterances of the Duke of Argyll, alleging that in demolishing these I had demolished Radicalism? I do not fancy that such line of attack would convince many Radicals.

The quotations given by Mr. Bradlaugh to establish his case are sufficient to show the nature of the private property which is attacked by all Socialists, and the principle on which Socialists are agreed.

"Messrs. William Morris, and E. Belfort Bax say: 'The land, the capital, the machinery, factories, workshops, stores, means of transit, mines, banking, all means of production and distribution of wealth, must be declared and treated as the common property of all' (Manifesto of the Socialistic League', p. 6); and that there may be no misapprehension as to what this means Mr. Bax writes: 'That for which the working classes have to strive is nothing less than for Communism or a collectivist Socialism, understanding by this the assumption by the people, in other words the concentration in the hands of a democratic State, of land, raw material, instruments of production, funded capital, etc.' ('Religion of Socialism', p. 78); and, again, the same writer says: 'Socialism has been well described as a new conception of the world presenting itself in industry as co-operative Communism' (p. 81)."

There is no word here of the destruction of all private property; but there is the claim for the appropriation by the community of all material necessary for the production of wealth. And this is the fundamental position of Socialism; on other matters there may be diversity of opinion, but on this there is none. With regard to this material it is that the claim for "Communism" is made; Mr. Bax above defines Communism as "the concentration in the hands of a democratic State" of this material, not of all wealth. This, again, is the "Communism" advocated by Marx. When he has stated his objection to "that system of production and the appropriation of products which rests on the antagonism of classes—on the spoliation of the many by the few", he goes on: "*In this sense* (italics mine) the Communists can reduce their whole theory to one expression: the abolition of private property" (p. 13). He then proceeds to rebut the accusation that Communists "wish to destroy property which is the product of a man's labor—earned by his own work; that property, which forms the basis of all personal liberty, activity, and independence—personally earned, personally acquired property". And showing that the proletarian's work produces capital, "a species of property which plunders wage-labor", he states that it is this which is to be made "common property". Historically, Communism has implied a condition of things very different from that advocated by Marx, and a Communistic society, always small, has really had a "common stock". Such an arrangement is only possible in a small community, and would be utterly unworkable for a nation. It may well be questioned whether Marx was wise in using in a new sense a term already applied to a form of social organisation which he did not desire to establish; still, he showed plainly the sense in which he was using it, and it is only just to take terms with the definitions attached to them by those who use them. I have myself used the term Communism in the older sense, in my pamphlet "Modern Socialism", quoted by Mr. Bradlaugh, but Marx's use of the word must be taken with Marx's limitations.

I am not able to defend the position taken up by Peter Kropotkin, the Anarchist school being opposed to the Collectivist in all questions of method and organisation; but I would point out that he does not apparently mean to make everything quite common property, since he says: "Our opponents say to us, 'venture to touch the peasant's plot of ground or the mechanic's cottage, and see how they will receive you'. Very well! But we shall not interfere with the plot of ground nor with the cottage " ("Expropriation", p. 5). So far as I understand the Anarchist ideal of social reorganisation, it includes a system of federated communes, each commune to have a common stock; but I have not succeeded in obtaining any clear idea of the relations supposed to exist between the communes.

I come to Mr. Bradlaugh's criticism of my own position on pp. 11 and 12. I agree that Socialism denies that there should be private property in wealth-material. But the objection that I distinguish "wealth" and "capital" is, if valid against me, valid against every writer on political economy. I did not invent a new, but accepted the current, distinction. And the distinction is not wholly fictitious. If one man owned in a country the whole material necessary for the production of wealth, no wealth could be produced without his consent; if one man owned all the commodities in a country, but the people could reach the material needed for production, they could make the commodities they required. Private property in the first case means submission to the owner thereof or starvation; private property in the second case, however absurd in such an exaggerated form, leaves the people free to feed and clothe themselves with the new results of their own labor.

The whole of the next paragraph (line 23, p. 7—line 10, p. 10) appears to me to be based on a radical misconception of the change proposed by the "Scientific Socialists". They do not propose to make a number of laws : "A man shall not work for himself"; "A man shall not save up his wages, and let out his savings at interest"; any more than they propose to make a law, "A man who is going to swim across a river shall not handcuff his wrists together and tie a 20lb. weight to each foot". What the Scientific Socialist proposes to do is to take over the land and the total capital of the country (plant, means of transit, banks, etc.) into the hands of the community; those who want to earn a living, i.e., all healthy adults, will have to utilise this material. Suppose the Northumberland Miners' Association desire to work the Northumberland mines, they would have to pay rent to the State (the whole community) for the right to work them; suppose the nail-makers of a town desired to utilise the factories in which they had worked as "hands", they would have to pay rent to the State for the use of land, factory, plant, etc. And now suppose that an individual nailmaker, dissatisfied with his work in the co-operative factory, determined to save some of his earnings and set up nailmaking on his own account. Need the State be convulsed, need his deserted fellow-workers of the factory cry out for a law to stop him? Not a bit of it. Unless the whole experience of the last century as to the advantages of division of labor and of large production over small be a delusion, the co-operative workers may look on at the individual capitalist with extreme serenity. If his nails cost ten, twenty, fifty, times as much as theirs to produce, who is going to be foolish enough to buy them, say at a shilling, when they can buy similar ones at a farthing? The capitalist now is the tyrant of the worker because he can say to him, "Work for me, or starve". The attempt of·a man to be a capitalist under Socialism would be entertaining, but harmless. He could not compel any man to work for him by threat of starvation on refusal. The human desire to get as much as possible for as little labor as possible will very rapidly put an end to profit-mongering, not because none will be willing to make profits, but because none will be willing to be made a profit of by another, when starvation does not·force him into submission. Once let monopoly in the material of wealth be destroyed, and the "natural forces" at work in society will settle the small matters without the interference of artificial laws.

Nor must it be supposed that I have devised this view of the subject merely to cut the ground from under the feet of Mr. Bradlaugh's objection. E. Belfort Bax, in his "Religion of Socialism", has dealt with a similar point in a similar manner:

"M. Leroy-Beaulien sneeringly complains that, under a Collectivist *régime*, no one would be allowed to mend his neighbor's trousers or shirt for a monetary consideration, inasmuch as he would then be employing his needle and thread for purposes of production, which would be a return to Individualism, and hence.illegal. Let M. Leroy-Beaulien reassure himself. All those who desire to make a living by an individualistic mending of shirts and trousers will be allowed full liberty to satisfy their aspirations so far as any

juridical coercion is concerned. We will not vouch for their
being much patronised, for the probability of repairs of this
character being executed better, more rapidly, and with less
expenditure of labor in the communal workshop is great. But
in any case, they would have their economic liberty to fatten
on" (p. 41).

Looking over the details of the paragraph which I have
subjected to the above sweeping criticism, some further
points may be noted. Machinery, tools, etc., would be
made when they were likely to be wanted, and stored till
wanted, as now; it is hard to see where the difficulty here
arises. The laborers now can unite in co-operative production to a small extent, but their attempts have failed,
one of the chief reasons being that their command of
capital is too small to enable them to compete with the
big capitalist. I have above spoken of the individual
worker starting on his own account, and so have partly
answered Mr. Bradlaugh's question on this head; if he
wants to get raw material and private means of production
he will have to save up and purchase them from the community, and so buy the razor to cut his own foolish throat.
No officer need trouble himself about the "individual's
ability to utilise the special means or material demanded";
all he has to do is to receive from the applicant the value
of that which he demands; the individual will have to
judge his own ability, and if he blunders he will have
only himself to blame. The difficulty of apportioning
pleasant and unpleasant labor may be met in many ways;
the unpleasant might be more highly paid, so that a short
term of one might balance a longer term of another.
Speaking generally, these matters will be settled by the
law of supply and demand. As men's tastes differ, and
technical education will have trained men for different
forms of work, taste and education will play a large part
in determining a man's work. Suppose a man is a weaver,
and finds that there is no vacancy for a weaver in the factories of the town he is living in, he might apply at the
municipal branch of the Labor Bureau—an establishment
for which every Socialist must thank Charles Bradlaugh,
and the full value of which will only be felt under Socialism
—and learn in what town there are vacancies in his trade.
If over the whole country there is no vacancy, he will have
to accept temporary employment in some other industry,

and he can leave his name on the books of the Bureau for the next vacancy. But are not all these questions based on the old idea that Socialism has a cast-iron scheme, with every detail mapped out on paper, and do they not rather imply that everyone is to be a perfect fool? We are not Utopian Socialists; we have no sudden cure-all for every ill which afflicts society; but we say that the private monopoly of the material of wealth means payment to idle individuals by the workers, and that any payment made by them for the use of this material should be made to the State, and used for the benefit of the community. The exact details of the working could only be given by one endowed with the spirit of prophecy, and many such matters will have to be solved by the common-sense and business experience of the administrators.

The worker's "control" over "the value of his work" does not mean that a man will have a right to "some portion" of a product to which he has added value. It means that where he has given so many hours of labor, and has received some symbol of exchange which represents their value, he may use that symbol of exchange as he pleases. Twenty workmen co-operate to produce a carved sideboard; it is not proposed that the workmen shall have the sideboard divided among them, so that one may carry his piece abroad (lines 34–40, p. 9), but that each shall receive a labor-note—or whatever the form of payment be—for the value given by work, and that each can use this as he pleases. The finished article might lie in the communal stores till wanted by an individual or a group who were prepared to pay for it as much labor as was required to produce it.

Mr. Bradlaugh, quoting Mr. Hyndman's proposal as to "collective ownership of land, capital, machinery, and credit", says :

"Mr. Hyndman's definition in the end means Communism or it means nothing. If the collective ownership of everything except labor, and the collective control of all the produce of labor for exchange, is not the total negation of private property, then words have no meaning."

But is this so? Mr. Bradlaugh does not consider that the capitalist monopoly of "everything except labor", and the capitalist "control of all the produce of labor for exchange" is the "total negation of private property", although it implies the continued confiscation of the results of labor, and results in a condition of things in which .931 persons out of every 1,000 die "without property worth speaking of" (Mulhall's "Dictionary of Statistics", from Probate Duty Returns, p. 279). But if capitalist monopoly of the wealth-material be compatible with private property, why should not collective monopoly of the wealth-material be equally compatible therewith? In neither case does the laborer individually own it, but in the present system it is owned by a class, and part of the laborer's produce enriches the class; under the proposed system it would be owned by the community, and part of the laborer's produce would go to the community, and he, as one of the community, would benefit by the utilisation of this collective wealth.

Mr Bradlaugh is technically right in saying that my statement that capital "under our present industrial system is the result of unpaid labor" is too sweeping; I should have said, "capital, with trifling exceptions, is", etc. Taking Mr. Mulhall's figures, which are somewhat higher than Mr. Bradlaugh's, of the total capital of savings in trade societies, savings banks, and societies of every sort, we find it put at £156,000,000. This gives less than £6 per head to the members of the manual labor class, and this only on the incorrect assumption that all money in savings banks, etc., is put in by them. But everyone knows that, to take but one example, the savings banks are largely used by small gentry, shopkeepers, governesses, etc., and not exclusively by the manual labor class. In speaking of "capital under our present industrial system", I was thinking of capital in the bulk, rather than of the small savings made by some lucky workers. If the tailor and the others make "a profit", that is if they get out of the laborer more than the fair equivalent of the labor they have given in making or preparing their wares for his use, then the profit, being taken from the laborer without equivalent, is a confiscation of part of the results of his labor. As a matter of fact few working tailors, etc., do more than earn subsistence by their own labor; the capital is made by the tailor and others who employ wage-laborers, and who, by taking from each a little more than is returned to him as wage, i.e., by not paying for all the labor, gradually or rapidly accumulate capital.

To the last paragraph, I do not think answer is needed. As Mr. Bradlaugh very fairly says, I analysed the facts on p. 15. I did not think it necessary to restate them on p. 16, in summarising the results as they bore on the question of Marx's three values.

I restate, in conclusion, my main objection to Mr. Bradlaugh's criticism of Socialism. He continually strikes at Utopian Socialism, not at Scientific. He never meets our main contention that private property in wealth-material must result theoretically in the servitude of the unpropertied to the propertied class, and practically does so result in every ancient and modern society; that it enables the idle to live on the industrious, by empowering them to charge the worker for the right to work; that it thus causes mischievous class distinctions, unjust acquirement of wealth without labor, equally unjust confiscation resulting in labor without wealth. He does not show us how these hitherto inevitable results of private property in wealth-material can be prevented. But until this central citadel can be carried, I and thousands more must remain Socialists.　　　　　　　　　　　　ANNIE BESANT.

SOCIALISM: ITS FALLACIES AND DANGERS.

ROUGH NOTES BY WAY OF REJOINDER.

I NEED hardly say that I acknowledge to the very fullest extent the considerate tone of Mrs. Besant's criticisms, and though I have in everything to adhere to the propositions advanced in my original paper, I trust that I shall not depart from the friendly lines on which this presentation of antagonistic views on a most important subject has hitherto proceeded. I desire to repeat and emphasise my complete conviction that my always brave and loyal colleague has in the whole of this most important

social movement been solely moved by her desire to
alleviate the hard conditions of life of many workers,
and to diminish the sum of human suffering. Where
disagreeing with her most, and when expressing this dis-
agreement, I desire that this may be fully remembered
by my readers.

Mrs. Besant, admitting that I have by my definition
made clear what it is I assail as Socialism, says that her
'first objection to my definition "is that it excludes the vast
majority of Socialists, if indeed it includes any," and she
goes to the length of asking me "in what Socialist work
can these or similar proposals be found". I answer that
until very recently they were to be found in the writings of
almost every French, English, and American Socialist. This
I have no doubt Mrs. Besant herself would admit, for she
states that historically Communism meant something different from "that advocated by Marx", and the words
Communism and Socialism were most certainly trans-
posable equivalents with Robert Owen, Cabet, Fourier,
Noyes, F. W. Evans, W. H. Hinds, and nearly all their
American and French contemporaries. And this is not
very ancient history; none of it dates back before the
nineteenth century; much of it was in vigor in the lifetime of the present writer. The initial and vital point of
difference between Mrs. Besant and myself—one which
governs the whole controversy—is that I allege that, in
express terms or in its practical working, Socialism must
deny or destroy all individual private property. Mrs.
Besant says this is not accepted by several Socialists she
names, *e.g.*, Marx, Engels, and Bebel in Germany; yet she
fairly enough quotes as follows from Marx: "In this sense
the Communists can reduce their whole theory to one
expression: the abolition of private property"; and saying
that "it may well be questioned whether Marx was wise
in using in a new sense" the term "Communism", Mrs.
Besant gets over the definite "abolition of private property" by italicising the words "in this sense". That is,
Mrs. Besant replies: Mr. Bradlaugh is wrong in attri-
buting to Socialism identity with Communism; Mr. Bradlaugh is wrong in identifying Communism with abolition
of private property—proof, Marx, a German Socialist of
eminence, did not hold those views. True, Marx used the
old word "Communism", but he so used it with a new

meaning. True, Marx said he meant "abolition of private property" as a correct summary of his Communistic views, but he said so with a limitation of the sense in which he used the words, which totally changes their meaning. Mrs. Besant must pardon me if I venture to uphold Marx's ability to express himself clearly, and to express some doubt either of his straightforwardness or of her appreciation of his meaning on this point. I notice that Mrs. Besant omits all reference to French Socialistic authors, and takes Gronlund as if the representative of American Socialism, which I venture to think is hardly the case. Mrs. Besant, naming Colins, should, I think, have added that, though Colins is unquestionably very able and very earnest, his "rational Socialism" finds comparatively few adherents in the Socialistic ranks. M. Naville, writing on Cabet in *La Nouvelle Revue*, and criticising the various modern schools of French Socialists, "Collectivists", "Anarchists", "State Socialists", says: "Quels que soit les noms dont elles s'affublent et les procédés qu'elles préconisent, toutes ces doctrines partent d'un même principe, toutes visent au même objectif: la transformation de l'etat social par la mise en commun des biens, par la creation d'une propriété universelle appartenant à tous et à chacun".

Mrs. Besant, objecting to my definition, asks: "How can there be a common stock for the whole nation?" and denies that this can be justified from any Socialist work; yet on the same page she requotes my extract from the Manifesto of the Socialist League that "land, capital, machinery, factories, workshops, stores, means of transit, mines, banking, all means of production and distribution of wealth, must be declared and treated as the common property of all". I am unable to distinguish between "common stock" and "common property", and fear that Mrs. Besant and myself are using words in such differing senses that useful discussion is impossible. Mrs. Besant says "the equal distribution of all produce is no essential part of Socialism". Unless there is some play on the word "equal", surely Mrs. Besant is here in direct conflict with the Socialist League and with the Social Democratic Federation. The organisation and control of distribution by the State and "the organisation of agricultural and industrial armies under State control" are both over-

and over again repeated as features in the programme.
Mr. W. Morris says that "capital, including the land,
machinery, factories, etc.," is to be put "into the hands
of the community to be used for the good of all alike".
A young man named Mahon, selected by the Socialist
League to be one of its representatives amongst the miners
lately on strike in Northumberland, in "A Plea for Socialism" addressed to those miners, and since published
from the offices of the League, says: "*The Socialist proposal* is to take the land and capital from the private
individuals who now unrighteously hold them, and put
them under the control of the community, and use them
for the benefit of the workers".   Mrs. Besant refers to
Colins and Agathon de Potter, but if I accurately appreciate Dr. Agathon de Potter he—for himself and for Colins
—is the interpreter of what is called "Rational Socialism",
which differs essentially from the Socialism taught by Mrs.
Besant.   Rational Socialism, to quote Agathon de Potter's
own comment on Mrs. Besant, "maintains that a part of
capital ought to rest in individual hands to constitute an
individual personal estate to encourage wage labor.   It
neither suppresses capital nor interest on capital, but it
renders both inoffensive by lowering the rate of interest
au minimum des circonstances and in forbidding loans *plus
que viagers*."   That is, interest would be kept down to a
minimum by the competition of the State as a lender,
and every debt would be extinguished in a fixed term
by a limited number of annual payments (A. de
Potter, *La Société Nouvelle*, pp. 302, 305).   Mr. Mahon,
in the address I have just quoted, says "the taking of
interest is wrong, no matter to what extent it may be
carried".

Mrs. Besant, in her reply to me, in effect says that I do
not understand Socialism, and that I consequently fail to
accurately represent it in my criticisms.   I quite admit
that, if Socialism and Communism are not convertible
words of equivalent meaning, Mrs. Besant's reply is well
urged.   Curiously enough, Mr. Tucker, an American
Anarchist Socialist, in other words says almost this of
Mrs. Besant, charging her with "stopping short of Communism in State Socialism", and therefore with failing
"to give the public any complete and satisfactory idea"
of what Socialism really is.   At the outset of my first

paper I admitted my difficulty in finding any general agreement amongst modern Socialists as to what was meant. I only pretended to make it clear what it was that I attacked under that name. Mrs. Besant says, "What the scientific Socialist proposes to do is to take over the land and total capital of the country". "Suppose the nailmakers of a town desired to utilise" any of this land or capital, "they would have to pay rent to the State". Suppose an individual nailmaker dissatisfied, he may, says Mrs. Besant, set up for himself when he has saved some of his earnings; "the co-operative workers may look on at the individual capitalist with great serenity". As I understand Mrs. Besant, Socialism says : "Capital is an evil, therefore it must be wholly taken away from the present possessors". I do not here discuss the possibility of so taking away all capital without a civil war, nor pause to comment on the terrible danger involved in the encouragement given to such a doctrine; but I suppose all capital taken away by the State from every individual capitalist. Then I understand Mrs. Besant to interpret Socialism as saying : we will not prevent an individual nailmaker from saving up his earnings and setting up as an individual capitalist nailmaker in competition with the co-operative factory, obtaining the uses of its materials of production by rental from the State. But supposing—which I cannot —that this can be reconciled with the organisation and direction of industrial armies by the State, does not this interpretation involve an utter abandonment of the principle that all private capital is an evil, and ought to be abolished? Mrs. Besant evidently does not think that there would be much reality in the permitted competition. She says: "The attempt of a man to be a capitalist under Socialism would be entertaining, but would be harmless"—meaning, probably, that she does not think that the individual already deprived of his previous savings would be readily able to even pay rent to the State, for the materials of production would only be attainable on hire from the State. But suppose that, in addition to being entertaining, the attempt really succeeded, and supposing that just as Robert Owen the poor mill hand did, by great thrift, individual energy, foresight, and enterprise, become Robert Owen the rich Socialist capitalist—some individual nailmaker did again acquire

new capital in lieu of that of which he had been deprived—is he to be allowed to keep it? If not, to say
that he may attempt is hardly serious. If yes, why
destroy the present capitalists and yet permit the creation
of new ones?

CHARLES BRADLAUGH.

A FEW WORDS IN FINAL REPLY.

ONE point at least has come out very clearly in the
friendly controversy between Mr. Bradlaugh and myself.
Namely, that what he attacks as "Socialism" is only
one form of Socialism; and I think I may add, taking his
list of names—Robert Owen, Cabet, Fourier, Noyes, F. W.
Evans, W. H. Hinds—not the form of Socialism which is
making its way in Europe and America to-day. It is true
that none of these men date back beyond the present
century, but in the science of sociology they are as much
out of date as authorities as the early writers of the
century on geology are in present-day geological science.
Nothing perhaps has been more remarkable in the present
century than the enormous advances made during it in all
branches of science; a veritable gulf separates the thinkers
of the early and of the later parts, and strictures levelled
against the teachings of the older schools are pointless
when turned against the doctrines of the new. Sociology
has shared in the general advance, and has passed from
a mere empiricism into a reasoned system. And most
noteworthy is it that the leading thinkers in this young
science—the birth of our own century—are, with the exception of Herbert Spencer, either tending towards Socialism
or are declared Socialists, and that they are being more
and more reinforced by the younger school of political
economists. And these thinkers are influencing the
course of political action, unconscious as are the politicians
of the moulding force. Fifty years ago a Radical drafting
a Bill for depriving non-cultivating landlords of unculti-

vated but cultivable land, would have parcelled out the land seized into small holdings which he would have sold to peasant *proprietors*; now-a-days, Mr. Bradlaugh, drafting his Bill, proposes to let the land to peasant *tenants*, paying rent to and holding from the State. The same sound Radical, attacking market rights and tolls in the hands of monopolising individuals and railway companies, proposes to abolish their charter rights, and to enable municipalities only to acquire authority over markets, so that rents and tolls paid shall go into the municipal exchequer instead of into the pockets of individuals. The same man is striving to prevent by law "free contracts" between employers and employed, in cases in which the employers use their position of advantage to make men take goods in lieu of money as wage, and to prevent them charging the men interest on money advanced before the agreed on pay-day. Truly, though Mr. Bradlaugh curses Socialism with his mouth, he is blessing it altogether in his legislation, and is making possible for us the way to the Promised Land.

In par. 3, is there not a little play on the word "stock"? I certainly understood "common stock" to mean common stock of commodities. I should not speak of a "stock" of "land, capital, machinery, factories", etc. The Socialist League sums up all these as "means of production and distribution of wealth", and claims these as common propert . Again, in the quotations from W. Morris and J. L. Mahon, it is land and capital that are claimed as common property. I am not aware that the Socialist League, or the Social Democratic Federation, has declared in favor of "equal distribution of all produce", and the phrase in the Socialist League Manifesto that every man will "receive the full reward of his labor" seems to point in the other direction, since all men certainly do not labor equally.

I agree in the statement of the view taken by Colins and Agathon de Potter on capital; they would have the State part-holder only of the capital of the country, and would thus extinguish the worst evils of the present system, which flow from the constant exploitation of the worker by the capitalist; with the capital owned by the State available to the worker, he would no longer be at the mercy of a private employer, and would only work for the latter when he thought he could thus do better for himself than by setting up on his own account with capital borrowed from the State. Socialism carried to this extent would be an enormous improvement on the present system; and the moderate views of Colins and Agathon de Potter seem to me to be of special interest in the present controversy, as showing how far is the Belgian School of Socialism from occupying the position assailed by Mr. Bradlaugh.

Mr. Benjamin Tucker, as an Anarchist, would naturally charge me with not going far enough; in his eyes Collectivist Socialism is inconsistent and weak, Anarchism being the only logical and perfect system of thought. So Mr. Auberon Herbert, an extreme Individualist, regards Mr. Bradlaugh's Individualism as a very poor weak-backed kind of thing, since Mr. Bradlaugh thinks that a majority may rightly impose a tax for a common object, whereas individual liberty demands that a man shall be left free to pay a tax or not as he chooses. Everyone who does not go to the extreme length of every opinion held by some individual nominally belonging to his party must be prepared for reproaches of this kind. But I can support Mr. Benjamin Tucker's strictures with perfect equanimity, as doubtless can Mr. Bradlaugh any levelled at him by Mr. Auberon Herbert. And in truth Mr. Benjamin Tucker and Mr. Auberon Herbert are men of very much the same type, and are living examples of the truth of the adage that extremes meet.

Mr. Bradlaugh misunderstands me in thinking that I represent Socialism as saying that "capital is an evil". Capital is an essential factor in production, and is therefore most certainly not an evil. The evil arises when individuals, monopolising the capital made by many, and excluding those who made it from all control over it, employ it as an instrument to exploit those who have none, and to utilise them as hands to heap up wealth for themselves. Capital as a tyrant over labor is an evil; capital as fertiliser and servant of labor is a good.

My reason for thinking that the enterprising individual nailmaker would be making an entertaining and harmless experiment, was, I think, given in my original statement. First, if his individually-made nails cost more to produce than the nails made by co-operative labor—that is, if division of labor be an advantage in production—he would not be able to compete with the co-operative workers in the open market. Secondly, he could not accumulate by exploiting his neighbors, and no man can accumulate large capital by his own work alone. Robert Owen the mill-hand became Robert Owen the capitalist because, when he had saved a little out of his own earnings, he could hire others to work for him, and then by paying them back less than the value they give him in work, he was able to save out of *their* earnings, and so increase his capital; this increased capital enabled him to employ additional workers, and he then saved out of the earnings of a larger number of people, and so grew rich. Under the present system the workers are compelled either to submit to this continued appropriation of part of the results of their labor, or to remain unemployed, *i.e.*, to starve. Under Socialism no such compulsion would be upon them, and a man's natural objection to be exploited may be trusted to for the prevention of exploitation as soon as the compulsion to submit to it is removed. Hence the serenity with which any such private attempts might be regarded.

All I have sought to do in my brief criticisms of Mr. Bradlaugh's objections to Socialism has been to show that they do not go to the root of the question of Socialism, that they do not even touch the central position of Socialism. Looking out at the future of the workers in this country, pressed as they are by increasing foreign competition, I can see no hope for them save in their control of their own labor, and their possession of all which is necesssary for the production of wealth. As chattel-slavery and serfage so, I believe, must wage-slavery perish, and then shall man's dominion over man disappear, and liberty shall be a reality instead of a name.

ANNIE BESANT.

PAMPHLETS ON SOCIALISM.

———◆———

WILL SOCIALISM BENEFIT THE ENGLISH PEOPLE? A Debate between CHARLES BRADLAUGH and H. M. HYNDMAN. Price 3d.

BY CHARLES BRADLAUGH.
OBJECTIONS TO SOCIALISM. Price 1d.

BY ANNIE BESANT.

MODERN SOCIALISM. Price 6d.

WHY I AM A SOCIALIST. Price 1d.

EVOLUTION OF SOCIETY. Price 3d.

REDISTRIBUTION OF POLITICAL POWER. Price 4d.

In the Press.

THE SOCIALIST MOVEMENT. (Reprinted from the *Westminster Review.*)

RADICALISM AND SOCIALISM.

———

LONDON:

FREETHOUGHT PUBLISHING COMPANY,
63, FLEET STREET, E.C.

WILL SOCIALISM BENEFIT THE ENGLISH PEOPLE?

VERBATIM REPORT OF

A DEBATE

BETWEEN

H. M. HYNDMAN AND CHARLES BRADLAUGH

Held at St. James' Hall on April 17th, 1884.

PROFESSOR BEESLY IN THE CHAIR.

[TENTH THOUSAND.]

LONDON:

FREETHOUGHT PUBLISHING COMPANY,

63, FLEET STREET, E.C.

1884.

PRICE THREEPENCE.

LONDON:

PRINTED BY ANNIE BESANT AND CHARLES BRADLAUGH,
63, FLEET STREET, E.C.

WILL SOCIALISM BENEFIT THE ENGLISH PEOPLE?

THE CHAIRMAN : Fellow citizens, we are met here to-night to listen to what I have no doubt will be a very interesting discussion. The subject is one of the highest importance. It is a subject upon which everyone who feels any interest in it ought to furnish himself with as clear ideas as possible. The speakers are both of them able representatives of their respective opinions. They are both of them well accustomed to expound them; there cannot be the smallest question about their sincerity, and the earnestness with which they hold those opinions. (Hear, hear.) Each of them is well acquainted with the other's position, and therefore, although one evening may seem to be but a very small space for handling so vast a subject, I dare say we shall find that they will soon know how to narrow down their controversy to the essential points at issue, and so we shall derive profit from the evening—greater profit than perhaps is usually derived from discussions of this character. I need hardly remind you that the usefulness of the meeting will depend a good deal upon a circumstance over which the speakers have no control, and that is the temper of the audience—(hear, hear)—their patience, their forbearance in listening to arguments with which they do not agree. Perhaps I shall not be wrong if I assume that a large portion of those present have come here with their minds pretty well made up already one way or the other. It would, however, I suppose, be too much to expect that they will not from time to time give expression to their feelings of approbation or disapprobation of the argu-

ments they may hear, but I would appeal to them not to
do so to such an extent as either to interfere with the quiet
hearing of those who may wish to listen quietly to what
is being said, or so as to curtail unfairly the space of tim
allotted to each of the speakers.   I may say that it is n ot
intended to-night to submit any resolution to the meetir g,
or to take any show of hands, and therefore there is no
reason whatever why it should be regarded as a trial of
strength, a trial of lungs, or exhibition of numerical
strength between the two different parties.   (Laughter.)
For myself, I may say I am in the Chair to-night because
both parties have done me the honor to believe that I
should endeavor to conduct the proceedings, as far as depends upon me, with impartiality—(hear, hear)—and
perhaps they thought I should find it all the more easy to
do so because they believe it is pretty well known that
I belong to a school of opinion which differs very considerably from the opinions of both Mr. Bradlaugh and Mr.
Hyndman. I shall not detain you any longer, but I shall
just explain to you the conditions on which it has been
agreed that this discussion should be carried on.   Mr.
Hyndman will first speak for half-an-hour; then Mr. Bradlaugh will speak for half-an-hour; then each of the
speakers will' address you for twenty minutes, and then
again for ten minutes; and that will conclude the proceedings.

Mr. HYNDMAN, who was received with loud cheers, said:
Mr. Chairman, friends, and fellow-citizens, in rising here
to-night as the delegate of the Democratic Federation to
maintain that Socialism will benefit the English people, I
desire to say at the outset that I do so in no sense as an
individual. (Hear, hear.) I come here as the delegate of
an organised Socialistic body. The cause for which I come
here and have the honor to champion is too high and too
noble to be mixed with personal considerations of any kind
whatsoever. I know very well that in meeting an opponent here to night who has been before the public for
very many years, who is a master of the art of addressing
public audiences, and thoroughly acquainted with all the
ways of debate, I do so at some considerable disadvantage.
I only ask those who are present, and who think that I do
not put the case of the Socialists sufficiently well before
this great audience, to supplement my shortcomings as I
go along; and to others, whether the majority or the

minority of those present who differ from what I have to
say, I only ask what I believe I should get without asking,
viz., for a fair and impartial consideration of the arguments
I have to lay before you. (Hear, hear.) Now, first, what
is Socialism? I will endeavor to give a definition which
applies to the active life of to-day. Socialism then is an
endeavor to substitute for the anarchical struggle or fight
for existence an organised co-operation for existence.
That, I say, in so far as it applies to the active life of to-
day. But it is something much more; it is a distinct
historical theory which accounts for the progress of man
in society by his command over the forces of nature, by
the economical development, the power which he has of
producing wealth. Thus the history of the past enables
us to understand the present, and in some sort to forecast
the future, but with that I have not to do at this moment.
What do we see around us? We see that never in the
history of mankind was there such power over nature as
there is to-day. Never had man before steam, electricity,
machinery—all these great powers with which to produce
wealth. Those powers are increasing in every country in
Western Europe and America at far greater rate than the
population is increasing. Therefore it is not necessary to
go to the amount of population to account for the contrasts
we see around us. If it were necessary to limit the amount
of population, let us begin with those who do not produce.
(Hear, hear.) If it is necessary there should be fewer
people in the country let a few of the idlers stop breeding.
Therefore when we come to these contrasts, which we all
see and deplore, with this enormous power and this enormous wealth on the one hand, and such terrible misery
and awful destitution upon the other, it must strike us all
—it has struck us all, or I take it we should not be here
to-night—that these contrasts ought not to continue.
(Hear, hear.) Why is it that on the one hand the producers
in this country are the poorest of the population? Why
is it that those who do not produce are the richest? How, on
the other hand, are we to give the producers a full share in
that which they produce, and to teach those who live in
luxury without producing, some better idea of existence?
On the answer, Mr. Chairman, to those two questions, I
take it, the debate we hold to-night will hinge. Now
then, first and foremost, men are born into this world,
hundreds and thousands of them, without any property

whatsoever—(Oh, oh)—or any claim to any property. We are all born without any property. They arrive at manhood and womanhood in that condition—thousands of them. What is their position? They have no property, no command over the means of production, either land, capital, machinery, or credit, either as individuals or as part of the organised community. Under what conditions, then, have they to live? They have not one thing which they possess but the force of labor in their bodies. Mind, what I am saying applies not only to the worker, not only to the distributor who is working on the railways, &c., but it applies in a very large degree to the small shopkeepers and clerks and those who live by intellectual labor. They have to compete against one another in what is called the labor market in order to be able only to exist. Under what circumstances do they so compete? The middle class economists all tell us that the law of that competition is that they get on the average the standard of life in the country in which they were born, and just so much as will enable them to hand on the same lot to their successors. There are some who get more; there are some highly skilled laborers who receive more than this, but there are others, as some perhaps here may well know, who for months never get a full meal, and there are whole classes who, as the official reports tell us, never get enough food to keep them clear of the diseases which arise from starvation. (Applause.) Such I say is the law under which they work. Now see what follows upon that. These producers of the community, the men who produce all the wealth in this England of ours, what do they get? Say that a man is receiving 5s. a day, which is considered remarkably high wages (the average of the country is about one-half of that), and he produces a value of £1 in that day, where does the 15s. go? It goes, as we know very well, to pay the landlord's rent, to pay interest on the capital, to pay profits, and it is labor value. The value of this man who is working very close to starvation wages produces the luxuries which we see around us. (Cheers.) That is the surplus value which is divided up by the idle or non-producing classes of the population. Now, what is the result to those who thus work? Are they not enfeebled by want of sufficient leisure, by want of power, by want of that which is taken from them under the forms of society in which we dwell? None can deny that it is so. We know that the brutal competition of one against the other, where there is plenty for all, means to the great mass of English people (and my opponent here to-night will not deny it), degradation to the English people, and worse degradation in the future than it is to-night. (Applause.) Consider the circumstances under which the work is carried on to-day. Say that a man is working, and a machine is introduced to the trade in which he is a skilled laborer, ought it not to benefit everyone that greater wealth can be produced with less labor? Certainly, there is no reason why it should not. Why are we known as organised individuals if we cannot take hold of what each of us invents and produce it for the benefit of all? It is not so used. It is used by a class against a class, and there is many a man who works as a skilled laborer to-day who, if a machine is invented whereby man may benefit, will be turned out to compete against his fellows on the street to-morrow. That is what I say is anarchy for those men, not order; and the uncertainty of the condition so produced, think of that. What uncertainty it is for a man not to know whether he will be able to keep his wife and his children because mankind is getting greater power over the forces of nature. Now, how does it tell on women? Are there not hundreds, nay thousands, of girls turned out into the streets to starve, nay, worse, to go to prostitution by reason of the invention of these machines. (Applause.) In these matters it is necessary to speak out. We Socialists do not blink the question. We go to the roots of the society we see around us. That is not all. Taking the system of production as it to-day exists, what do you see? An increasing difficulty in buying what you may call good goods. There has been the age of stone, there has been the age of bronze and the age of iron, but it strikes me we are in the age of adulteration. If a careful summary were made of the process of production for profit under which our present civilisation exists, it strikes me a fair representation of it would be a keg of bosh butter, a bale of shoddy cloth, and a wooden ham, and that might go down to posterity as a fair summary of what our system is tending to. (Hear, hear.) Remember that workmen who produce these adulterated goods have no interest in these adulterations, which injure their health, lower their vitality, and damage the market upon which they are dependent for their livelihood. (Ap-

plause.) What do you say to that, then, for a system of
production which is based on falsifying the very 'goods
which the men have to produce? I say again it is
anarchy, not order, when you use the force of nature
to produce rottenness instead of pure goods. (Cheers.)
Again, what do we see around us to-day? A universal
crisis in every industrial centre. There are men out of
work at Shields, and there are many in the East End of London who are unable to get anything to do, and it is getting
worse. That state of things is not confined to this country,
but it is all over the world. What is the reason of this
great industrial crisis that comes once in every eight or
nine or ten years? How do you account for it? We have
our explanation, and it is this. We say—and remember
what is the case to-day—there is wheat piled up in the
elevators of Chicago and in New York. There is food
enough in America. Is there no one in London who wants
a loaf? Is there nobody who would give a day's work for
some of that wheat in our great industrial centres? Plenty
of them; but you cannot bring the two together. There
are gluts of commodities such as boots and shoes, and yet
there are plenty of people with bare feet who would be
glad to do a day's work in order to get them. Consider
what this means. It means that you cannot bring the two
sources of wealth together, the labor and the goods which
have been produced. Why? Because the class that owns
the means of production cannot produce to a profit, which
profit the very glut itself prevents. (Hear, hear.) What
is the reason, again, of that? It is this—that whereas
mankind in the factories or upon the farm, and men all
through our great industries, are working in social union,
exchange is conducted at war; those who take the commodities after they are produced continue to produce more
and more in order to undersell one another, and the worker
has no command over the market, the result being this
great financial crisis, which throws hundreds and thousands
into misery day after day. (Applause.) We say that can
only be remedied as the production is social, so the exchange
must be social too; that the workers must control the system
of exchange in the interest of the whole of the community;
that it must no longer be conducted for the advantage of
a class; that the competition for gain above, and competition for bare subsistence-wages below, must fade into
a great organisation where both are conducted for the

general good. As we are talking and discussing here we can see very well that the State itself, the organising State of the middle class, has been obliged to come in in order to remedy in some sort the anarchy which exists around us. Take the Factories Acts. Why were they introduced? I do not think my opponent would deny that they were most valuable measures, that they have done some good, and protected women and children somewhat. So infamous was the slavery under unrestricted competition that it was necessary to stop the degradation which was going on. Again, people were growing up in ignorance. Parents did not see that their children were educated in any way whatever. It became so serious to the community—so manifest was it that it was necessary to intervene, that the School Board was introduced, and it has not gone half far enough in my humble judgment, but nevertheless the rights of parents to bring up their children in ignorance were interfered with by Parliament, and were put a stop to as far as they then could go. There is an interference on the part of the State. Again, in the question of employers' liability for injury done to their workmen, the State again comes in, and it is acknowledged on all hands by the middle class economists, whom we Socialists oppose, that this is beneficial to the community. (No, no.) I say yes. I say it is acknowledged by Professor Thorold Rogers, if that gentleman will look at his writings. It is acknowledged by Mr. Henry Sidgwick in his last book—let him look at his writings. It is acknowledged by Henry Fawcett, of whom I will have something to say directly. It is acknowledged by Mr. Walker, the American—by all the leading middle class economists of the present day. ("Herbert Spencer.") He is not an economist, to start with, and no one ever contended he was before this gentleman in the hall. (Oh, oh.) You may say oh! but it is so. To go on; I say these interferences have been commonly acknowledged as beneficial and necessary, and it is my belief that at the present moment it would be impossible to put an end to either of these measures. I must hurry on. Again, we are no Utopians. We cannot take up society by the root and plant it elsewhere. We have not the slightest wish to take a trip to Venus, or take a little jaunt to Saturn. We have no idea of that sort at all, neither do we think we can raise up a little oasis of co-operation in the midst of a great wilderness of competi-

tion. We have no such idea whatever. Every attempt
made in this direction has been a failure, and we do not
intend to try it again. They were failures because they
did not take account of what was going on around them,
of having an association which should dominate over all
in the interest of all. We are in no sense Utopians. We
take the history of the past in order to analyse the history
of the future. That being so, what do we see in the
sphere of State organisation? I have spoken about State
prohibition. You see already a State Post Office, not
organised in the interests of the workers in the Post
Office—for they compete for starvation wages, like everybody else. (No, no.) A gentleman behind me says: "No,
no," but I should think no one would dispute that when
the Postmaster-General said: "If you do not like your
wages, I can get somebody outside to do it just as cheap
or cheaper." Thus they are working at starvation wages.
The Post Office produces to the country £2,500,000 a-year,
or thereabouts. We say that organisation should be used,
not for the benefit of the middle class to reduce their taxation, but for the benefit of the workers, and to improve
them. (Applause.) We go farther; we go to each of the
other departments that are used by the State, the Telegraph, the Savings Bank, the various departments under
their control, the dockyards and factories—all these should
be handled by salaried servants, but instead of being
handled for the upper class and the middle class, they
should be worked for the benefit of the workers, and for
the benefit of all. (Loud applause.) We desire it not
under the control of a class, but under the control of a
Democracy, where every adult woman and man shall be
entitled to a vote. (Hear, hear.) This is no control of
class. The State ceases when every man and every woman
is the State himself—(hear, hear)—when it is the right and
the duty of all to labor, and none is able to thrust off on
to another class the right of maintaining them from their
cradles to their graves. I say that such a Democratic
community as that ceases to be a State; it means an
organisation for all and by all. Such an organisation we look
to as the force of the future. The Democratic Federation
(whose delegate I am to-night) has put forward a series
of stepping-stones for this organisation. We believe that
the propaganda we have carried on has brought many
questions to the front, and is bringing them day by day.

We say the work we have done has been already to a large
extent beneficial, and that Socialistic ideas are abroad
among the people at this hour. Sir, we are accused of
preaching discontent and stirring up actual conflict. We
do preach discontent, and we mean to preach discontent;
and we mean if we can to stir up actual conflict. (Hear,
hear.) I have never known any progress in the history
of the world where the men who were striving for it were
not accused of setting class against class. There is class
conflict going on without our feeling it; it is going on in
every country in Europe, and it is bitter in England. It
is here to-day though it is below the surface, but thirty or
forty years ago it appeared in our cities, and we desire to-
day, that it shall be the conflict of argument as far as
possible; an organised conflict wherein all shall benefit
and none really suffer. Such proposals as those which I
have here, and which I have not time now to dilate upon,
are objected to, particularly the one for feeding children
in the Board Schools, and every child that goes there in
my opinion ought to be well fed. What does this over-
pressure arise from? From want of physical vigor. If
you overwork the brain the body will break down to a
moral certainty. (Hear, hear.) So with regard to housing
of the poor; the compulsory construction of artisans'
dwellings in our cities all through the country. Why
should that not be? Is not that for the benefit of all?
Assuredly it is. The small amount of injury which might
be done means really justice to the whole community. I
may have another opportunity of going seriatim through
these proposals of ours, but I desire in the few minutes
that are left to me to point out that our system in no way
hampers individuality—nay, it is the first system where
individuality for all has ever been possible. (Hear, hear.)
Sir, I can imagine nothing more horrible than to see, as I
see day after day, able men, far more capable as I believe
than I am myself, crushed down by society, bound to keep
their noses to the grindstone every day of their lives, unable to use individuality, unable to use the powers they
have been gifted with, unable to do a stroke of work for
the emancipation of man, because they are obliged to work
in order to keep themselves. (Cheers.) Is that individuality? It is slavery; and one of the worst and most degrading forms of slavery that the world has ever seen. If
you go to the match-box-makers in the East-end of London, if

you go to the north and see the people at work in the mills, or to any of the numberless sweaters' dens, what do you find? Individuality? No! not a particle of it. (Cheers.) Very well then. We say, light labor for all. We know right well that three or four hours' work a day is more than sufficient to cover luxury and comfort for every man. (Hear, hear.) We say that this can only be done by the collective ownership of land, capital, machinery and credit, by the complete ownership of the people in this great country of ours. I say, therefore, that Socialism will benefit the English people. (Hear, hear.) I contend then that it will benefit them physically—("Prove it")—tha, it will benefit them in this way, that it will benefit every child to be brought up in full physical health, benefit him and her to be taught to labor not against their fellows ;. will give them an intellectual education, it will give them a moral education as against beastly competition for greed of gain. (Applause.) It will do more than this. All th world looks to us because here capitalism and landlordism are more supreme than elsewhere. They know they cannot move unless we men in England move ; they know that here is the nexus of the greed for gain that dominates this planet ; that if we Socialists can organise, as we shall organise, a power that it will benefit not our own people but the organised industry of the civilised world, and I say that such an ideal, such a national ideal, to keep before our men and our women amongst us, the emancipation of men and the enfranchisement of women, the right of those who live by labor to enjoy the fruits of that labor in common for the benefit of all, and to get for our country the leadership in this great crusade for men, is the noblest thing which will benefit every man and woman that has a part in it, and will carry us down to posterity as those who worked for the greatness and glory of mankind and the human race to countless and countless generations. (Loud applause.)

The CHAIRMAN: I now call upon Mr. Bradlaugh.

Mr. BRADLAUGH, who was received with loud cheers, said: Friends, the distinction between myself and my antagonist is this. We both recognise—I am not quite sure from his speech how far we actually clearly recognise—we both recognise many social evils. He wants the State to remedy them, I want the individuals to remedy them. (Hear, hear. A voice: "Which individuals?") I will tell you,

and I want the evil of interruption remedied by your
individually holding your tongue. We recognise the
most serious evils, and especially in large centres of population, arising out of the poverty already existing, aggravat-
ing and intensifying the crime, disease, and misery developed
from it. My antagonist wants to cure that by some
indefinite organisation. (A voice: "Not indefinite.") It
may be definite to you. It is not to me yet—(hear, hear)—
and I will show you so when I follow what he has said.
I want to remedy the evil, attacking it in detail by the
action of the individuals most affected by it. I do not
wonder that men call themselves Socialists. The evils are
grave enough to make men willing to take any name that
they may connect with a possible cure. What I shall try
to do is to show that the cure does not lie in the direction
pointed out in the speech we have listened to, and I have
to complain that we have had no definition of Socialism,
that the two very vague phrases which commenced the
speech were as far from being a definition as any phrases
can possibly be. (Hear, hear.) Unless we can understand
one another there is no use in discussing with one another.
I shall try at least to make the position I take clear, and I
will begin by distinguishing between social reformers and
Socialists. Getting the vote for women may be done
without being a member of the Democratic Federation,
and there are no political or social evils which have been
referred to in the speech of to-night, nor any one of the
remedies for them, that were not discussed so long ago that
they may be found in the old Chartist Circular of 1840.
(Hear, hear.) I do not mean that they are less worth
discussing now, but I do mean that they have not the
newness that has been claimed for them in the speech to
which we have just listened. Social reform is one thing
because it is reform; Socialism is the opposite because it
is revolution—(applause, in which Mr. Hyndman joined)
—and that I am sorry to see is approved by my antagonist.
Revolution, as he says, to be effected by argument if possible. Aye, but by what if argument be not possible? (Force.)
Yes, that is the term. (Applause.) Force. Yes, that is
the curse, and that is why I deem it my duty to be here at
the expense of much misrepresentation, for the purpose of
diverting and turning away this argument of force which
holds weapons to our enemies, and which hurts and damns
our cause. (Applause.) Let me here point out that which

has been already stated roughly in the speech to which we have listened, namely, that no Socialistic experiment has yet ever succeeded in the world. (Oh, oh.) None ever! The temporary success—(interruption)—if you cannot listen to argument against you, how do you hope to convince the majority who are hostile to you? (Hear, hear.) I was saying that no Socialistic experiment had ever yet been successful. Some have seemed to be temporarily successful, but only so long as they have been held together, either by some religious tie, and then they have broken up when the effect of the tie has failed, and of this there are numerous illustrations; or by personal devotion to some one man, and then they have broken up when that man has grown weary, or when his life has ceased; or when directed by some strong chief or chiefs, holding together only so long as the direction lasted. Then they have only been temporarily successful, while they have been very few in number. When their apparent success has tempted many to join them, then they have broken down, and I will tell you why. As long as they were few, they did not lose the sense of private property; they did not lose sight of the advantage they were gaining by their individual exertions. The small community owned its property hostile to, or at least distinct from, that of every property around it, and therefore each one knew every addition he had made to the common stock; the stock was so small that he could count his increased richness. I have complained that we have heard no definition of Socialism, and the complaint would be unfair indeed unless I were prepared to give what I believe to be a definition. I will do it at once. I say that Socialism denies individual private property. (Hear, hear, No, no.) I will show you that it does in the last words which fell from the speaker when he had forgotten to speak cautiously, and it is not unnatural—I shall probably do the same—it is not unnatural that the enthusiasm of such a meeting as this should induce one not to speak cautiously. I am glad he did not, because he spoke accurately then from his own position. I say that Socialism denies all individual private property, and affirms that society organised as the State — (No) — those who say "No" will remember at present I am not debating with them. (Hear, hear.) They possibly may be more intelligent, but this gentleman (Mr. Hyndman) is the representative for the moment—(hear hear)—and affirms that society organised as the State should own all wealth, direct all labor, and compel the equal distribution of all produce. I say that is what the vague words amount to. What does the collective ownership of all the means of wealth, and of the results of labor mean, if it does not mean that? What does the organised direction of work through the State mean, if it does not mean that? If the words are only counters to jingle in the ears of the hungry, then they are not only no good, but may result in serious mischief. (Hear, hear.) I say that a Socialistic state would be that state of society in which everything would be held in common, in which the labor of every individual would be directed and controlled by the State, to which State would belong all results of labor. I urge the importance of exact definitions. (Hear, hear.) The gentleman says that he represents a body which has issued some programme. One of the persons signing that programme writes himself, and he actually complains that the opponents of Socialism want too much definition and too much explanation of what is to be done, and he says that scientific Socialism gives no details. Dare you try to organise society without discussing details? It is the details of life which make up life. (Cheers.) The men who neglect details are lost in a fog, they have no sure path. You might as well build a house without bricks as discuss a scheme without details, and I object to vague phrases which may mean anything or nothing, and I object to being told that this is to be done by a revolution, to be effected by argument if possible. (Laughter.) We ought to know what it is to be done by if argument is not possible, and I will show you that argument will be impossible within a very few moments. The question is: "Will Socialism benefit the English people?" and by "benefit" I mean permanently improve the condition of, and by "the English people" I mean the majority of the English people. ("All.") I would say "all" if I could, but the man who says "all" is very likely to benefit none. (Laughter.) The practical way is to benefit the majority with the least injury to any. And I object that if a Socialistic State could be realised it could only be done by revolution; that it would require in effect two revolutions, one a revolution of physical force and the other a mental revolution, and I will show you that both of them are impossible. (Hear, hear, and interruption.) Permit me to say, even if you

are wiser than myself, you had better hear me first—to
laugh at me before hearing me may be Socialistic, but it
is not common sense. (Laughter and cheers.) I object,
if the two revolutions could be effected, and if Socialism
could be realised, that then it would be fatal to all progress by neutralising and paralysing individual effort, and
I say that civilisation has only been in proportion to the
energy and enterprise of the individual. (Hear, hear.)
Now I have said that in order to effect Socialism in this
country—and I am only dealing with this country—it
would require a physical-force revolution, because you
would want that physical force to make all the present property owners who are unwilling, surrender their private
property to the common fund—you would want that physical
force to dispossess them. You say "by argument if possible"; but how many property-owners are there? I say
that the property-owners are in the majority, not in the
minority. (No, no.) I am not going merely to say it, I
am going to prove it. (Applause.) I am going to prove
that the property-owners in this country are in the enormous majority. What is a property-owner? A property-
owner is that person who has anything whatever beyond
what is necessary for the actual existence of the moment.
All savings in the Savings Bank, the Co-operative Store,
the Building Society, the Friendly Society and the Assurance Society are property; and I will show you that there
are millions of working men in this country who are in
that condition. (Applause.) It is not true that the majority are starving. It is bad enough that any should
starve—it is terrible enough that any should starve; and I
and one other in this room at least have given evidence of
our sincerity in the discussion of this question. It is from
no ignoring of poverty, of the misery and the terrible crime
which grow out of it, that I speak; but I say you are hin-
dering the cure of it to pretend that the bulk are in that
condition, when it is comparatively the few. Property-
owners belong to all classes—the wage-earning class are
largely property-owners. (Oh, oh, and laughter.) I will
prove it—do not laugh till you have heard the evidence.
Ignorance does not give you the right to make a revolution.
In old times, before the science of medicine was studied,
quacks were ready to come forward to cure every disease,
and they did it with thorough honesty, with thorough confidence, and with thorough incapacity. Unless we test the

symptoms we may not agree even about the disease.
(Cheers.) I say, then, that physical force revolution must
fail because the majority are against you, and I say even
if it succeeded by the desperate energy of those owning
nothing who directed it, that then the crime of it and the
terror of it, and the mischief of it, and the long-enduring
demoralisation of it, would more retard and hinder progress than do any possible good—(great applause)—and I
allege that those who pretend when they are in a minority,
that science has given them the means to equalise strength
by the use of weapons and explosives, which were not
known in other times, are criminal in the highest degree.
(Bravo and interruption. A voice : "Coercion.") I would
try to coerce you by appealing to your brains, but if you
have not any I cannot help it. But I say that a Socialistic
State, even if it could be realised by force, could not be
maintained unless you make a mental revolution—a revolution in which you alter all present forms of expression—a revolution in which you efface the habit of centuries of education—a revolution in which the use of the
words "my house," "my coat," "my watch," "my
book," all disappear. (Oh.) "Oh!" you say; but why
may I have a gold watch? The man in the next street
has none. Is there to be common lot? Then where the
distinction? You say, "These are details," and I say,
Yes, they are details, they are the details that you have
not studied. (Applause.) I say that every form of expressing private property would have to be unlearned,
and for that you must cancel all your literature,
you must unteach all your teachers, you must un-
educate all your schoolmasters and re-educate them, and a
new dictionary will have to be invented. (Hear, hear.)
"Hear, hear," yes; but in the meantime what becomes of
society? Will you direct it? and who are "you"? (Laughter.)
I object that in a Socialistic State there would be no inducement to thrift, no individual savings, no accumulation,
no check upon waste. I say that on the contrary you would
have paralysis and neutralisation of endeavor, and that in
fact you would simply go back, you could not go forward.
(Hear, hear.) I urge that the only sufficient inducement
to the general urging on of progress in society is by individual effort, spurred to action by the hope of private
gain; it may be gain of money, it may be gain in other
kind, it may be gain in the praise of fellows or sharing

their greater happiness; but whatever it is, it is the individual motive which prompts and spurs the individual to action. (Hear, hear.) In this Collective Socialism, the State would direct everything, and there could be no freedom of opinion at all, no expression of opinion at all except that which the State ordered and directed. (Rubbish.) You say "Rubbish," and I think you correctly express your own thoughts, but at least do not anticipate mine. (Laughter.) If I want to lecture now I hire a hall if I can; I get people to come if I can; I pay for announcements if I can; my private risk enables me to do it, or that of those who stand by me, it is the same thing. In a State where the State owns the lecture hall, who shall have it? May I or some other who thinks he can speak? Will the hungry pay for the gas wasted on my empty room? How is it to be arranged? Will some committee decide whether there shall be such a lecture or not? Do not say these are foolish details; they are details of your system which you have to face. A public meeting, who may convene it—how many may concur in it—who shall provide the building—who pay for it? Or a pamphlet; at present I buy paper and print it if I can get a printer to trust me, or have the means of paying him; he prints it for his private profit at his private press. There will be no private presses, and no private printers, no private money to pay for it, or if there be, then your collective holding is a sham and a delusion. (Cheers.) How is a newspaper to be conducted which requires large capital? May it be conducted hostilely to the State? Will the State advance funds for the paper to advocate that you may make a revolution to overturn it? (Loud laughter and applause.) How will you arrange for museums and theatres, music halls and places of public resort? (Oh.) You may say "Oh," but there must be some amusement in life—if you live as dead as the Shakers, you will be as pale as the Shakers. They are honest, but they are gloomy. (Question.) They are honest, but they are sad, and they are only limited in number. Now that is done by private enterprise. How will you induce a great actor to stop here, or a good singer? He may get paid in other countries in the world for his private benefit, but here he must do it for the common good. How will you get great actors or singers at all? Will you train them? Shall the State select them early in life? Now people speculate in a special kind of education, and incur the risk, the individual risk, in the hope of gaining individual profit. (Hear, hear.) If you say these are nothing, then you have not stopped to consider it at all. How are you to deal with the railways? I prefer that all monopolies should be controlled by the State, which gives the monopoly. (Applause.) But that is not Socialism. ("Yes, it is.") That is not Socialism, for the railway is not everybody's property to use as everybody pleases; persons can only purchase the right of travelling upon it for the distance they want to go by parting with a portion of their individual earnings. How, when the State owns railways, is it to be managed? May I go to Aberdeen if and when I please? (Laughter.) Is the poor man who stops to earn my journey, or do you not think of any of these things at all? Omnibuses and cabs, how are they to be regulated when the collective property belongs to the organised State? How will you get your cabmen and chimney-sweeps? If you organise labor, you must pick all these men, and who is to be the "you" to pick them? How is the distinction to be made between employment on skilled and unskilled labor? Individual effort regulates all this; State effort would crush it all. You talk about foreign produce. How are you going to get it? You will have no markets here. ("Why not?") Why, if all things are owned by everybody, nobody can sell to anybody. (Laughter.) Are you going to send unpaid buyers abroad to use their great skill without reward to buy cheaply for you, and who are "you"? What may the State buy abroad—may it be luxuries for everybody, or only for some? and if for some, why only for some? and if no luxuries at all, how are you going to get people to act if there is a dead level which nothing can go beyond? Is the State to provide a private laboratory for scientists, and private libraries for students, to give the artist the proper means for study, for painting, or for music, or for sculpture, and if not, how will excellence in these be won? Or are these to be neglected? and if yes, what becomes then of the beauty which I think some one near me is in favor of. (Laughter, question.) There would be no encouragement to make beauty. You say "Question;" but it is the whole question. If you knock all beauty out of life, then life will not be left worth living. (Cheers.) I am told that property is to be held collectively, and one of the points in connexion with tha

is the nationalisation of the land. (Hear, hear.) Let me
show you whom you have to deal with, then. You have
to deal with some millions of people, not a handful, as
some say—not a mere handful of marauders, as some say.
For example, you have 1,057,896 persons in this country
holding small plots of land, the bulk of these probably in
centres of population, plots from under an acre up to fifteen
acres. How are you going to get them to give it up?
(Hear, hear.) And ought you to try? They are not
marauders. 500,000 of them are members of building
societies now, working men, and probably another 200,000
of them have been. (Hear, hear.) Are you going to fight
them, or are you going to leave them their private property, and only own collectively all the rest? In some
words which my able antagonist will recognise it was said:
"Force, or the fear of force, is unfortunately the only
reasoning which can appeal to a dominant estate, or which
will even induce them to surrender any portion of their
property." (Hear, hear.) You say "Hear, hear;" but
you must use that force against ten millions of the population. I will show you that ten millions of the population are
in possession of recorded property. Here are 1,057,000—
they represent at least four millions—(No, and cries)—
they have wives and children. You do not regard wives
and children. I do. (Cheers, and interruption from a
steward of the Democratic Federation.) You, who are so
indecent when you are here as a steward on the other side
to preserve order, at least set some example. The gentleman who now interrupts was good enough, at a recent
meeting, to suggest that I should have the first rope when
revolution came. At least let him be decent here. I say
the nationalisation of the land, if proposed, would render
at once bankrupt every life assurance company in the kingdom. They have some seventy-five millions invested of mortgage on landed property. You speak of a few thousands.
Why, in the ordinary savings' banks, in 1883, you have
1,900,000 depositors; in the Post Office Savings' Bank
2.706,612 depositors. [The Chairman here called "Time."]
Fight them! (Loud and prolonged cheering.)

Mr. HYNDMAN, who was again received with loud cheers:
Mr. Chairman, I must confess when I entered this hall I did
not expect that I had to explain all the details of bottle-
washers, cooks, and cabmen in the remote future. (Hear,
hear.) I must honestly say that it never entered my mind

that my opponent would adopt that line of argument. He has adopted some other lines of argument more, as it seems to me, germane to the matter, and with those I shall deal. I will commence, however, by saying that he correctly stated in a certain way the difference between us when he said that the difference was between the collective power and the individual power, but, as I pointed out in my opening address, when all have the vote, all are the State. (Hear, hear.) They could elect therefore for certain purposes all those whom they desired to organise their labor. It is just as possible for the worker in a factory, in a mine, or on the land to elect those who shall organise their labor and that they should exchange the products of that labor with those around them, as it is that somebody to-day should take upon himself, owning that property, to organise their labor and take from them the third part of the labor value they produce. (Cheers.) But, sir, my opponent said that I claim a novelty in this business. I claimed nothing of the sort. (Hear, hear.) Nor have I in anything I have ever written or said claimed any novelty whatsoever. What I say is this, that we Socialists to-day are the direct inheritors of whole generations of those who have worked before us, and more especially are we indebted to those who worked prior to 1848. Such men as Robert Owen —(hear, hear)—a noble and glorious man. He was unable to see the full historical development, but he worked hard for co-operation as far as he could see it. Such men as Bronterre O'Brien again, a really great man. (Bravo.) He demanded the nationalisation of the land, and denounced the villainy of capital under which the working class, as I contend, suffer to-day. Again, there were such men as Oastler, Stephens, Feargus O'Connor, to a certain point, and many more men who worked hard for the cause which we call Socialism to-day. It is perfectly true that for the organised scientific Socialism we are indebted to another great man, a foreigner this time, who lived thirty years in our midst; we are indebted to Dr. Karl Marx for that organisation, but I say that he himself was deeply indebted to these Englishmen, and acknowledged his indebtedness in everything he ever wrote, and that being so I claim no novelty. We claim a direct inheritance, and we stand here as international Socialists; beside that international Socialism we must have. But I am told the difference is between revolution and reform.

(Hear, hear.)　The revolution is going on to-day.　(Hear, hear.)　The revolution is here amongst us.　The very fact that we are here debating Socialism to-night, organised revolutionary Socialism, is itself a revolution. (Hear, hear.)　I say that two or three years ago it would have been impossible to have had this hall crowded by an audience perhaps evenly divided between those who agree with Socialism and those who are opposed to it, and I say that that in itself is a revolution of opinion, a mental revolution of that very kind that my opponent says we ought to bring about.　And what is that mental revolution?　It is a reflexion of, the revolution that is going on below in the forms of production to-day.　The revolution is going on day by day; electricity is supplanting steam, and steam is supplanting in other directions the old mechanical powers, and that constant competition of machinery with the skilled working man is producing a revolution in his lot, and rendering it more and more insecure.　Therefore, I say that is not reform; it is revolution.　(No.)　It is revolution, and we make ourselves the mouthpieces of that revolution, and desire to carry it out.　(Applause.) Again, I said " by argument if possible," and my presence here as a delegate to-night shows that we are anxious to convince.　Why, Sir, amongst our body there are many men who are wealthy to-day who are anxious to step down from their position of advantage.　(Oh, oh, laughter, and repeated cries of " Name, name.")

The CHAIRMAN : Gentlemen, be so good as to allow the speaker to continue without interruption.　If you take up his time, I shall be obliged to allow him longer time than the twenty minutes allotted to him.

Mr. HYNDMAN : Now, with relation to force, my opponent says that we are all for force.　Is there no force used to-day at all?　(Hear, hear.)　Has he not himself been the victim of force?　(Applause.)　I take it, Sir, that the force of to-day is constantly used within the letter of law, but in spirit illegally, in order to enforce the views of the dominant class.　(Hear, hear.)　We are told that argument, therefore, must fail, and that if argument fails, then we will resort to force.　Now, what is the position?　We know perfectly well that in the long run, unless you succeed by argument, force eventually does decide it.　But we should be madmen, we should be fools indeed, if we were to-day, when we have the right of public meeting, the free right of argument, if to-day we were to go before the English people, in the minority we are, and advocate force. We endeavor to convince them, and we say we are opposed to force because we believe force can destroy, but cannot reconstruct. We appeal to you not to bring force on yourselves, not to drive men to desperation, men many of whom are at present living in misery; but take hold of society around you and organise it for the benefit of all. (Applause.) Now, I am told further that Socialism denies all individual property alike. What did I say? I said, first of all, that we had the right, if we could get it, to the means of production. Very well, what does that mean? It means that in place of a class having control of the land, the machinery, the capital, and the credit, that the community should take them. I pointed out how in the Post Office, how in the railways, how in the factories, how in the shipping, it would be perfectly possible to continue the same system to-day. But who are the shareholders in the railroads: do they ever do any good in the world? They are simply using the labor of the dead in order to get the labor of the living. (Cheers). I say that the whole railway system to-day might be organised just as well for the benefit of the community, and far better for all the workers in this country, than it is to-day under the control of shareholders and Boards of Directors. I have been told that I am lost in a fog and that we are quacks, and a variety of other things. Such matters as this I never pay any attention to. I remember, sir, the phrase of a famous Frenchman who on one occasion, when an antagonist said that he was a fool, an idiot, a dolt, and a variety of other things, said: "I understand by all these pretty compliments that my antagonist does not agree with me." (Hear, hear.) I knew that, sir, before I came here. But I am accused of saying that the majority are starving. I never said such a word. I never said anything at all like it. What I said was that the majority of the population who had to compete with one another in the labor market either as producers, distributors, or as men who use their intellectual powers for others' benefit, were competing against one another for a subsistence wage, and I say further that when my opponent states that there is this large amount of property he seems to forget that it is not so, and if he will refer to the *Economist* of February 23rd, 1884, he will discover that the savings banks are not a criterion of the wealth of the wage-earning class. The return shows that the savings are owned by others. And with regard to this building society business which is brought forward, and the amount of land held by building societies, a great many of those lands are mortgaged heavily to the capitalist class; and in addition to that with regard to the large number of owners whom my opponent quotes from the Blue-books, I would ask him to look at the "Financial Reform Almanack," and see how those Blue-books have been fudged up, and how a single owner sometimes figures as eight or ten. But do you suppose that even those who hold building allotments are going to be dispossessed or injured? Suppose they get a full return for all the labor which they do, they would get in each year three or four times the amount of their building allotment. As a matter of fact the value of the labor which they get in the shape of wages is not more than one-third or one-fourth of the value which they produce. Now, that being so, how much greater return that is to them than the paltry building allotment, even supposing they were not mortgaged back to the capitalist class, as so many of them are. And again, how in any way does this small ownership benefit them? Take a period of distress like this, what happens? Do you not know that working men wage-earners throughout the country are forced to have resort over and over again to their savings, to sell out every little thing they have to tide over the period of depression? Look how it is to-day. How quickly that property fades away in times of depression. The little they have got together is soon gone, and very little indeed it is, not certainly enough to induce them to reject any system whereby they can obtain the means of production and relieve themselves from the domination of a class. I am told that there will be no incitement to thrift, and that no individual will be interested in doing anything for the advantage of the community, or to elevate himself. Sir, I think I may deny that any great thing has ever been done for direct personal gain. (Hear, hear.) I believe that a higher end and aim than that really has influenced mankind in every great advance that has been made. (Loud applause.) I appeal, sir, to higher motives that have governed mankind, not to low personal greed and profit which leads each man to strive to cut the others' throats for personal advantage.

I have yet to learn that Newton or Simpson or Darwin or Faraday worked as they worked for the sake of individual greed or individual advantage. (Applause.) They did not; they worked for the good of the human race, and because they worked for their fellows around them. Faraday himself lived on £400 a year, when he might have made four millions in his lifetime if he had chosen to patent what he did. (Oh, oh, and cheers.) He was the greatest chemical and electrical genius in his time, and he deliberately determined to give up his life to the sciences he had made his own. That has been so over and over again in the history of mankind. (Hear, hear.) All the great advances have been made by men, even under our present individual system, who were really imbued with the collective idea. It is said there would be really no high education. Why, sir, what education has been got for the people to-day has been really got by the interference of the State. (Hear, hear.) Even to-day they cannot get high education. Why? Because the upper and middle classes have laid their hands on the endowments intended for the benefit of the poor, and taken them to their own advantage. (Cheers.) That is what class domination does. The universities—to whom do they belong to-day? To the upper and middle classes. The higher education throughout is, as a whole, shut out from the poor, and I say again that until that organised Democratic State comes in to interfere our education will be the sham that it is to a large extent to-day. And amusement again! It would be out of our proceedings, and therefore I cannot appeal to it, but I say how much amusement is there for working-men to-day as a whole? How much enjoyment? How much can he use his time? I have spoken of this before, of the individuality. My opponent says all individuality will be crushed. I say individuality is crushed to-day. (Hear, hear.) And not for one class, but for all to a large extent. There are many of us who are crushed. Although some may have means, their intellectual development has been hampered from their earliest youth by the society around them, for they have not been able to emancipate themselves from these fetters that are around them in every direction. I say it cramps human intelligence to be perpetually thinking whether there will be bread-and-cheese for to-morrow. I say that so far from accumulation not being made, why under

every old communal form, far inferior to that which we are
working for, people were always a year or two years
ahead of their subsistence. Is that so with us? Not at
all. My opponent himself admits that there are many who
are constantly on the verge of starvation who are yet ready
to work. Very well. Then I say such individuality as that
means degradation, not elevation; it means injury, not
progress. (Cheers.) I think I have dealt in the main
with my opponent's arguments. (Hear, hear, and laughter.)
He has asked me to state how a newspaper could be brought
out under the new system. Well, what difficulty is there
in the organization of a body of men to bring out a newspaper? It is just as easy under any system of society as it
is to-day. At this very moment there is being introduced
into one of the largest printing offices in London a mechanical type-setter. A nice result that will be for the compositors, if there are any here, whereby a man sitting at a
table could play the types into the places it is necessary for
them to go into! ("Why not?") I say it is a great
advantage, but it is a very nice thing for the compositors
who would be thrown out as unskilled laborers on to the
street under our present system, but who would be benefited
by the newspapers coming out with much less labor under
the new system, which we champion. That thing applies
in every direction. I say that if all are liable to work; the
object of all will be to lessen the amount of necessary
work, whereas to-day the object of every class which is
living by profit is to increase the amount of work in order
that they may increase the amount of profit. But again,
and with this I will conclude. I would say, how is it that
the workers have got what little they have got? ("Through
Trades Unions.") Now, what are they but small communal societies? (Hear, hear.) They are societies in
which the individual sinks himself for the common advantage, and that is the only way in which they have
gained anything at all. That is the best evidence, that by
a wider extension of the same system all those who really
produce and are useful members will gain a similar
advantage. (Applause.)

Mr. BRADLAUGH (who was again received with loud
cheers): I regret that my antagonist imagined that some
words which I used to the persons who interrupted me
before I could get out my sentence, were intended to apply
to him. I could have had no right to apply it except to

the person who called my sentiments rubbish before he heard them; not one of those words had any application or was intended to have any application to the gentleman I am discussing with.

Mr. HYNDMAN: Then I beg your pardon.

Mr. BRADLAUGH: I am told first, that I have to consult the "Financial Reform Almanack" upon the Blue Books relating to land-owning. It is hardly necessary for me to do that, because I analysed the returns eleven years ago, and published an analysis of them long before they appeared in the "Financial Reform Almanack," although that is a very admirable publication. But no analysis would change the fact that 1,057,896 persons own small properties, 852,438 of them holding less than one acre —(A voice: "They are mortgaged")—and when I am told that they are mortgaged, it is perfectly true that the essence of a building society's plan is that the men who have not got the £200 to pay for their houses, are paying it out of their earnings by weekly or monthly instalments into the building society, the money being advanced at the commencement to enable the purchase to be made. And therefore the fact of their being mortgaged does not affect the statement I made. It is a lessening mortgage, and more than half-a-million of such small properties have been cleared during the last twenty years. The fact of their being mortgaged does not affect the argument, and if it does as to those who are mortgaged, how will you deal with the rest? Then I am told that the savings are not put in by the working classes, but by others. But which others? There are 4,500,000 depositors —who are the others? Is it the few thousand owners of capital who have done it? But you cannot make 4,500,000 of them. I will read the figures. There are and there were paid into the Savings Bank in 1883 (not the Post Office) £127,799,536; how could that be done by men only earning bare subsistence? It is not true. I do not care for the *Economist*. (Laughter). No, I have a knowledge of the people at least as good as any *Economist* writer. I should suggest that when you have 2,300,000 persons members of friendly societies, that every one of those persons belongs to the working-classes—(hear, hear)—and when you have 500,000 persons members of co-operative societies, I suggest to you that three-fifths of them belong to the working-classes—(hear, hear)—and when you have

half-a-million of people members of building societies, I
suggest to you that half of them at least belong to the
absolute artisan classes. (Cheers). And I say that if you
consider the words "working-classes" to mean persons
who exist by the sale of their labor, then the whole of
those belong to the working-classes—(hear, hear)—and
although it is perfectly true that the 4,500,000 depositors
in the Savings Banks may include many children and servants, yet out of those figures I have read to you, you
cannot have less than two and a half millions adult males
—there are more than that—representing at least 10,000,000
in population. (Hear, hear). And what are the figures?
The figures are of absolute savings left in the Savings'
Bank at the end of the year—Post-Office Savings' Banks,
£36,194,000; ordinary Savings' Banks, £45,403,569; and
then we are told that thrift is no good, because in the bad
times it is soon used. But if there is nothing, then in the
bad times it is starvation. (Applause). I am told that
man is blinded by thinking of bread and cheese for
to-morrow. It is not true. (Hear, hear, and Oh, oh).
It is not true. (Cheers and counter cheers). I am asked
what good these building societies have done. I refer you
to the great borough I have the honor to represent. I tell
you that the building society plots have removed hundreds
of them from squalor into cleanliness, and a whole district has grown up larger than the whole of the old town,
in which men who were dwelling in filth and misery have
now by their own individual exertions earned them
clean, healthy, moral homes. (Cheers.) You ask me what
is the good of it, and I answer you that in Lancashire,
during the twenty-five years that I have been familiar
with it, in the West Riding of Yorkshire, during the
twenty-five years I have known it, hundreds of cleanly
homes have sprung up in almost every district—thousands
through those counties—and I say that that has made
them more moral. I say that while they take no thought
of bread and hunger for to-morrow they will be paralysed
and indifferent, that they will have wasted themselves and
their lives, and I say that while they tried to surround
their wives and children with comfort, and acted with
thrift in providing for the morrow, they were making a
new race which will hinder the revolution you invoke.
(Loud applause.) You say, use argument if possible, if
not force must go. Eh! I read: "gunpowder helped to

sweep away feudalism with all its beauty and all its chivalry, when new forms arose from the decay of the old. Now far stronger explosives are arrayed against capitalism." I say it is not true; in this country there is no such array. I say it is a wicked lying libel to print it of the working men for whom I have the right to speak. (Prolonged applause.) I say that in the struggles in which labor takes part they would injure none. I say that they have grown out of the mad deeds of the old trades' unions, only possible when men were outlaws and had no rights; and I say they rely on the platform to-day, on the press to-day, and on the organisation of their great bodies and unions to-day, on their congresses to-day, and they regard that man as their worst enemy who dare put into the hands of the capitalist foe things like that. (Loud cheers, and a voice: "Read a little further.") I will read as far as I please. I have now another. I am told about shareholders in railways, and I find a proposal that they shall be expropriated with or without compensation—(hear, hear)—without compensation, and the national debt is to be extinguished. (Hear, hear.) Well, but you will then destroy every trade society in England —(hear, hear)—every life assurance company in England, every benefit society in England. Every savings bank will be ruined, for they have their money invested in Government securities and in these railway securities. You do not care for that, but I do, for I belong to the English people. And then you tell me when every man has a vote the State ceases. It does not. It is quite possible for every citizen to have a vote, and a very bad State to be left at the polling. (Hear, hear.) I am in favor of Democracy. (Oh!) Aye, and I ask for the vote for all. (Cheers.) I asked for the vote when some of you were opposing it. (Cheers.) I am told that force is used against me, and that I am a victim of it. I do not look much like a victim. (Laughter, and a voice: "You are, though.") No, I am not. I am winning liberty for those that come after me by showing respect to the law, and by fighting within the law. (Loud cheers.) And then you say that you appeal to higher motives, not to greed of gain. (Hear, hear.) I do not appeal to greed of gain alone. I pointed out one might be moved by the desire to be known or to be praised, and to deserve it. I pointed out all that in the speech I put to you. It is not true that there is only the greed of personal gain. But it is good and desirable to have that greed if you can make those around you less miserable, less starving with the gain that is won. You say you do not say the majority are starving. Why then do you pretend that the few take and that the bulk who earn are left without? (Hear, hear.) If those words have no meaning do not use them. You are right to modify them here, but you are wrong to print extravagant programmes which deceive the people. Take one illustration for example. Here you say that the total annual earnings of the country are £1,300,000,000, you say that of that the landlords take £1,000,000,000, and that the producers get £300,000,000. Where do you get your figures from? I find that the classes paying income tax pay income tax on £580,000,000 of income, and out of that these are incomes under £200 to the extent of about £26,000,000. There are incomes under £300 to the extent of about another £26,000,000. If all the rest are capitalists, which they are not, it would only leave £528,000,000, as against £772,000,000 of the total, £1,300,000,000. It is no use flinging about vague figures and big words. It is no use appealing in vague phrase to the future. The present is here. Do not talk of organising the State after you have destroyed this. Take the broom and sweep one street clean by individual effort, and do not blow bubbles in the air. (Loud applause.) I am told that the lines and argument I have used have surprised. That is hardly my fault— (hear, hear)—and it should not have been your misfortune; because I have delivered nearly every proposition I have put to-night in the course of a careful six lectures, some of which have been noticed in the journal with which I see your name connected. But why are these details not worth dealing with? Why do you jeer at the bottle-washer? Surely the bottle-washer is as good as the prince. (Hear, hear, and cheers.) I belong to the bottle-washers, and I want to know how our bottles are to be washed. Then you say, under the Socialistic State a number of men may organise a newspaper then as they do to-day. That is not true. They organise a newspaper to-day by clubbing together their private property, but they will then have no private property to club together. There will be no private paper-maker to buy paper from, no private printer to print it for them for hire. Everything will be held by the State, and can only be used under the

direction of the State. You have not answered any of the
the propositions I put to you, and unless you answer them
I cannot suppose you are prepared to deal with them.
(Cheers.) I regret that I did an injustice in suggesting
that the propositions you put you claim to be new. I
thought I heard it, and it shows I misunderstood. (Hear,
hear.) But I had thought there was some claim for the
newness in the speech which opened the debate. But if
you refer me for your views to Bronterre O'Brien, Feargus
O'Connor, and Robert Owen, you cannot unite those three
opposite men in any harmonious social system; the whole
of their plans and most of their ideas were opposed,
and nobody would say he inherited the whole of
their policy knowing it, if he gave his antagonist
credit for knowing any thing about it. Well now,
I would ask you here, and I ask all who have to
deal with this, to consider the question which is really
raised: "Will Socialism benefit the English people?"
(Cries of "Yes," and "No.") It is no use saying there
are people in filth and misery, poverty and crime. We
know it—we deplore it, and to the best of our ability, even
if wrongfully, we have tried for thirty years to awaken
men to the knowledge of it. You say organised society
will remedy it. That may be true, but you do not show us
the plan of organisation you propose. You say everybody
having a vote they will do right, but I have seen countries
where everybody has had a vote, and they have done
wrong. (Hear, hear.) You do not venture to say whether
you would have private property or not. You say first you
mean collective ownership, and then say you are not against
the private property of these people. You cannot blow
hot and cold. You must be for the annihilation of all
private property, or else your Socialistic system is of no
avail. You say that reform is revolution, that electricity
superseding steam or gas is revolution. It is a misuse
of words. New agents modify old conditions, modify
and do not destroy. It is progress, not destruction. It is
perfectly true that everything which benefits the human
kind by saving labor, injures some temporarily at the time
this benefit first comes; but those who judge worthily and
widely judge by the general benefit of the human race, and
you appeal to the worst passions when you try to excite
men amongst the audience who may be compositors, and
who may be driven out of employ by machines. It is what

was done in the old blanket-weavers' days. It is what was
done in the old days in Lancashire and Lanarkshire. It is
what has ever been done by men who deal with these great
social problems without belonging to and having their
hearts in the welfare of the people. (Loud cheers.) Instead of making the State all-powerful, I would make the
individual so strong for good that the State would have
little left to do. (Hear, hear.) Every State interference
with liberty is only defensible to-day because of the corrupt
social state which we have got to remedy. (Cheers.) We
are not beginning with a new plan, we are dealing with an
old society; and when you talk of International Socialism,
the wants of every nation differ, their wrongs differ,
their needs differ, their traditions differ, and their aspirations differ. You cannot bring twenty honest earnest men
of diverse countries together in any part of the world to plan
reform but what you find their schemes, suggestions, and the
whole of their trains of thought are different from one another.
Then words suggesting force have no right to be used with
the possibility of bad deeds behind them. The hungry are
always ready to strike—(hear, hear)—and if you tell property owners we will not take from you by force if you give
up willingly, it is the doctrine of the highwayman, who says:
"Your money, or your life. I will not take your life if
you give me your money, but I shall be compelled to shoot
you if you do not." (Great applause.) I am glad, short
as this time is, that at least we have met to exchange some
thoughts upon this question; but when the speaker says
that two or three years ago such a discussion would have
been impossible, it shows that he does not know the history
of the country to which I belong. (Hear, hear.) Archibald
Campbell, Robert Owen, Lloyd Jones, debated this very
question before crowds as big as this thirty, thirty-five,
and forty years ago, and those who say "No" simply do not
know the history of their own country. (Hear, hear.) We
are for reform. Revolution means destruction first. We
will cure gradually. If we try to cure the whole immediately, we must poison and destroy. We have to deal with
generations of ill and habit that cannot be swept away by
the stroke of a magic wand. It wants great patience, great
endurance, bearing great obloquy. All those who preach
class war do not know what life should be. Class war is
murder; class war is fratricide; class war is suicide; and
those who rail at the bourgeoisie may have won the right

by hard toil, in mine and vein, with bar, pick, and shovel to do it; but if not, they should think long before they attempt the railing. (Loud cheers.)

Mr. Hyndman (who was again cheered on rising): Mr. Chairman, friends, and fellow citizens, before going to any further arguments of my opponent's, I will conclude the sentence which he left unconcluded. (Hear, hear.) He says he quoted the passage: "Gunpowder helped to sweep away feudalism with all its beauty and all its chivalry, when new forms arose from the decay of the old; now far stronger explosives are arrayed against capitalism, whilst the ideas of the time are as alive with revolution"—that cannot be doubted, I think—"as they were when feudalism fell. To avoid the like crushing anarchy of to-day"— I gave some instance of it in my opening speech—"and the fierce anarchy of to-morrow, we are striving to help forward the workers of the control of the State as the only means whereby such hideous trouble can be avoided, and production and exchange can be organised for the benefit of the country at large." (Cheers.) Now, Sir, I utterly deny that that passage bears the interpretation which my opponent put upon it. (Cheers.) I say, Sir, he should not, knowing what followed, have stopped where he did. I do not think it was quite fair—(hear, hear)—and I now put it to you whether that does not alter the sense entirely of the passage where he stopped. (Applause.) I say we are working here—aye, working every day. He has worked many years in his cause, and I thank him for what he has done. He has done great good—I know that. But I say we are working to-day because perhaps we see a little farther than he does. (Laughter and cheers.) He has spoken of the great advantage in his own town. I do not happen to know the town of Northampton; but he has spoken of Lancashire, and says the people there are producing a new race, a race stalwart and gallant——

Mr. Bradlaugh: I never said so.

Mr. Hyndman: I beg your pardon, sir, a new race which should withstand the revolution we were approaching. I say, take the blue book of 1875, and let him study the degradation, the physical misery of the popular centres, and then say what do you say of the new race. I lived in Stockport twenty-five years ago, and I have been back there several times since, and I state positively that the people of to-day are punier and more stunted than they were twenty-five years ago. (Cheers.) I say the factory work, as admitted to-day by the report of every certifying surgeon, means degradation to the women and children who work in those mills, and I say, if that is the new race let us have the old one. Remember it is only by re-organisation that you can stop this miserable degeneration that is going on absolutely to-day. (Hear, hear.) Again I am asked with regard to the figures which were given, where do you get them from? I will tell you, from Mr. Giffen and Mr. Mulhall. Mr. Giffen puts the annual income of the country at 1,200 millions sterling, Mr. Mulhall at 1,247 millions sterling, to which you have to add the amount which comes to this country from foreign countries in return for various investments we have there. Now then, in the year 1869 Mr. Dudley Baxter, quite as good an expert as either Mr. Mulhall or Mr. Giffen, put the earnings of the wage-earning class at 255 millions sterling out of a smaller income, and Mr. Giffen himself, only six years ago, put the earnings of the wage-earning class at £338,700,000. When he denied that in the *Times* I sent the figures to show that he did say so, but the *Times* would not print my letter against Mr. Giffen. That shows how it is. Therefore, I say, going from the figures, upon the system my opponent urges, the working class get about one-fourth or one-third at the outset of the total produce and wealth of this country, and I say that all the talk about building societies, and all the talk about the enormous investments that they have, must read like bitter irony to men who see 800 millions of their wealth being taken from them by the social arrangements of to-day. (Cheers.) Again, Sir, I am told that Bronterre O'Brien, Feargus O'Connor and Robert Owen differed. I know they did; but do not we inherit the learning of Aristotle and Plato, although they were absolutely opposed? Certainly we do. (Hisses and cheers.) We are indebted to both. What I say is this, that Feargus O'Connor, as I told you, differed from the other two very much, but O'Brien and Owen were both of them Socialists although in a different way. (Laughter.) We are deeply indebted to the men who preach the nationalisation of the land as O'Brien did and as Spence did, and we are deeply indebted to Robert Owen who showed how if the State were to take possession capital might be dominated. He himself did not work that out because he could not, but he showed how it could

be done. (Laughter.) Read his works any of you who
doubt—read his "Combination between Land and Capital"—but where he failed was that he had not seen the
historical development which leads up to State domination,
but the State domination not under the control of a class
as it is to-day, but under the control of the people for the
benefit of all. I never said that universal suffrage of itself would right anything. It is this very mental change
which must be wrought, the mental change we are trying
to bring about. I say the organised power of the community
must be used with the definite forces which now dominate
them. I never contended for a single moment that universal suffrage was alone enough; time, education, organisation, better knowledge are all necessary in order
to bring about that which we desire, but you will
not bring it about by simply exalting the individual.
As I pointed out to my opponent, the one good thing the
working classes have done, they have done as Trade Unionists, by combination, by sinking the individual against the
class which is organised against them. They must dominate it by organisation. My opponent admits the corrupt
social state; but this very social state is all round us. I
am told there is no social war. Is there no social war?
What happened at Kidderminster the other day? Unfortunately it was attended with violence, but it was begun
by the capitalist. They began by substituting female
labor for men's labor in order to make more profit. Was
not that class war, using a man's own wife against himself?
(Cheers.) Why, Sir, under the present system a man's
foes are indeed those of his own household. His own wife
and children are brought in to compete with him on the
labor market. Now, I say that this is class war, that we
see the way in which the war is going on, and we desire
that that class war shall inure to the benefit of the
community and all those above all who work. But I am
told that in dealing with these things I omit points that
Mr. Bradlaugh puts to me. I say that these small matters
are as nothing compared to what I have already proposed:
to give food to all children in school, to the control of the
land by the people, and by permitting the whole of this
country to be used, not as it is used to-day for a comparatively small minority, especially the agricultural land.
Take the condition of the land. Look at the great landowners who dominate over us. Look at the Duke of Bed-

ford and the Duke of Westminster, and men like those. Is that the result of individuality my opponent wishes to see? I say let us municipalise the land—let us apply it to all classes by cumulative taxation, as we advocate. (Cheers.) Again, if you take the question of railroads and the National Debt. The National Debt was imposed and the railroads were sold to the shareholders by a class. The people were never represented. They never gave their assent to this enormous debt. They never gave their assent to this most egregious monopoly. They have never been asked yet whether they approve of these enormous monopolies. They have never been asked whether they approve of this indebtedness. I say let it be put to them. Let this question be put boldly before them—whether they are willing to sanction what has been done by a class or whether they are not. That is what I say we are attempting to do, and we shall achieve it. (Cheers.) I am told we are appealing to the hungry. We are not. We are appealing here to-night to the educated and the intelligent, and the men who have something, because we say hungry men make revolutions and riots, but they never made and organised revolution yet. It is the best educated and organised and capable men who have always made revolutions in our country. The revolution of 1641 to 1649, one of the greatest revolutions in history, was made in the interest of the middle classes, but how was it made? It was made by strong, stalwart, well-conducted, well-fed men. I say those revolutions were beneficial, and I say that such a revolution to-day, although God forbid it should come by force, I trust will come with the organised education of all. (Cheers.) But I say that such a revolution will enhance individuality, it will relieve people from this crushing domination of a class, and will enable each man to exhange through Government banks and Government distributive centres. Then men may have and own the fruits of their labor whereby they may all benefit. Therefore I say that what we look to is a thoroughly organised England wherein each man will work for all, where there will be free exchange of the fruits of labor without any profit, and where we shall hold up a really organised centre for mankind. (Applause).

Mr. BRADLAUGH (who was again received with cheers): I did not gather that the words which were read in any way explained or modified these words: " Now far stronger explosives are arrayed against capitalism," and I should have liked to have known, in the mind of one of the signers who happens to be speaking this evening, what that meant. If it did not mean that a stronger explosive than gunpowder was a weapon which could and might be arrayed in this war, then it has no meaning whatever. (Hear, hear. A voice: "It meant moral force.") A moral explosive! (Laughter.) A moral explosive stronger than gunpowder! There must have been an explosive in a vacuum there, I am afraid. (Laughter.) Then I am told that the times are as rife with revolution now as when feudalism was destroyed. It is not true. It is simply the repetition of words without meaning, or which if meant, are not true. No evidence was given of it, and to use vague phrases of this kind is utterly and wholly misleading. There is a respect for law amongst the people now that did not obtain at all then. There is an industry and saving now that did not exist at all then. I will remind you that on every matter which has been contradicted, when challenged upon it, no sort of evidence has been given. I asked who were the "others" than working folk of the 4,500,000 depositors; not the slightest explanation is given. My definition of Socialism has not been touched—never even objected to; yet if it be the true definition, it is fatal to the whole of the argument that has been put to us. (Hear, hear.) Then it has been put upon me that I have said there is no class war. I never said so. I rebuked those who try to make a class war. (Hear, hear.) There is too much class war, and I have done my best in my short life to try to diminish it—(a laugh)—and those who laugh are probably incapable of comprehending either the disadvantage or the work. (Cheers.) At least they do not convey to me the notion that Socialism involves courtesy in its communication with opponents. (Oh.) I am glad to have another illustration of the truth of what I am saying. (Question.) Then I am told it is not true what I have said about Lancashire and Yorkshire, but here again the point that I urged was not grappled with. I said the houses were better, newer, cleaner, and the only answer made is as to the places they work in. I dealt with the homes built within the past twenty years [Mr. Hyndman expressed dissent]; it is no use shaking your head; it was the homes I mentioned. I said that more human homes had been built and healthy surroundings provided, in which a man found the opportunity of making his wife and children more comfortable. It is true that there are many factories very bad, but it is not true of the whole of them; it is not even true of the majority of them erected in the present generation. (Hear, hear, and Oh.) I have been in hundreds of them. My speech will go amongst Lancashire and Yorkshire men who work in those mills, and who will know whether what I am saying is true or not. (Cheers.) In every new mill built in the last twenty years the best resources of science have been utilised, because owners of capital have found that under comfortable conditions more is got from the labor, and therefore they do it. (Hear, hear.) Ah! but if that is true, it gives the lie to the position taken. (Ridiculous.) You say it is ridiculous. Your saying it is ridiculous is simply to say you are ignorant of the classes you propose to organise. Then I am told that Trades Unions work on Socialist lines. (No.) Yes, that was said—by combination and co-operation. But combination does not necessarily involve socialism, nor does co-operation Each co-operative society owns its own property; each trade society watches its own interests; and it is because they are their own interests that they try to watch them. (Applause.) What they have learned is that, by the different trades meeting together in congresses year by year, they may not waste their efforts in fighting against one another, and may turn them to the real utilisation of their advantages in the struggle for life. Then I am told "we want the control of the land." But how? And what will you do with that 1,000,000 of people? You have said nothing about that. You say that the nation has not approved of the railways being constructed as they are; but that does not give you the right to steal them. There are poor people who own shares as well as rich ones, poor people whose livelihood depends on them. You ought to deal with details, and if you are incapable of details, you have no right to try and move the people towards overturning what exists. (Applause.) You say that you have not appealed to the starving, I say you have told the whole of the wage-earning class that they are starving. You say: "To-day the worn-out wage slaves of our boasted civilisation look hopelessly at the wealth which they have created to be devoured only by the rich and their hangers-on." (Cheers.) I tell you that is not true. I have always claimed that the rich take too much (hear hear); but it is not true that they take all. It is not true that the State has educated the people. The people, in many fashions, have educated themselves. They won cheap papers against the State; they sold the unstamped press, and broke through against the State. Lancashire men and Yorkshire men did it. From Stockport's neighborhood, which you say you know, thirty men lay in gaol one Christmas day in the fight for a free press and to win this education. (Great cheers.) When you used the three names and spoke of the system from them, and I show you the systems contradict each other, all you say is we inherit all their wisdom. So every generation inherits the whole of the wisdom of the generations which go before; but that is not Socialism. It was individual effort that gained the wisdom and left its record. The individual Aristotle who reasoned, the individual Plato who wrote, the individual Bronterre O'Brien who taught, and these men would have been crippled and gagged in your Socialistic State, which would have left them no platform, no voice. (Applause.) I know, in appealing to the miserable, they may be moved by their misery, but you will not cure their misery by vague preaching. You say you desire revolution—you say you are clamoring for it. These are the words you use. You say: "We are urging it on;" and I say it is the duty of every honest man to delay and prevent revolution. (Great cheers.) Revolution if it must come is terrible, if it must come it is horrible, revolution means ruined homes, it leaves behind the memory of bloody deeds. (Cheers and groans.) I speak for the English people, which through generations of pain and toil gradually has climbed towards liberty, the liberty of which they have won some glimpses, and which they are claiming still. I speak for the people—who are ready to suffer much if they may redeem some, who know that the errors of yesterday cannot be sponged away in a moment to-day, and who would try slowly, gradually, to mould, to modify, to build, and who declare that those who preach international Socialism, and talk vaguely about explosives, are playing into the hands of our enemies, and giving our enemies an excuse to coerce us. (Prolonged cheers.)

Mr. HYNDMAN: Friends and fellow-citizens, it is now my pleasant duty to ask you to accord a hearty vote of thanks to the honored English gentleman who occupies the chair. He is a man whose whole life has been devoted to working in the interests of the poorer classes of this country, a man who twenty years ago took the chair when no other man dared, a man who in conjunction with his friends stood forth on behalf of Trades Unions when they were abused and denounced by all the upper classes of this country. I say we owe him for his presence here to-night and the admirable way in which he has conducted this meeting, our sincere thanks, and I ask you to join with us in giving him a very cordial vote.

Mr. BRADLAUGH: I have pleasure in seconding that vote. I have learnt may lessons from your chairman twenty-five years ago, lessons which have served me, and I desire to tender him my thanks while I second the proposition that you give him yours. I desire to thank you who have listened patiently to some things that have offended you.

The resolution was carried with acclamation.

The CHAIRMAN: Gentlemen, I am very much obliged to you for the very kind way in which you have given this vote of thanks. My duty to-night has been an extremely easy one. As you have seen, the meeting has conducted itself in the most orderly manner, and the credit of it is entirely and alone to you and to the good temper with which the two disputants have carried on the discussion.

Will Socialism Benefit the English People?

A WRITTEN DEBATE BETWEEN

E. BELFORT BAX AND CHARLES BRADLAUGH.

LONDON:

FREETHOUGHT PUBLISHING COMPANY,

63, FLEET STREET, E.C.

1887.

LONDON:
PRINTED BY ANNIE BESANT AND CHARLES BRADLAUGH,
63, FLEET STREET, E.C.

WILL SOCIALISM BENEFIT THE ENGLISH PEOPLE?

FIRST PAPER BY E. BELFORT BAX.

MODERN Socialism may be defined as a new view of life (*i.e.*, of human relations) having an economic basis. Although its theory has been already many times expounded of recent years by myself and others, it may be deemed necessary on the present occasion for me to go over the ground once more. The economic goal of modern or scientific Socialism, no less than that of the Utopian Socialism of Owen, Fourier, St. Simon, etc., which preceded it, is the equal participation by all in the necessaries, comforts, and enjoyments of life, and the equal duty of all to assist in the necessary work of the world. But while the Utopian Socialism believed this to be attainable by mere individual initiative and example without any special reference to the condition of the world as a whole, Modern Socialism finds the earnest of its ideal in the facts of social evolution[1]— and it is on this rock of the ages, with its many-hued strata of economic-formation, that the modern Socialist builds his faith.

Society, it is generally admitted in the present day, began

---

[1] We are so much accustomed to the idea of Evolution in the present day, that we can with difficulty understand its absence. Hence the fallacious antithesis made between Evolution and Revolution. The true antithesis to the notion of social Evolution is not that of Revolution, but the idea of the possibility of isolated individuals or groups being able to change society, so to say, abstractly and of their own initiative, irrespective of the general current of human progress.

B 2

to expand under the ægis of a limited, unconscious and
crude tribal Socialism, in which property was in common,
and morality and religion consisted in devotion to the
social unit.   This in the course of progress lapsed, owing
to its credulity and limitation in scope, and was gradually
supplanted by Civilisation with its basis of Individualism
in economics, morals, religion, etc.; the latter in its turn
is, as Socialists believe, now after many a century, in the
moment of its completest realisation, destined to undergo
a transformation in which its fundamental principle will
be sacrificed and the old solidarity again assert itself,
purged ·from its imperfections, and with the seal of completeness and universality upon it.

Such, in a few words, is the skeleton of the historical
theory of Socialism.   With what we may term the first
transformation of society (from Tribal Communism to
Civilisation) it would be beside the present question to deal
further.   I therefore, having stated the fact, pass on to
consider in more detail the development of the completest
form of Civilisation, viz., modern Capitalism, with the
nature of the process by which Socialists believe its transformation into a real social order will be effected; and
lastly the reasons why such social order must benefit the
English people no less than every other people.

Modern Capitalism, and the civilisation which is its
expression, is the most extreme antithesis in every respect
of tribal society.   All the ties which formerly bound the
individual to his group are ruptured.   Modern society is
based on the nominal independence of the individual as
unit.   Let us briefly trace the development of this independence on its economic side from the Middle Ages down-
ward.   The earliest distinctive form of mediæval society,
that of the feudal estate, was for the most part an industrial whole, the links connecting it with the outer world
being few, and seldom indispensable to its existence.   Well-
nigh everything produced on the estate came from its soil.
The *villein* and his sons tilled the ground, reaped the
harvest, and hunted the wild animals, raised domestic
stock, felled the trees, built the dwelling, etc.; his wife
and daughters spun the flax and carded the wool, which
they worked up into articles of clothing; brewed the
mead, gathered the grapes, made the wine, etc.   Division
of labor and a system of exchange in a society on this plan

were obviously unessential. This system, as everyone knows, continued the dominant one throughout Europe for centuries. But in the course of time it gradually gave way before the growing town industrial organisation of the guilds. Each man here worked to maintain himself or his family at a *particular* handicraft, by exchanging or selling the product of his labor. In this way specialisation of labor and a more extended commerce arose. But the mediæval burgher was neither free nor a capitalist in the modern sense. Though only indirectly, if at all, under the domination of a lord, he was under the very strict *surveillance* of his guild. The guild, by regulating the number of his apprentices and the quality of his material and work, took good care that he should not develop his individualistic instincts. The burgher class of the Middle Ages was nevertheless the forerunner of the modern middle class. As the mediæval system broke up, the guilds gradually declined. A floating class of journeymen wage-laborers came into existence and flooded the towns, while the burgher class became restive at the restrictions of their own guilds, of which wealthy cliques soon obtained the entire control, while a new middle-class established itself outside the chartered cities. This development, essentially the same throughout the progressive races, is typically represented in England. The symptoms of the dissolution of the economical conditions of the Middle Ages were, the uprooting of the people from the soil, and the abolition of the old feudal and communal rights, the dissolution of the monasteries and the old feudal establishments, the opening up of a world-market, the new inventions, etc. Such was the soil out of which modern Capitalism grew, as expounded by Marx in the second volume of "Das Kapital" (English translation.) Modern Capitalism, and therewith the modern "middle-class", its embodiment, dates from the sixteenth century. Its industrial course has been marked by three phases: (1) simple co-operation of a number of handicraftsmen under the lead of a wealthy burgher; (2) the manufacture or workshop system; and (3) the "great machine industry" which arose at the end of the last century and has been expanding itself in scope and intensity ever since. With this, its last phase, production for use has given way completely before that production for profit which breeds to-day the commercial rottenness we see around us. Wares of all kinds are now produced for a forced sale, by means of their cheapness—"gluts" succeed to "booms"—till trade depression becomes permanent. The small capitalist is continually being thrown upon the labor market by inability to hold his own in the competitive arena. Capital tends thus to become concentrated in fewer and fewer hands, while the reserve army of labor tends steadily to augment. The result is increasing riches for the few and increasing poverty for the many. The "increase of national wealth" at the present day means increase of misery for the mass of the people.

The economical change toward complete Individualism, the issue of which is the modern capitalistic system, has been accompanied by political, moral, and religious changes intimately connected with it, but which, important as they are, I can only notice very briefly here. (1) The break-up of the feudal states helped to consolidate the power of the Crown. This it was which completed that economical revolution in breaking down the local centres or feudal groups with their common lands, traditions, customs, and jurisdictions, isolated the individual, and laid the foundation of the modern centralised national systems of Europe. (2) The economical backbone of the landed class as a class being broken, the political power passed both by gradual process and revolutionary crisis into the hands of the new capitalist or monied classes. This was partially effected in England by the "glorious Revolution" of 1689; in France more completely by the Great Revolution of 1789. From the sixteenth century downwards political history is the history of the middle or trading classes in their efforts to free the individual from the fetters of feudalism and monarchy, to the end that on the one side there might be a body of free and landless laborers, and on the other a body of moneybags free to exploit them. To effect the end in view political power was necessary, and though obtained in this country, in principle, in 1689, or even at the Commonwealth, was not finally and fully realised till the Reform Act of 1832.

(3) Then again, the individualistic tendencies of bourgeois economics are reflected in its religion and ethics. As I have elsewhere shown, Christianity is through and through individualistic. But during the Middle Ages its

individualism was subordinated to the current communal and pagan tendencies it took on from the barbarians, and the form it assumed was largely colored by these tendencies. Hence Catholicism has been in many respects the least objectionable form of Christianity, precisely because its spirit is the least Christian. Just as every member of the local community of peasants had a right as such to the common land, etc., so every member of the universal church or community of saints had a right as such to the heavenly pastures. The Reformation, the religious side of the rise of capitalistic individualism, affirmed salvation to be a matter solely of personal concern. It tore the individual away from his spiritual moorings, just as it had torn him away from his temporal moorings, and left him to shift for himself. It pretended to be a restoration of primitive Christianity, and this was true as regards spirit if not as regards doctrine. For primitive Christianity was also the ideal expression of the dissolution of communal life—in this case the civic life of the classical world. Protestantism has always accentuated the doctrine of individual responsibility to the deity; religion under Protestantism became personal and matter-of-fact, *i.e.* eminently bourgeois.

(4) With ethics proper it has been just the same. The highest Protestant conception of goodness is, not zeal for social ends but a maundering self-introspection, having personal holiness for its end.

The results of commercial individualism we see at the present day on all hands, and nowhere in richer luxuriance than among the "English people", unless it be in the United States, where the economic development has gone further even than in this country. Let us only look around at the material aspect of things—the universal empire of shoddy goods, jerry buildings, foulness and squalor. As one enters London or any other large city, what is it that greets the eye? A vast agglomeration of filth in every conceivable variety of form—railway works, factories, slums—indicative of human misery that no tongue or pen could adequately describe. Had Dante lived now and wanted material for his vision of hell, he would only have needed to take the South-Eastern train on landing at Dover, and depict the place he saw as he entered the English metropolis. And for what ostensibly is human nature, and for what are the vast majority of human lives ground down to being thus *the slave of the mere process of production and distribution?* Forsooth, in order that a relatively small class may live either without labor at all or with the labor of the gambler[1]—which latter the literary *flâneur* glorifies under the name of the *aleatory.*

In my own eyes, statistics have no great value, experience showing that they can be made to prove any proposition in the hands of a clever manipulator. To my thinking, a day's journey through the slums of a great city proves more than tons of statistics. One fact outweighs a thousand figures. But since I am not writing altogether on my own account, but also on behalf of the Socialist League, and many persons like to see figures in an article of this kind, here are some. First you have H. M. Hyndman's figures: £1,300,000,000 annual revenue of the country, of which £300,000,000 only accrue to the working classes who produce it, the remaining £1,000,000,000 going in various proportions to the non-producing classes. I am not aware how Hyndman arrives at these figures, but I have never seen them seriously controverted, and they seem to me to express admirably the ratio one would *expect* to obtain, on a rough estimate, judging from the facts of modern social life. Then you have the statistics carefully compiled by G. B. Shaw in Fabian Tract No. 5.[2] These give a similar total, but the proportions as £800,000,000 to the non-producers and £500,000,000 to the producers. In a footnote, however, to page 9 of the document in question, the amiable and witty author significantly remarks that these statistics assume regularity of employment and take no account of deductions for ground-rent, which being interpreted must mean that a sum not very much less than £200,000,000 has to be taken off the lesser and added to the greater amount, so that after all we are brought back approximately to the Hyndman figures quoted above. But, as I before said,

---

[1] It is amusing and instructive, as illustrative of bourgeois humbug, to listen to middle-class paterfamilias and his holy horror of Monte Carlo and similar establishments, where gambling is at least honestly and straightforwardly carried on, while this same worthy himself thieves and gambles every day in "business" or stock-exchange speculations.

[2] Mr. Bax is in error in ascribing Tract No. 5 to the pen of G. Bernard Shaw.—A. B.

such figures as these have no value to me except as a
"cut-and-dried" statement of the fact obvious in itself
without the aid of any figures at all—to wit, that society
is composed of two fundamental classes, a relatively small
class of monopolists that possesses the bulk of the wealth
produced, and a very large class of producers that con-
sumes only a fraction of that wealth. These classes, of
course, shade off into one another, but the fact of their
existence and of the antagonism of their interests still
remains an indubitable truth.

It is this great curse of civilisation which Socialists
would fain see abolished. Many would doubtless gladly
have a wave of barbarism sweep this rottenness away as it
swept away the effete classical civilisation. But the Socialist knows that this would only mean the martyrdom of
nineteenth century progress, or something like it, having
to be gone over again. There is no effective putting back
the clock of human evolution. No, Civilisation can be only
definitively overthrown by Socialism. The state-world, the
civitas, can only become a social world, a *societas*, by a
revolution generated in the fulness of its own development. The means of the present exploitation of labor, the
cause of the present horrible state of things is monopoly.
Its *modus operandi* is the extraction of surplus value from
the laborer by compelling him to work a whole day while
receiving only so much of the results of his labor as is
necessary to keep him in bare subsistence. Remove the
monopoly from the hands of individuals, and you do away
with the possibility of surplus value. The above revolution then consists in the assumption by the people themselves, organised to this end, of the means of production,
distribution, and exchange (as explained in the Socialist
manifestos), and in the working of them in their own
interest, that is, in the interest of the whole community.
This would, of course, soon result in the extinction of that
"private enterprise", whose exploits consist in destroying
all the worth of life under pretence of enhancing it,
but really in the interests of individual greed. That
"stimulus of personal interest" which spreads like a
cancer through artistic and literary productivity, flooding
the world with cheap and nasty work, would be finally
cut up by the roots. Industry would be regulated
consciously with a view to the needs of Society so far

as ascertainable. Wealth would be produced for *use*, and not for *profit*.

With the abolition of classes, consequent on the abolition of monopoly, national rivalries, at present mainly reduced to questions of commerce, would come to an end. The break up of the present State-nationalities of Europe would be one of the first results of Socialism, which is nothing if not international. The sphere of politics would be gradually merged in that of industrial direction. With no independent nations there would be no national interests, as such; with no classes there would be no class-interests, as such. Bourgeois civilisation at an end, there would be no longer any object in maintaining the sham of a creed to which the modern proletariat as a class has has never attached itself, and in which nine-tenths of the educated middle-class have not only ceased to believe by their own confession, but for which even the sentimental attachment they may have had some decade and a half back, is rapidly waning. Finally, with the consummation of individualism in Economics comes the destruction of individualism in Ethics, whether in its brutal form of (so-called) Utilitarianism or self-interest, or in its inverted and apotheosised form of introspective maunderings having "personal holiness" as an end. Both must give place to an Ethic in which social and individual interest have ceased to conflict, which has as its foundation the principle that the *perfect individual is realised only in and through the perfect society*, and which hence abandons the morbid striving after individual perfection for the healthy endeavor after social happiness. Politics will thus become ethical and ethics political. Personal will be no longer divorced from public character. Social order will supervene on anarchy.

Will Socialism benefit the English people? Will fresh air benefit the suffocating man? Will food benefit the starving man? Will rest benefit the weary man? If not, perhaps Socialism will not benefit the English people. Otherwise, the question "Would Socialism benefit the English people?" would seem to partake of the ironical.

Mr. Bradlaugh's Reply to First Paper by Mr. E. Belfort Bax.

1. The question which ought to have been discussed between Mr. Bax and myself is, "Will Socialism benefit the English People?" Having carefully read the opening paper by Mr. Bax, on whom is now the duty of affirming the proposition that Socialism will benefit the English people, I am afraid that such a discussion is unlikely to be effectual if conducted on the lines of that opening paper.

2. The first step should, I submit, have been to make clear precisely what it is that Mr. Bax means when he uses the word "Socialism"; and then there should have been some attempt to show how such Socialism could be put in practice in this country; what were the beneficial results to the English people to be expected as the consequence of such Socialism in practice; and why any such benefits, if secured by the English people, were to be regarded as solely or mainly attributable to Socialism. In the first step Mr. Bax has, I think, failed; the other points he has not even touched, unless the very vague generalities I shall notice presently are considered by him sufficient.

3. Mr. Bax says that he defines "Modern Socialism" "as a new view of life (*i.e.* of human relations) having an economic basis", and he adds that "the economic goal of modern or scientific Socialism" "is the equal participation by all in the necessaries, comforts, and enjoyments of life, and the equal duty of all to assist in the necessary work of the world"; and he afterwards affirms that Socialism is to be realised "in the assumption by the people themselves, organised to this end, of the means of production, distribution, and exchange, and in the working of them in the interest of the whole community".

4. But it is no definition to say that Socialism is a new view of human relations upon an economic basis unless the "view" and the "basis" are both clearly explained, and this explanation has certainly not been given by Mr. Bax in the paper to which I am now replying. He does speak of the "economic goal", but can scarcely mean that the "goal" to be arrived at is with him the equivalent for

the "economic basis" from which the Socialistic system
starts.

5. Then Mr. Bax says that the economic goal of the
the Socialism which he ought to affirm, "no less than the
Utopian Socialism of Owen, Fourier, St. Simon, etc.", is—.
I will omit the "etc.", as much too vague for serious discussion, and will ask Mr. Bax, does the "no less" mean
that the Socialism he affirms is at least that of, or at least
the equivalent of, those of Robert Owen, Charles Fourier,
and Claude Henri St. Simon? That is, does he mean that
the Socialism which he maintains includes and accepts the
whole of what he calls the Utopian Socialism of these eminent persons, and in addition affirms something else (and
if yes, what?) which makes it "modern or scientific" in
lieu of being "Utopian"? I must not be understood as
admitting that the theories of Robert Owen, Charles
Fourier, and St. Simon are identical or even workable
together.

6. Mr. Bax objects that Utopian Socialists, such as
Owen, Fourier, and St. Simon, believed equal participation
by all "to be attainable by mere individual initiative".
This seems to me inaccurate, but as it is scarcely relevant
to the issue I only note the point as perhaps enabling me
to distinguish the Socialism Mr. Bax now affirms. I understand Mr. Bax, in this, to maintain that Robert Owen
and his friends were Utopian because they tried to reduce
Socialism to actual practice in groups, and that Modern
Socialism is practical in entirely avoiding any such experiments. If I am wrong in this interpretation perhaps Mr.
Bax will state precisely what it is that he means, as I fear
I do not quite know what he intends by the concluding
sentence of his first paragraph.

7. If Mr. Bax attaches any importance to the words,
"special reference to the condition of the world as a whole",
with regard to any attempt now or in future to establish
Socialism in England, I shall be glad to have this explained, the more so as I see that he declares that Socialism
"is nothing if not international". Does this last phrase
mean that no plan of Socialism could succeed in England
unless that plan were also adopted by other European
countries, or does the condition of the world, as a whole,
involve that Socialism must be accepted in Africa before it
can succeed here?

8. As I see that Mr. Bax is of opinion that "the break up of the present State nationalities of Europe would be one of the first results of Socialism", I would ask him to state distinctly what other results, if any, of Socialism he anticipates in England as occurring prior to the expected break up of European State nationalities? I would further press him as to what he means by the break up, say, of the Swiss, Italian, French, and German nationalities? and what kind of governments, if any, he looks for as likely to be existing, or which he may desire to exist, in each or any of these countries respectively after such break up? and whether he anticipates that such break up of State nationalities would be a slow and peaceful process? and if yes, why? or whether he regards such break up as in any case likely or desirable to be rapidly effected? and if yes, how? and whether if State nationality is to cease in England, as one of the earliest results of Socialism, he will briefly state the form of government, if any, which he hopes for in this country, and how he thinks it can exist without representing State nationality, or at least some federation of State nationalities.

9. If I rightly apprehend the note by Mr. Bax, he denies the possibility of any social change being effected by isolated individuals or groups. It is true he limits this denial by the words "abstractly, and of their own initiative, irrespective of the general current of human progress"; but the first word, "abstractly", is here meaningless, and on the last eight words it is only necessary to say that the general current of human progress has been made up of innumerable instances of isolated and individual effort ultimately co-operating and coalescing for the desired end, and thus ensuring the progress. To be told that the modern Socialist builds his faith on a "rock of ages" with "many-hued strata of economic formation" is marvellously pretty, but it has the disadvantage of not being necessarily clear in its meaning to the hearer or reader.

10. Not finding a definition of Socialism in these words of Mr. Bax, I will state my own view. I define Socialism either as affirming (1) that organised society should own all wealth, direct all labor, and compel the equal distribution of all produce, or as affirming (2) that organised society should take possession of land, capital, all means

of production, distribution, and exchange, should control all labor, regulate all distribution, and conduct all exchange. That is, I understand a Socialistic State to be one in which everything would be in common as to its user, and in which all labor would be State-controlled. I therefore identify Socialism with Communism. Does Mr. Bax accept either of these definitions?

11. Mr. Bax says that there is to be "the assumption" (does this mean the taking away from the present owners? and if yes, by what means and on what conditions as regards the present owners?) of the "means of production, distribution, and exchange"; and that there is then to be "equal participation by all in the necessaries, comforts, and enjoyments of life" (this, I suppose, means that under scientific Socialism everyone is to have an equal share of everything); and that the people are to be "organised to this end". I would ask Mr. Bax to tell me whether in so using those words he means that the organised people should take into their possession as a common stock and then own all wealth, and equally participate in all produce, and if not, what distinction he draws? I would also ask him whether he includes all conceivable wealth under the words "means of production, distribution, and exchange, necessaries, comforts, and enjoyments of life", or whether he means to except any of the results of production? and if he makes any such exception, why?

12. In his third paragraph Mr. Bax promises to state "the nature of the process" by which the transformation of what he describes as capitalism into "a real social order" will be effected, and further promises then to give "the reasons why such social order must benefit the English people". I hope that he will not think me rude in saying that I find no trace in his paper of any attempt to fulfil either promise.

13. There is one statement of Mr. Bax, *i.e.*, that "civilisation can be only definitely overthrown by Socialism", which if Socialism could widely prevail would very possibly be accurate. I am unable, however, to see that the definite overthrow of civilisation either in England or everywhere is shown by Mr. Bax to be probably, or even possibly, beneficial to the English people. Mr. Bax adds that the "State world" is to become a "social world" "by a revolution generated in the fulness of its own development".

I would respectfully ask Mr. Bax to explain to me how and when he thinks this English State is to become some kind of English society other than a State? and in what way this is to be effected "by a revolution generated in the fulness of its own development"?

14. Mr. Bax affirms that Socialism "would of course soon result in the extinction of that private enterprise "— that is, in the extinction of some private enterprise he objects to. I venture to ask him whether Socialism, if realisable, would not certainly result in the complete extinction of all private enterprise, or what kinds of private enterprise he thinks would resist and survive? and why?

15. If I pass almost without examination, and with but very slight contradiction, Mr. Bax's inexact presentment of history, it is because I believe it absolutely irrelevant to the question, Will Socialism benefit the English people? and this is the only question I intend at present to discuss.

16. When Mr. Bax says that "Christianity is through and through Individualistic", I would ask him—if it be in any degree material to the issue between us—to explain how such a proposition is reconcilable with Acts ii., 44; iv., 32.

17. I see in Mr. Bax's paper occasional, but not precise, references to other works from his own pen and to the writings of others. I would respectfully ask him to requote here any words or statistics which he may think necessary to his argument. I have hardly the time for research outside my own bookshelves, and without exact reference might not light upon the intended passage; and our readers might some of them be in similar difficulty.

18. Mr. Bax makes the following statement with great confidence, and as if one of indisputable fact:

"The small capitalist is continually being thrown upon the labor market by inability to hold his own in the competitive arena. Capital tends thus to become concentrated in fewer and fewer hands, while the reserve army of labor tends steadily to augment. The result is increasing riches for the few and increasing poverty for the many. The 'increase of national wealth' at the present day means increase of misery for the mass of the people."

I very much doubt whether any portion of the paragraph is true as to this country, except the one that the "army of labor tends steadily to augment". This I have always maintained, and have no doubt that the evils of society resulting from the tendency of population to increase until positive checks operate are of a most serious nature. I would, as to the rest of the paragraph, ask Mr. Bax to refer me to the particular trades in which, during the last twenty years in England, the small capitalists have in any large numbers been so thrown upon the labor market. Also I would ask him whether the individual possessors of capital in England are not more numerous in proportion to population than they were forty years ago, and whether there is not now less pauperism in proportion to population in England, than there was forty years ago. Mr. John Morley, speaking at the Cobden Club dinner, said :

"In the years 1874-5 to 1884-5 the incomes between £200 and £1,000 per year have increased by 30 per cent., though the population has only increased by 10 per cent. Incomes over £5,000 a year have decreased by 10 per cent. You come to this as a general conclusion—that the lower the income the more rapid has been the rate of increase."

Does Mr. Bax dispute these figures? I admit that with the increasing education of the past thirty years there is an increasing consciousness of suffering and augmented discontent with unfair life conditions. I have done my best to increase this consciousness and discontent in order to compel ameliorating changes. I admit that with the increase of population in great centres you have limited areas of exceedingly acute misery, disease, and crime, which are probably in excess of what was possible in small centres of population; but I deny that there is increase of misery for the mass of the people, and assert on the contrary that the condition of the masses in England has certainly improved during the past fifty years. As the burden of proof is on Mr. Bax, I invite him to give me the exact figures and references on which he relies to prove the allegations I traverse. I quite admit that it is true that there are unduly large landed estates and unduly large fortunes in a few hands. The land evil may, I think, be dealt with by legislation under existing institutions. The undue accumulations of capital are a little more difficult to check, but even this may be only a question of limiting power of bequest, of imposing cumulative tax on inherited personalty beyond a certain figure, or of higher and graduated income tax in excess of a certain amount. I would also submit that the large accumulations of our richest capitalists form only a small portion of the gross national wealth. Mr. Bax quotes, on the authority of Mr. Hyndman, some figures as to which he admits that he does not know how they have been arrived at, but which he says he has never seen "seriously controverted". I do not know whether Mr. Bax means that he does not regard objection from myself as serious, but he will see that in my debate with Mr. Hyndman, p. 30, I specifically challenged these very figures, and Mr. Hyndman, though alluding to this, p. 34, never disputed the returns I relied on. I have not seen the other statistics referred to by Mr. Bax. If they are material, I should be obliged by his giving them in detail in his next paper, as the lump totals given do not enable me—even if I understand them—to do more than challenge their accuracy. I say "even if I understand them", because Mr. Bax writes that money not earned by producers—that is, the estimated increased value—should be added to the income of the non-producer—that is, that something not brought into existence should be reckoned as part of the income of someone who cannot be benefited by this non-existent quantity. Mr. Bax may mean something by this. Will he kindly explain?

19. I exceedingly doubt whether Mr. Bax is right in saying that in England "the break-up of the feudal states helped to consolidate the power of the Crown". And if he did not mean this to apply to England, it is irrelevant to the issue we are discussing. Nor is it true that the history of this country from the sixteenth century to the present time "is the history of the middle or trading classes in their efforts to free the individual from the fetters of feudalism and monarchy, to the end that on the one side there might be a body of free and landless laborers, and on the other a body of moneybags free to exploit them". In any case Mr. Bax omits to show any connexion between these alleged past sins of the English trading classes and the proposition he has undertaken to affirm.

20. Mr. Bax says:

"The means of the present exploitation of labor, the cause of the present horrible state of things, is monopoly. Its *modus operandi* is the extraction of surplus-value from the laborer by compelling him to work a whole day while receiving only so much of the results of his labor as is necessary to keep him in bare subsistence. Remove the monopoly from the hands of individuals, and you do away with the possibility of surplus-value."

This paragraph is an accumulation of inaccuracies. It assumes that at present some unnamed individuals have a monopoly either of all labor or of certain unspecified kinds of labor. Neither of these assumptions is true. It assumes that there is always or generally a surplus-value of considerable amount which the laborer has earned, to which he is morally entitled, but which he does not get. This is sometimes true, but seldom to the extent suggested by the form of the statement. The margin of profit over cost of production is usually very small. Then Mr. Bax says that by Socialism you "do away with surplus-value", but he does not explain how manufacture will be possible if no part of the result of labor is to go for plant, the expenses of conduct of the works, outlay for raw material, cost of exchange and distribution, which must necessarily be incurred, whether any particular industrial enterprise is exploited by an individual, by a corporation, or by a community.

Mr. E. Belfort Bax's Second Paper.

I am sorry that Mr. Bradlaugh is dissatisfied with my opening statement of the Socialist position, wherein I sought to show the historic evolution of the present system of society, more especially with reference to England, and thence to deduce the Socialistic as the only issue possible to benefit the English people. But Mr. Bradlaugh, I am sure, is aware of the disadvantage under which the opener of a debate on a subject like the present labors. As it is, I had to trespass on his courtesy by taking up more space than was originally agreed upon for my still necessarily incomplete survey. To judge from Mr. Bradlaugh's remarks, he would have had me eliminate *holus bolus* the historical side of the question. This I could under no circumstances have done. The Socialism I am defending is indissolubly bound up with the past as well as the present of human society, and is incomprehensible except as the result of an historical development. I must therefore respectfully urge upon Mr. Bradlaugh to deal with the historical side of my article, as upon this the theory of modern Socialism largely hinges. I am quite willing for him to confine his attention to England, since this country may quite well be taken as typical; but I must protest against one of the most important parts of my argument being waved aside with the epithet "inexact", or with mere bald denials of the facts contained in it.

I will now proceed to deal with Mr. Bradlaugh's paragraphs *seriatim*. Nos. 1 and 2 I have animadverted upon in opening these remarks. (3 and 4) I contend that my definition of Socialism is perfectly clear—*i. e.*, as clear as any definition can be which does not assume the proportions of an exposition. I do not see that Mr. Bradlaugh's definitions are as definitions any clearer than mine, but with them I will deal in the proper place.

No 4 consists of a play upon the words "goal" and "basis"—this at least is all that I can make out of it. The economic "basis", I thought I made tolerably evident, was that historic development of industry up to modern capitalism, which Mr. Bradlaugh objects to discuss; the "goal" is of course the Socialism which we contend is its outcome. My whole article consisted in an endeavor to state the "basis" and the "goal". The statement of the "basis" Mr. Bradlaugh has ignored; the statement of the "goal" he has understood variously, but never, I think, according to the ordinary sense of the words used by me.

(5, 6, 7) The relation between Utopian and Scientific Socialist theory is that they are both products of the same intellectual movement at different stages, just as astrology and astronomy, alchemy and chemistry, are alike products of the scientific spirit, the one of its infancy, the other of its maturity. The attempt to reform the world by founding model communities or otherwise by groups of individuals is analogous to the attempt of Goethe's Wagner to "distil" a human being out of a retort. Mr. Bradlaugh is right in taking me to imply that this quasi-practicality is at least one distinctive feature of Utopianism.

(7, 8, 9) By Socialism being "nothing if not international", I certainly meant that there is no possibility of the definite establishment of Socialism anywhere without a concurrent movement among the proletariat of the whole *civilised world*. I cannot regard England or any other

c 2

western country as isolated from the general movement of
civilisation. The condition of the civilised world as a
whole is the immediate basis on which modern Socialism
founds. This basis is the capitalistic system, the growth
and nature of which I have already sketched. By the
"break up of nationalities" I refer to the existing centralised State-systems of Europe. At present, although for
obvious reasons each nationality has to work out its own
Socialist movement more or less independently, yet this
independence is recognised by all Socialists to be only pro-
visional—that the centralised State of to-day will eventually be merged in a federation of all socialised communities.
The *centre* of the larger (as opposed to the smaller or
communal) social organisation will be shifted from the
nation to the group of nations constituting the socialised
world. But, says Mr. Bradlaugh, how long after the first
establishment of Socialism will this political readjustment
take place? Will a period of six weeks and three days
elapse, or seven weeks, or how long? I am very sorry,
but I really cannot inform him. The two events may be
simultaneous or they may not, according to the circumstances under which the crisis of the social revolution
accomplishes itself. I can only affirm the fact of the logical connexion of these events, and that the one must follow
sooner or later upon the other. Would the "break up"
be a slow and peaceful process? asks Mr. Bradlaugh.
Possibly yes, but probably no.

(9) Mr. Bradlaugh rightly conceives that I deny the
possibility of any social change being effected by isolated
individuals or groups. The word "abstractly", which
he alleges, however, to be meaningless, contains the gist
of the whole note, which affirms the impotence of individual
effort *abstracted* from social condition. In answer to Mr.
Bradlaugh's strictures I may say that "isolated and individual effort" has never been (and never can be) effective
save as the expression and outcome of an underlying social
movement. It is the social circumstances and intellectual
atmosphere of his age which make the individual what
he is. The mere aggregate of individuals existing at a
particular moment does not constitute society, any more
than the mere aggregate of cell and tissue here and now
constitutes the man—in both cases, it is the structural
synthesis, the organic *form*, which determines the *reality* of

the *thing*. I am sure if Mr. Bradlaugh considers the matter he will see that his "innumerable instances" of individual initiative, as contributing to progress, simply resolve themselves into cases of individuals having given *voice* and *definiteness* to tendencies already *born* of that social and more particularly economic development which maintains itself as *one* movement irrespective of the individuals, generations, and even races, through which it is manifested. My contention is that if people cut themselves off from the main stream of this development their action is futile.

(10, 11) I submit that Mr. Bradlaugh's first definition of a "Socialistic State" (which he would substitute for my own) is much too vague to be of any use for purposes of discussion. As it stands certainly no modern Socialist would accept it. His second is open to less objection, and taking the words in their ordinary meaning, I should not be indisposed to adopt it[1], as it is little more than a blurred re-statement of my own definition. The explanatory rider is of course indefensible. "*Everything* common as to its user" forsooth!—that's just what it wouldn't be. Mr. Bradlaugh really seems to credit Socialists with the fatuous absurdity of advocating a general scramble for hats and coats. The *use* of a thing as to its being "individual" or "common" must be entirely determined by the nature of the thing itself—whether it is a palace or a pair of boots, for example. It is quite true that Socialism by implication affirms that personal possession shall be limited to objects of personal use, but certainly does not imply that every pockethandkerchief, coat, hat, stocking, petticoat, chemise, "shall be common as to their user". The remark, however, is obviously only one of those touches of playful humor which for those who can appreciate them lend a charm to so many of Mr. Bradlaugh's speeches and articles; and I should not have essayed to refute it but for the fact that the British public is so dense at seeing a joke. Again, as to all labor being State-controlled, it is only necessary to say that after Mr. Bradlaugh had performed his share of the work necessary to the maintenance of the community of which he was a member, he could labor as uncon-

---

[1] In saying this, I assume that "all labor" means all social labor, not the labor an individual might perform for his own amusement.

trolledly as he pleased under a Socialistic *régime*. With regard to Socialism and Communism, I may say that the words Socialism, Communism and Collectivism are with me interchangeable, and mean economically the communisation of the means necessary to production, distribution, and exchange—and nothing else. You may of course affirm if you like that this would eventuate in the communisation of the product to a very large extent, but this would be an after and indirect, and not an immediate and direct, result of Socialism.

(11) By the "assumption of, etc," I mean the taking away from the present owners by any means, constitutional or otherwise, as circumstances may dictate, of the means of production, etc., now in the hands of private persons or syndicates. Socialism only proposes to confiscate wealth used for production on a large scale *i.e.*, as capital, in the fullest sense of the word

(12) *How* the new social order is to be inaugurated, to wit, by the taking over of capital in the above sense, I certainly thought had been sufficiently indicated by me in more than one place. As to the benefits thence resulting to the English people, I also thought I made sufficiently clear that since the capitalist system, with its results as described, is so fully developed in England, that *ergo* the English people must especially benefit by its abolition.

(13) Civilization means primarily the domination of property as held privately, with the corresponding distinction of a propertied, dominating class, and a propertyless, dominated class. It is seen fullest developed in the modern capitalist world—with its empire of profit-mongering. Hence the abolition of capitalism implies the abolition of the last phase of the civilised or State-world which is based on the above class-antagonism.

(14) The private enterprise I referred to is that which has material personal gain for its end. I see no reason why under Socialism any *other* form of private enterprise should be extinguished.

(15) I must again ask Mr. Bradlaugh to deal with the historical side of my paper.

(16) That the early Christians as a matter of temporary convenience, believing the end of the world to be at hand, chose to form a mutual benefit society, does not affect in the least the principles and ultimate tendencies of Chris-

tiānity. That its principles were not Communistic would
be, for that matter, sufficiently proved by Acts v., 4, if
Mr. Bradlaugh regards the book of "Acts" as having any
special historical value. As our friend William Morris
remarked to me the other day, the vaunted Communism of
the primitive Christians is essentially the same as the
donation of a thousand pounds by a Birmingham manufacturer to a cause he takes an interest in. The self-
sacrifice might have been greater in the former than in the
latter case, but the transaction is identical in kind.

No. 17 I will bear in mind, though as regards the
statistical Fabian Tract, I have seen it in a place I should
ha e thought not altogether inaccessible to Mr. Bradlaugh.

(18) I must confess I was somewhat staggered by Mr.
Bradlaugh's challenging my statement that the large
capitalist swallows up the small one. This everyday
occurrence seemed so incontrovertible, and has never to
my knowledge been questioned by anyone. Probably Mr.
Bradlaugh's own constituents at Northampton could tell
him something about this in connexion with the boot-
making industry. I will, however, endeavor to satisfy his
passion for figures by procuring some on the subject in my
next article. Meanwhile, surely Mr. Bradlaugh will admit
that goods can be thrown on to the competitive market
cheaper and more rapidly when produced with large
capital than with small, and if he admits this he admits
that the result described *must* ensue. Is there not now
less pauperism in proportion to population than forty years
ago? Very possibly less pauperism, but certainly more
poverty. The middle classes have taken care to suppress
pauperism and reduce the rates at the same time by well-
nigh abolishing out-door relief and making the workhouses
worse than prisons. What has Mr. Bradlaugh to say
about the perennial unemployed question?

Space presses, but I shall revert to No. 18 in my next,
unless Mr. Bradlaugh should prefer to restate the points
there raised by him in his reply to this.

(19) Mr. Bradlaugh "doubts" but does not criticise
certain historical truisms put forward by me. He also
alleges that I have failed to show their connexion with the
subject in dispute. But surely before one can judge
whether Socialism will benefit the English people it is

desirable to show why its antithesis, capitalistic individualism, *hasn't* and *won't* benefit the English people.

(20) Mr. Bradlaugh further characterises a paragraph of mine as "an accumulation of inaccuracies". I can only say I am prepared to stand by it to the very letter. I never said anything about "monopoly of labor". The "unnamed individuals" constituting the capitalist class have a *monopoly* of the means by which alone labor can become economically productive, which of course gives them a *command* over those who possess nothing but their labor-power. The margin of the final profit may, as Mr. Bradlaugh says, be very small or *nil*, and yet the rate of exploitation or of the production of surplus-value may be a hundred per cent., as Marx has conclusively shown ("Capital", vol. i., c. ix., p. 201 *et seq.*). I am surprised to find this confusion between the concepts surplus-value and profit in a person of Mr. Bradlaugh's acuteness. However, there it is. Then, again, the final sentence. On the hypothesis that the whole community owns and works the means of production, etc., for its own behoof, by whom, I would ask, are the "expenses" named to be incurred? Surely there is here also some confusion of ideas.

In conclusion, if I might do so without giving offence, I should like to ask Mr. Bradlaugh to formulate his objections in a more comprehensive and less detached fashion. It is easy to fire off thirty or forty questions in two columns, which it would take thirty or forty columns to answer properly. With fair play given me to reply to a series of such articles as Mr. Bradlaugh's last, I have my misgivings lest the English people might have established Socialism before I had succeeded in convincing Mr. Bradlaugh that it would benefit them.

MR. BRADLAUGH'S REJOINDER TO MR. BAX'S SECOND PAPER.

(1) Mr. Bax says that I have ignored the "basis" of Socialism; but, having again referred to the first paragraph of his first paper, I find that, though he speaks of "an economic basis", he nowhere in that paragraph, or as far as I can see elsewhere, explains what he means by these words. He says his whole article is an endeavor to

afford such an explanation. I, after a careful rereading, am unable to gather the supposed explanation from either of his papers, and therefore will ask him to kindly state briefly, and as clearly as he can, what it is that he holds to be the "new view of life (*i.e.*, of human relations), having an economic basis". As he puts these words as affording his definition of the Socialism which he affirms is to benefit the English people, it is absolutely necessary—especially as various schools of Socialists differently define the word—that I should know precisely what he means, if I am to discuss the probable effects of the Socialism intended by him, and the making clear our meaning will certainly be for the advantage of our readers.

(2) It is true that Mr. Bax says that "the condition of the civilised world as a whole is the immediate basis on which Socialism founds". But here, again, I do not understand what he means. If he means that there is sameness of condition for the working classes in any two civilised peoples, I must traverse this. Type, temperament, climate, soil, general life conditions, political conditions, social conditions, transmitted predispositions, vary considerably in every nation, and you cannot usefully lump these into a whole in order to propound a political or social theory for the English people. The wants, the miseries, the comforts, the means in possession, the facilities for gaining a livelihood, the legal hindrances, the amount of liberty enjoyed, differ in almost every country. So also there is an enormous difference as to the available means of reform and amelioration at the disposal, or within the probable command, of various peoples.

(3) Nor am I quite sure how much of the world Mr. Bax intends by "the civilised world", for he elsewhere explains "civilisation" to mean the existence in the same country "of a propertied dominating class and a propertyless dominated class". This curious definition is wide enough to include nearly every country in the world so far as I have any information.

(4) It is the more necessary that I should press Mr. Bax for a clear and concise definition of what he means by Socialism, because his objections to the definitions put forward by me in par. 9 of my last paper hardly render his own view more clear. I gave two definitions,

(1) " that organised society should own all wealth, direct all labor, and compel the equal distribution of all produce ". This, says Mr. Bax, is "much too vague ". While I can understand that it may not be the definition Mr. Bax thinks accurate, I avow it seems to me tolerably clear and explicit. He adds that " as it stands no modern Socialist would accept it ". But is this last declaration quite true ? The definition is divided into three subheads : — That organised society should (*a*) own all wealth ; (*b*) direct all labor ; (*c*) compel the equal distribution of all produce. I shall be obliged if Mr. Bax will state as against each subhead the respects in which he thinks it vague and inaccurate.

(5) As to my second statement of Socialism, *i.e.*, " that organised society should take possession of land, capital, all means of production, distribution, and exchange, should control all labor, regulate all distribution, and conduct all exchange ", I understand Mr. Bax to accept these words with the qualification that " ' all labor ' means all social labor, not the labor an individual might perform for his own amusement ". I do not quite appreciate the qualification, and should be glad if Mr. Bax would state some instances of the labor a man or woman might perform, and the raw material on which he might work, in a Socialistic State, without being under the control which Mr. Bax says is to be applied to " all (other) labor ". The acceptance of the definition involves of course the advocacy of the possible dispossession by force, that is, after a civil war, in which those who at present have possession of land and capital and of the means of production, distribution, and exchange, would resist the dispossession.

(6) Though accepting the words just quoted, Mr. Bax objects to the " explanatory rider" that " everything would be common as to their user ", but I understand him to say that " personal possession " would be limited under Socialism " to objects of personal use ". Does he regard, say, an eight-roomed house, and a one acre garden attached, as an object of personal use ? or would a four-wheeled cab and the horse and equipments be objects of personal use ? Can Mr. Bax state any formula which he thinks may distinguish the objects of which the user would be common from those of which the user would be personal and private ? If everything is not to be common as to its user,

how can there possibly be the "equal participation by all in the necessaries, comforts, and enjoyments of life"? Does Mr. Bax think that a man wearing Lancashire wooden clogs can equally participate in the enjoyment of my long and supple leather fishing-boots?

(7) Mr. Bax frankly enough says that "the words Socialism, Communism, and Collectivism are interchangeable, and mean economically the communisation of the means necessary to production, distribution, and exchange", and he concedes "that this would eventuate in the communisation of the product to a very large extent". That is, to a large extent he agrees with me that Socialism would mean Communism as to the products, as well as to the means of production. I would ask him to explain how and why he thinks this communisation of products would operate to a large extent, and how and why the operation would be stopped at any point?

(8) To par. 5 of my paper, Mr. Bax offers no real answer. In his first paper he affirmed that the "economic goal of modern or scientific Socialism, no less than that of the Utopian Socialism of Owen, Fourier, St. Simon", "is the equal participation by all in the necessaries and comforts of life". Questioned by me specifically as to this (par. 5), he gives an answer which, if it means what it says, declares that the Socialism of Robert Owen, Fourier, and St. Simon, stands to the Socialism of Mr. Bax as astrology does to astronomy. If this be true, it is difficult to characterise Mr. Bax's first statement without being rude.

(9) More than once Mr. Bax challenges me to deal with what he describes as the historical side of his opening paper. So far as his paper does not purport to state the history of the English people, I decline to do so, it being outside the question I have agreed to debate. For the rest, I am unable to find that Mr. Bax has furnished any historical statement which I can identify with English history. He has presented a very ably-written romance, sometimes consonant with fact, sometimes utterly conflicting, the whole is put in language often exceedingly poetic, but I prefer to break up what he beautifully describes as "this rock of the ages, with its many-hued strata of economic formation" into plain and prosaic statements of fact which may be identified as to meaning,

and which if material to the issue may be challenged or
verified. Mr. Bax objects to "being waved aside with
the epithet 'inexact', or with mere bald denials", but I
answer that the affirmer of a proposition is bound in such
a debate as this to put forward at least some evidence in
support of the statements challenged. To answer that
what I consider his romances are "historical truisms" is
scarcely convincing.

(10) In answer to paragraphs 7, 8, and 9 of my reply to
Mr. Bax's first paper, he states "that there is no possibility of the definite establishment of Socialism anywhere
without a concurrent movement among the proletariat of the
whole civilised world". If those words really mean anything more than a vague expression of opinion, they would
mean that "the definite establishment of Socialism"
cannot be possible in England until there is a concurrent
movement (whatever that may mean) amongst the peoples
of all Europe, of the greater part of America, of some
parts of Asia and of Africa, and of some parts of Australia.
This makes the possibilities of the definite establishment
of Socialism in England so extremely remote as to considerably diminish the usefulness of our discussion. I
desire to discuss here the probable influences of Socialism
on the happiness of the English people during the present
and immediately succeeding generations. I do not desire
to waste time in this debate in arguing as to remote
possibilities of what may or may not happen some centuries
hence.

(11) Mr. Bax says that by the "break-up of nationalities", which he alleged in his opening paper "would be
one of the first results of Socialism", he means "that the
centralised State of to-day will be eventually merged in a
federation of all socialised communities". He very fairly
says that he cannot say when this is likely to happen.
But as this is to be one of the "first results of Socialism",
it is surely a little unpractical to discuss the conjectural
happiness of the English people, if it is admittedly contin-
gent on the happening of an event in any case improbable
—perhaps impossible—and as to the time of the happening
of which Mr. Bax cannot even hazard a conjecture, except
that it is to be "one of the first results" of the establishment of Socialism in this country. As the break-up of
nationalities, which Mr. Bax affirms is to be one of the

first results of the establishment of Socialism in England, is declared by him to be probably not a peaceful process, it seems to me therefore clear that in this respect, at any rate, whenever it happens, Socialism is not likely to benefit the English people. All violent changes result in great immediate misery to the poorer classes affected by and taking part in such changes. All violent changes have hitherto been followed by periods of reaction, and have often, in consequence of the demoralisation attending armed conflict, temporarily placed the masses under the control of a military dictator.

(12) Mr. Bax says that "assumption, etc.", does mean the taking away from the present owners "of the means of production, etc.", and that this taking away is to be "by any means, constitutional or otherwise, as circumstances may dictate". This is so very large that it includes the violent taking, at the mere discretion of the takers, and Mr. Bax is requested to explain who is to judge what it is that circumstances are likely to dictate in relation to property in the hands of others to those who as yet have it not. I cannot conceive that the encouragement of assumption of property by violence is likely to improve the general happiness of those so taught to acquire. I can conceive that it may totally demoralise the public mind. Mr. Bax does not answer any of the other questions in paragraph 10, and yet a clear understanding on those points is most vital to the issue between us.

(13) Mr. Bax does say that "Socialism only proposes to confiscate wealth used for production on a large scale". Does he really mean by this that Socialism will allow private wealth to be used for production on a small or on a moderate scale? Does he mean that under Socialism there may be small employers paying wage to those they employ? Unless he means this, his limitation of the confiscation proposal is absurd.

(14) Mr. Bax says that the only private enterprise Socialism sees reason for extinguishing is "the private enterprise which has material personal gain for its end". Will he please give me some illustration of personal enterprise in labor upon raw material which does not come within this definition.

(15) Mr. Bax originally said that Christianity was through and through Individualistic. When I in par 16

showed him that as to property this was not all true, he does not attempt to in any way explain the positive words of Act ii., 44: "And all that believed were together, and had all things common"; or of Acts iv., 32: "And the multitude of them that believed were of one heart and of one soul: neither said any of them that ought of the things which he possessed was his own; but they had all things common"; except by the bold declaration that these words "do not affect in the least". He says that the principles of Christianity were not communistic is proved by the fact stated in chap. v., verse 4, that Ananias might have kept his property if he had not joined the Christian community and had not professed to give up to that community all his possessions. I cannot see the force of this as a reply. Mr. Bax apparently forgets that he introduced into this debate the principles of Christianity as affecting the ownership of goods. My only course was to point out that his statement was inaccurate and misleading. It is no part of my duty in this discussion to express any opinion on the special historical value of any of the Christian books.

(16) Instead of expressing surprise that I challenge his statements as to the increase of the number of small employers and owners of small accumulations, Mr. Bax should remember that the onus is upon him to prove the whole of the statements he makes, and I especially wait for him to do this on the facts and figures alleged by him and challenged by me in paragraph 18. The vague reference to "the bootmaking industry" here clearly marks Mr. Bax's absolute unacquaintance with the subject. I ask him to take on this Kettering, Leicester, London, Northampton, including the country villages, Norwich, and Stafford, and compare these with their condition forty years ago.

(17) Mr. Bax admits that there is very possibly less pauperism in proportion to population than there was forty years ago, but he alleges that there is more poverty. I ask him to prove his allegation not by loose statements, but by giving precise and detailed facts relating to the counties, towns, and cities, with names of each, in 1847 and 1887. Mr. Bax asks me what it is that I have "to say about the perennial unemployed question". Unless Mr. Bax can show that Socialism will provide employment in England for the unemployed of this country, the answer would not be relevant to this debate, and in any event should be

given by Mr. Bax as part of his case.   My general views
on the unemployed population are fully stated in the
volume containing the verbatim report of the defence of
myself and co-defendant in the case of Reg v. Bradlaugh
and Besant.   I do not see that they make in any way in
favor of the proposition which Mr. Bax undertook to
affirm and do not therefore burden the debate by repeating them.

This paper is already so long that I reserve until my
next my rejoinder on surplus value.

MR. BAX'S LAST PAPER.

I regret that Mr. Bradlaugh's second paper should not
have contained a more distinct criticism of the modern
Socialism set forth in my opening article than it does.   Mr.
Bradlaugh in his last complained that I had not made
myself clear to him on certain points.   These I endeavored
to explain in a few sentences.   He now again says he does
not understand what I mean.   Briefly, then, once more,
the "economic basis" of modern society is production for
profit, through the monopoly of the means of production
by the named and unnamed individuals constituting the
capitalist class, in its various sections.   The "economic
basis" of Socialism is the collective ownership of these
means of production by society as a whole, and their working not for the *profit* of individuals or classes, but for the
use of society as a whole, both collectively and individually.
I believe, as I before said, that the tendency under Socialism would be increasingly towards a collectivisation of the
product, but when, how, and the precise proportions in
which this would take place I do not pretend to prophesy.
In fact, when Mr. Bradlaugh pursues me with four-wheeled
cabs, wooden clogs, and his long and supple leather fishing-
boots, and says, what of these? who shall ride in this cab?
who shall wear these boots? how do you know that he
who wears the boots will like the boots he wears? there is
only one truthful answer I can make him, and that is, "I
don't know, and I don't care"; and in saying this I am
sure I express the sentiments of the immense majority of
modern Socialists.   Such conundrums have not the slightest practical interest at the present time; and if Socialism

pretended to answer them it would thereby proclaim its own absurdity and worthlessness. If Mr. Bradlaugh wants to discuss such interesting details as these, I commend him to the Positivists, who will further inform him how many times a man is to tap his forehead or scratch his left ear (I forget which) before going to bed in the society of the future.

And this brings me to the point where, with due respect to Mr. Bradlaugh, I should like to signalise what I think is the cause of Mr. Bradlaugh's failure (as I cannot but deem it) even so much as to touch the question at the root of the issue between us. Mr. Bradlaugh seems to be looking out in my exposition for something he doesn't find, and he is disconcerted because he doesn't find it. Hence his unwillingness to deal with the historical and other points put forward by me, and his anxiety to wave aside so many things as "irrelevant to the issue between us". This latter practice or proceeding reaches its acme of eccentricity, if I may so call it, when Mr. Bradlaugh intimates his opinion that the question of the unemployed has nothing to do with Socialism, and challenges me to prove that Socialism would benefit the unemployed! Now I submit that though human nature can stand a great deal in controversy, yet there is a limit to all things under the sun. And I do think that Mr. Bradlaugh might have borne in mind the elementary fact that Socialism *by its very definition* excludes the possibility of there being any "unemployed" to benefit. The "unemployed" belong to present society, and it clearly devolves upon Mr. Bradlaugh as the champion of present society as against Socialism to deal with this great problem of modern times. He may say, of course, that Socialism is wrong and impracticable; but granted Socialism, and *ex hypothesi* there is no such thing as an "unemployed" class. However, I will not press this point.

The question then arises, what is this "something" Mr. Bradlaugh is trying to find in modern Socialism, and can't? I think I am not far wrong in saying that what Mr. Bradlaugh is looking for is (1) a handy and portable conspectus of future society, which, when found, he might proceed to pull to pieces at his leisure; and (2) an attempted application of such a scheme to the English people *as* English— *i.e.*, considered as an isolated whole and without reference to the rest of civilisation. Unfortunately, in neither of these respects can modern Socialism oblige Mr. Bradlaugh. The Socialist of to-day does not profess to carry in his pocket any ready-made detailed scheme for the future of human society. Such schemes he regards as mere quackery nowadays. All he professes to do is to proclaim a law, or a system of laws, if you like, of social evolution. He shows the development of society in the past, exhibits the logical tendency immanent in that development, and deduces therefrom the main principle of the next stage of social progress. For this reason an international Socialism, with the means of production and distribution concentrated in the hands of society, as advocated by modern Socialists, could not have taken place in any previous period of the world's history. As to the details of the arrangement, whether immediate or ultimate, these no human being can see. All we say is, let the working classes, organised to this end, take over the means of production, distribution, and exchange; first the land, railways, mines, factories, credit establishments, and the larger warehouses and retail stores, which stand ready organised to their hand; at the same time let the executive proceed to establish new workshops, warehouses, and stores on a large scale in those trades where they do not already exist, and so undermine the smaller establishments possessed and worked by individuals, and which might for that matter *remain unmolested* until this happy consummation. Beyond this we do not profess to make any definite proposal as to production or distribution. The rest must be left to time and circumstances to work itself out. (The above is, I think, in itself, a sufficient answer to Mr. Bradlaugh's paragraph 7. It will be seen from this why I regard Mr. Bradlaugh's first definition as inadmissible on all the three sub-heads he mentions.) Before leaving this question of " detail ", I should like to illustrate the common absurdity of requiring a detailed plan of the new society in its complete form, of its pioneers to-day, by asking Mr. Bradlaugh if it would have been very reasonable to have expected a member of the Long Parliament (let us say) to give a detailed exposition of the political and social relations of the modern commercial world ? The Puritan townsman of the seventeenth century undeniably represented the principle of the supremacy of the middle classes as against Feudalism,

D

and yet we know how little he could have pictured to himself the ultimate issue of this principle as presented in
nineteenth-century England. Yet the parallel is feeble,
seeing that *his* principle had already made some practical
headway, and the change from the social life of the seventeenth to that of the nineteenth century is immeasurably
less in scope than that from a fully-developed capitalistic
civilisation to a fully-developed Socialism.

To come to the other point. Modern Socialism is unable to deduce the social change it deems imminent, from
the idiosyncracies of a particular people, or to conceive
Socialism as applied exclusively to any one people. The
modern European States (with the various colonies which
are their offshoots) had their origin in loose feudal con-
federacies with little or no national cohesion. (I should
not have insulted Mr. Bradlaugh with references for this
elementary historical fact but for certain remarks in his
last paper; as it is, I refer him, as regards England, to
almost any page of Green, Freeman, or Stubbs.) *We* regard the modern *national* stage as merely transitional; Mr.
Bradlaugh, on the contrary, seems to regard it as a sort
of thing that was in the beginning, is now, and ever shall
be. Already we see the nationality idea becoming a mere
cover for financing operations, market-hunting, and capitalist competition generally. The "differences" of type,
temperament, etc., are but surface-differences compared
with the fundamental laws governing the development of
all human society. The most diverse nationalities were
once united under the very inelastic civilisation of Roman
antiquity. Western Europe, irrespective of race, was,
again, dominated by the feudal system; the whole civilised world is now alike under the iron heel of modern
capitalism—*i.e.*, profit-mongering and wage-slavery. Mere
racial differences may be quite well left out of account in
dealing with the deeper problems of social development.
If Mr. Bradlaugh would deign to notice my brief historical
sketch, he would find the essential identity, irrespective of
nationality, of Western development from Feudalism to
capitalism there indicated. Nay, even the Socialist movement has already taken hold in greater or less degree of
the workers of the whole of modern civilisation from the
Pacific to the Volga. A few years ago there was no Socialist movement either in England or America; it is now

daily advancing by giant's strides. **Mr. Bradlaugh** makes a difficulty as to what I mean by the well-known phrase modern or western civilisation. I mean of course the economic, political, social, and intellectual life of Europe and its colonies, including the greater part of America. In economics this means modern capitalism, with its railways and great machine-industry; in politics, middle-class "constitutional" government (monarchical or republican); in social relations, the particular compound of vulgarity veneered with culture sometimes termed Philistinism; in religion, the organised hypocrisy which assents to, or does not reject, a body of dogmas, rites, and ceremonies the plain meaning of which is obsolete or no longer believed in by the educated classes. But, says Mr. Bradlaugh, how about Russia, there is no constitutional government there? No, and everyone recognises the Russian despotism as an anachronism—that is, as something out of place in nineteenth-century Europe. There are, of course, "backward" countries in Europe that fail as yet to reach the standard of completed bourgeois perfection, as realised in England and in other important Western nations. The attainment of this, however, as we have often seen, is only a matter of a few years. But modern capitalistic civilisation, I may observe, *re* par 10, is not the only form of civilisation. There have been other and more immature forms of civilisation, the "economic basis" of which has been serfdom or chattel-slavery. Some of these survive still in a stationary or decaying state—notably in Asia, and here and there in Africa. These (with the barbaric and savage populations of the globe) may be left temporarily out of account. They are outside the main stream of modern social development.[1]

As regards Mr. Bradlaugh's paragraph 3, I would like to ask him in what *purely* barbaric or savage community he

---

[1] To mention one point only, as regards nationalism. Under nationalism the capitalist can play off the imported foreign workman against the native, or can transport his capital to other lands, where he will find a crowd of starvelings to do his bidding. This could not happen were the national barrier broken down. When Mr. Bradlaugh looks at the interconnexion of modern industry and commerce throughout the modern world-market, he must surely see that the establishment of Socialism in England implies the immediate co-operation of at least the nations constituting the van of civilisation.

finds a dominant *class* of exploiters and a dominated *class* of exploited within the community, it being understood that we are not talking of cases here and there of rapacity on the part of individual chieftains ; or what is more to the point, I would ask him to explain how my definition of civilisation can be made to apply to the internal economy of those primitive tribal communities, by the gradual consolidation of which all centralised nations were formed, and the last remaining survivals of which may be seen in the Russian Mir, the Swiss Allemen, the Hindoo "village", etc., etc.[1] (*cf.* Maine's 'Village Communities" and other works, Laveleye's "La Propriété Primitive", Maurrer's "Deutsche Markverfassung", also Mommsen's "Römische Studien", and first volume of "Roman History", etc., etc.) *Apropos* of this I might quote Emerson's words with one alteration : "Society is *civilised* (Emerson said *barbarous*) until every industrious man can get his living without dishonest customs". When this latter is the case we shall have Socialism.

Mr. Bradlaugh's paragraph 8 evidently implies more than it says. I am sure Mr. Bradlaugh would not feel inclined to be rude without thinking he had some very good cause. Notwithstanding, as I really cannot see the terrible *lapsus* I am supposed to have made, I must still adhere to both my statements as to Owen, Fourier, and Co., to wit, that though the *end* of modern Socialism is, broadly speaking, similar to that of Utopian Socialism, as I understand it, yet that as a science or theory of Society it stands in much the same relation to the latter as modern chemistry does to alchemy, or astronomy to astrology.

In paragraph 9, Mr. Bradlaugh again discredits the historical side of my opening paper without discussing it. He says I ought to bring forward some evidence in support of the statements challenged. This I should have been most happy to do, if I had known what *were* the statements challenged. But seeing that Mr. Bradlaugh admits my account to be "sometimes consonant with

---

[1] The not unfrequent existence of slavery in its cruder form in barbaric societies, while apparently contradicting my contention, does not really do so. The captive taken in war is reckoned a chattel precisely because he is not in the tribal society, within the limits of which alone social life is as yet recognised. There is no exploitation of tribesman by tribesman

fact ", I had surely a right to expect that he would name
the points where, in his opinion, it was "utterly conflicting" therewith, and briefly state his reasons for so
thinking. It .seems to me this would have been more
germane to the issue (seeing the importance modern
Socialism attaches to its "historical basis") than pro-
pounding impossible riddles as to the precise point where
communisation of the product will begin and end in future
Society, problems which obviously can only be solved by
experience, and upon which modern Socialism does not
profess to dogmatise.

One last word on the point about Christianity inci-
dentally raised in my first article. What I meant was
that the *essential principle* of Christianity, that upon which
its whole theory of life and conduct is based, is an assumed relation between the individual soul and the
divinity directly revealed in it and to it. The *end* of the
individual's being and conduct is his union with this
divinity ; all moral action is in the last resort subservient
to this as its supreme source and object. My aim was to
place this morality in contrast at once with the old tribal
morality of the early world and with that of modern
Socialism, the object of which was and is, not the perfection and apotheosis of the individual soul, but the welfare of the social body. I still contend that isolated
passages in the Acts (which, *bien entendu*, may or may not
represent historical facts) do not "in the least affect" my
position. A policy pursued under special circumstances as
a matter of convenience cannot be taken as affirming a
principle. I may say, however, before leaving the subject,
that I can find not the slightest justification in the text for
the gloss Mr. Bradlaugh has put upon the Ananias inci-
dent in his last paper.

And now, then, for the promised facts and figures relative
to Mr. Bradlaugh's paragraph 18 in first paper, and the
progressive concentration of capital in fewer hands. Does
Mr. Bradlaugh know that (1) in the bakery trade a complete transformation has taken place within the last few
years; that whereas every baker used to bake his own
bread, now there are hundreds of bakers in London who
sell but do not bake bread ? (The reason of this is that
large firms like Neville are able to bake bread and deliver
it cheaper than retailers can bake it.) (2) In the fancy

bakery trade I am told the same fact is still more notice-
able, where firms like "Huntley and Palmer" and the
"National Bakery Company" are ousting the small
capitalist completely out of the field.   Moreover in this, as
in other departments, it is becoming general for large
grocers to supply cakes and biscuits made by the firms in
question, thereby completely crushing the small specialist
retailers.   (3) Take, again, the refreshment trade, and the
same process will be found to hold good, as evidenced by
the success of the "Aërated Bread Company", "Lockhart",
etc.   (4) I am informed by a correspondent of large experience in the glass-bottle trade that he is convinced that
the whole of the smaller makers must before long "go to
the wall".   One of the largest glass-bottle makers in
England has absorbed, to his personal knowledge, eight
small factories within a few years, and no new ones have
sprung up to take their places, or are likely to do so.
(5) Again, Joseph Chamberlain's (or rather Nettlefold's)
screw-making business has, it is well known, very nearly
crushed all other screw-makers out of existence.   Lipton's
is also a case in point.   (6) The business of transportation
shows precisely the same phenomenon, large men crushing
small men, and large companies crushing small companies.
An immeasurably larger amount of the carrying trade, as
everyone knows, passes into the hands of the few large
shipping companies than into that of all the small firms
combined.   The instances pointed out, I think, fully bear
out my friend, Alexander Donald (who has for two or three
years past been specially investigating this matter at first
hand and in detail) in writing : "The facts (relative to this
subject), which have not been reduced to tabular form by
anyone, simply because the bourgeoisie don't want information on the subject, leave no doubt as to the truth of
your statement".
    I will not weary the reader by running through the
gamut of the various trades and industries, which, so far
as I am aware, all without exception tell the same tale ;
but here are a few official statistics :—From 1863 to 1869,
there were 4,782 new limited companies started ; from
1870 to 1876 there were 6,905 ; from 1877 to 1883 there
were 8,643 : and in 1883 alone there were 1,634, the largest
number ever started in one year.   Of course, a considerable portion of these fail ; in the sharp competition there is

among them it is the fittest to cope with existing conditions only, which survive. But here again the main element of success is practically unlimited capital, wherewith to "hold on" and to "push". I would ask Mr. Bradlaugh to consider the amount of concentration of capital all this means, for statistics in this case, where every company is officially registered, must obviously be rigidly accurate. The same remark applies to the figures respecting bankruptcies and compositions with creditors, which form part of the obverse of the same medal. Here are a few taken hapazard :— The bankruptcies and "compositions", which in 1870 were 5,002, in 1875 realised 7,899, and in 1879 attained the enormous total of 13,132.

Of course, I must accept Mr. Bradlaugh's statement that the boot-making districts are better off to-day than forty years ago. I must only call Mr. Bradlaugh's attention to the fact that forty years ago the industry of the country was only beginning to settle down from the acute crisis caused by the introduction of the great machine industry. Now no one denies that the sudden and severe misery caused by this subsided for a time, during the flourishing period of British manufactures and trade, otherwise the Cobden-Bright school of politicians could never have got the ear of the English working-classes as they did. It may well be that the after-glow of this period of "leaps and bounds" lingers still in some industries and in some districts. Our contention is that, taking things all round, and setting aside this as well as temporary trade "booms", etc., the tendency toward a polarisation of wealth and poverty is making itself apparent in a yearly accelerating ratio. When Mr. Bradlaugh asks me to furnish statistics of every important town in Great Britain in 1847 and in 1887, he is, I respectfully submit, making a somewhat unreasonable and unnecessary demand upon me. My opinion of the value of such statistics considered *per se* is not such as would induce me to undertake elaborate researches on that head. On this point I am entirely of Carlyle's way of thinking. Figures, which appear so orderly and beautiful and convincing, are but abstractions; they are only serviceable as a shorthand registration of a conclusion arrived at by other means. The, in most cases, insuperable difficulty of initial verification, the difficulty of finding out the precise data on which they are based, the facts they suppress and the facts they express, render them practically valueless. Statistics have a fraudulent appearance of an accuracy which they can only possibly possess in a very few special cases. Hence the superstitious belief in figures on the part of the modern mind. For my own part, no number of statistics would have ever made me a Socialist, and no number of them would *un*make me one; so Mr. Bradlaugh must pardon my declining to treat the statistical side of this question as possessing any but a purely secondary and formal interest.

In concluding my share of this debate, I must again apologise for the length of this paper, only pleading the largeness and importance of the subject in excuse. At the same time, I should like to express my sense of the uniform courtesy of Mr. Bradlaugh in the conduct of his side. The subject "Will Socialism Benefit the English People?", as I believe, is necessarily decided in the affirmative by an understanding of what Socialism (in its modern sense) means, and can only be profitably discussed on this issue. Hence the direction I have endeavored to give to the debate.

FINAL REPLY BY MR. BRADLAUGH.

Although I can hardly think that in these letters there has been any real debate of the question, "Will Socialism benefit the English people?", yet, as my opponent has been throughout courteous and credits me with showing like courtesy, it is possible to hope that our good-tempered exchange of phrases may not have been as wholly useless to others as I am afraid it has been to myself. In this last reply it would, of course, be unfair for me to open out any other facts or to state any other issues than those already within the purview of this correspondence.

In his second paper Mr. Bax referred me to Karl Marx on capitalist production and the rate of surplus-value ("Capital", Vol. I., chap. ix., p. 201, *et seq.*), as if in some way showing error on my part. Having carefully re-read the words of Mr. Marx, I do not see that the contention as to surplus-value—a contention which I cannot accept as there stated—helps Mr. Bax at all. His assertion in his first letter, that in consequence of monopoly a surplus-value was unfairly extracted from the laborer, I answered in paragragh 20 of my first letter. Mr. Bax rejoined that he did not say "anything about monopoly of labor"; that his use of the word "monopoly" was not intended to include monopoly of labor, and only referred to the monopoly of the means of production; but as he says that this monopoly gives the command, i.e., control, that is, the monopoly of the control of labor, I scarcely appreciate the correction. Mr. Bax writes as if, under community enterprise, no expenses would be incurred in production; but this is surely not arguable, and can hardly be seriously meant. He says the surplus-value may be 100 per cent. and the profit *nil*. This is impossible unless you regard the labor as the only necessary element in realising value, and treat the other matters necessary to efficient production, and stated by me in paragraph 20 of my first letter, as being purely imaginary. "Surplus-value" is a mere phrase jingle unless it means value added in the production over and above all the cost of production.

Mr. Bax says that

"the 'economic basis' of modern society is production for profit, through the monopoly of the means of production by the named and unnamed individuals constituting the capitalist class in its various sections".

And that the

"'Economic basis' of Socialism is the collective ownership of these means of production by society as a whole, and their working not for the *profit* of individuals or classes but for the *use* of society as a whole, both collectively and individually".

It is worth noting on this (1) that while it is true that the artificially created land laws of this country have given in England a practical monopoly of metal and mineral raw material to the comparatively limited number who have the control of the bulk of the land, and while it is also true that of wealth, other than landed, the distribution has in a few instances thrown enormous accumulations into individual hands, it is not true that there is otherwise any "monopoly by any distinct class of the means of production as against all workers"; and (2) that it is not quite easy to understand how the English people could work say cotton, wool, coal, and iron, and their results, for foreign consumption otherwise than by manufacturing for profit. The land monopoly created by law may be broken down by law. The unfair distribution may be gradually corrected without destroying present society as proposed by Mr. Bax.

Mr. Bax jests with the questions stated for his consideration in paragraph 6 of my last paper, and his serious answer to me is that having at the outset declared his Socialism to mean "the equal participation by all in the necessaries, comforts and enjoyments of life", he neither knows nor cares what the expression means or how it would work itself out. This may be enough for Socialists, but it is hardly useful to an enquirer or satisfactory to a critic. Robert Owen—whom Mr. Bax names as agreeing with modern Socialists in teaching "equal participation", but whom he has here never verbally quoted—held, as Mr. Bax holds, that in a Socialistic State all things should be in common; but Robert Owen held this in the ordinary meaning of words, and never pretended that such doctrine was not the absolute negation of private property.

When Mr. Bax affirms that

" Socialism *by its very definition* excludes the possibility of there being any 'unemployed' to benefit",

it is not very easy to consider him serious. I at once concede that if writing in a decree, or formulating in a constitution, that no men, women, or children should ever be hungry would avoid the necessity for procuring by labor the means of subsistence, Mr. Bax would have a strong case, but even Mr. Bax cannot mean this. If Mr. Bax merely means that as he proposes to abolish employers there would be no unemployed, this is more ingenious than ingenuous. In the programme of the Social Democratic Federation, formally accepted by Mr. Bax for the purposes of this debate, I find

" organisation of agricultural and industrial armies under State control on co-operative principles",

as one of the proposals of that Socialist body, and I do not gather how or why the Socialistic State in England is to be presumed always to be able to employ in productive work the whole of the population; or how, without such productive work, it is to be always in position to provide

the whole of the population with the necessaries of life.
Mr. Bax says:

" The Socialist of to-day does not profess to carry in his pocket
any ready-made detailed scheme for the future of human
society ".

But as Mr. Bax advocates the destruction of the present
state of society, even by force, in order that the Socialistic
scheme may be worked out in practice, he ought to have
been ready to at least outline some probable or possible
working scheme, especially as he undertook to affirm that
this scheme would in its actual working benefit the English
people.

If the Socialist has no detailed scheme for the future,
why did Mr. Bax, as one of the preliminaries of this debate,
explicitly, and without reserve accept the following declarations of the Social Democratic Federation.

" The land, with all the mines, railways, and other means of
transit, to be declared and treated as collective or common
property.

" The production of wealth to be regulated by society in the
common interest of all its members.

" The means of production, distribution, and exchange to be
declared and treated as collective or common property."

If there is no plan of treatment what becomes of clauses
1 and 3? If there is no plan of the regulation of the produce of labor, what is the meaning of clause 2? If Mr.
Bax has no detailed Socialistic scheme for the future of the
English people, how is it possible even to guess whether or
not Socialism will in its attempted practice prove beneficial
to the English people? His latest explanation of the
assumption of wealth and the then conduct of enterprise,
in reply to paragraphs 12, 13, and 14 of my second letter,
deserves examination.

" All we say is, let the working classes, organised to this
end, take over the means of production, distribution, and
exchange; first the land, railways, mines, factories, credit
establishments, and the larger warehouses and retail stores,
which stand ready organised to their hand; at the same time
let the executive proceed to establish new workshops, warehouses, and stores on a large scale in those trades where they
do not already exist, and so undermine the smaller establishments possessed and worked by individuals, and which might

for that matter *remain unmolested* until this happy consummation. Beyond this we do not profess to make any definitive
proposal as to production or distribution."

Large properties and industrial enterprises are to be
taken over, that is, are to be taken away from those who
have them, and this whether the owners are single individuals or hundreds, or associated small owners or shareholders. Nothing is said of any compensation on this
taking over. In the programme of the Social Democratic Federation, railways are proposed to be taken "with
or without compensation". The smaller manufacturers
and tradesmen are to be "undermined", that is, gradually
ruined, and Mr. Bax gravely argues that this will—either
in the process of ruining or as an ultimate result—benefit
the English people. To do him justice, really Mr. Bax
does nothing of the kind. Although in his debate he
undertook to prove that Socialism would benefit the
English people, he now says:

"Modern Socialism is unable to deduce the social change it
deems imminent, from the idiosyncrasies of a particular people,
or to conceive Socialism as applied exclusively to any one
people".

But was it not a pity then to engage to debate the
question, limited to the English people, as it expressly
was by its wording? Mr. Bax now explicitly admits, that
is, that Socialism must be world-wide or non-existent, and
he has no suggestions as to how many centuries must
elapse before world-wide Socialism may be feasible.

On statistics, Mr. Bax is simply marvellous; he introduced statistics in his first paper, he gives more statistics
in his last; challenged upon the accuracy of his figures,
and utterly unable to verify them he boldly and blandly
writes:

"The, in most cases, insuperable difficulty of initial verification, the difficulty of finding out the precise data on which they
are based, the facts they suppress and the facts they express,
render them practically valueless. Statistics have a fraudulent
appearance of an accuracy which they can only possess in a very
few special cases. Hence the superstitious belief in figures on
the part of the modern mind. For my own part, no number of
statistics would have ever made me a Socialist, and no number
of them would *unmake* me one."

It, of course, simplifies discussions on Socialism, when

the Socialist states facts and figures, but refuses to verify them, and *per contra* denies the right of his antagonist to go into details in any of these matters.

In his first paper Mr. Bax said :

"The small capitalist is continually being thrown upon the labor-market by inability to hold his own in the competitive arena. Capital tends thus to become concentrated in fewer and fewer hands."

In paragraph 18 of my first paper I challenged this, and at last Mr. Bax gives a statement which he considers proof : (1) There are fewer bakers who bake as well as sell ; (2) that in glass-bottle manufacturing a few large manufacturers swallow up the small ones ; (3) that Nettlefold's have nearly crushed out all other screw-makers ; (4) that the carrying trade passes into the hands of large companies ; (5) that a friend of Mr. Bax says that the facts (admittedly not reduced to tabular form by anyone) leave no doubt as to the truth of Mr. Bax's assertion ; (6) that limited companies are on the increase.

1. If Mr. Bax's statement as to bakers were true, it would not show that there were not as many or more vending bakers with small capital, or that the sale of bread-foods by others than the actual bakers had on balance thrown small capitalists back on the labor-market. It might show that there had been economy in the manufacture of some bread-foods. Mr. Bax gives no figures, and perhaps limits his remarks to London. The Census for 1881 (General Report, p. 42) alleges an increase in the purveyors of bread and vegetables of 12·5 per cent. since 1871. These include the fancy bakers and pastrycooks.

2. Mr. Bax gives nothing beyond his mere statement, and therefore furnishes no means of testing it. The Census for 1881 (General Report, p. 41) says that glass manufacture has increased 10 per cent. since 1871. It is, however, a small manufacture, only employing 19,338 men and 1,692 women.

"Of the 21,630 persons engaged in it, 5,984 were enumerated in Lancashire, 3,591 in the West Riding, 2,884 in Durham, 2,769 in London, 2,089 in Worcestershire, 1,752 in Warwickshire, 1,151 in Staffordshire, and only 1,410 in all the other counties."

3. I am unable to test this statement, of which Mr.

Bax offers no evidence, and which, if true as to one small industry, would have very little weight. The Census (General Report, p. 49) says that in 1881 :

"The makers of bolts, nuts, rivets, screws, and staples numbered 8,017, and had also increased very greatly, the uncorrected total in 1871 having been 5,726 ".

So far as it goes, this is directly the opposite of Mr. Bax's assertion.

4. The Census 1881 shows an enormous increase of persons engaged in the carrying trade, and as a railway or steamship company is made up of very many shareholders of unequal holdings, Mr. Bax's present statement in nowise helps as evidence of his original assertion that " small capitalists are being thrown on the labor market ".

5. I do not know anything of the investigations of Mr. Alexander Donald. I do know that a gentleman of that name did attend some lectures delivered by me, and advanced, as if facts, some most extraordinary statements, which clashed with all accessible statistics. Whether or not this is the same gentleman, his statement is vague, and his animus against the *bourgeoisie* (a class to which he and Mr. Bax both belong) weakens the value of his too general corroboration.

6. The increase of *bond fide* limited liability companies for manufacturing purposes is direct evidence against Mr. Bax. It proves the existence of a large number of persons with small capital clubbed together for enterprise too large to be usefully undertaken except by such association.

To roughly sum up the argument. The definition of a Socialistic State now advanced by Mr. Bax in his three letters, is that State in which "the working classes organised to that end [the manner and method of the organisation, and the character, duties, and responsibilities of the organisers being unstated] shall take over [that is seize and appropriate, and probably by force] the means of production, distribution, and exchange " [nothing being said as to what is to happen to the present possessors in case they should not agree to, or should resist, this transfer]. There is then to be " collective ownership of these means of production by society as a whole " [all details as to the manner of the exercise of this ownership being positively refused], and all working is to be " not for profit of indi-

-viduals or classes, but for the use of society as a whole, both collectively and individually " ; all the matters specified .are to be common property, but there is still to be private property in some wealth, not specified. There is to be " the equal participation by all in the necessaries, comforts, .and enjoyments of life ", the production of wealth is to be regulated, and industrial armies are to be controlled. But, according to Mr. Bax, the foregoing does not mean, and no modern Socialist would admit that it means, that organised society should own all wealth, direct all labor, and compel the equal distribution of all produce. Mr. Bax must pardon me if I can only construe words in their ordinary everyday meaning, and if I express my regret that he should have been party to signing Socialistic manifestoes, which, as read in their natural sense, mean one thing, without adding a caution that the Socialist declarations were intended in a non-natural sense.

Mr. Bax has no scheme either for the taking possession, or for the common owning, or for the controlling, or for the regulation, or for the equal participation, and he frankly says that he neither knows nor cares what will be the detailed results. Yet he contends that this Socialism will benefit the English people.

There are very many points of interrogation, and of traverse, in my first and second letters, which Mr. Bax has passed in silence. These are so numerous that I content myself with recalling the fact, which I leave to the judgment of the readers.

NOTE BY E. BELFORT BAX.

THERE are one or two points in the foregoing articles upon which I should like to add a remark or two by way of elucidation :

(1) With regard to the three great periods of modern industry referred to on p. 5, it should be observed that simple co-operation (the assemblage of a number of workmen under one roof under the direction of a capitalist) was the prevailing form of production from the middle of the sixteenth to the middle of the seventeenth century, when it began to be superseded by the

manufacture or workshop system, with its organised division of labor, which continued in uninterrupted sway till it reached its highest perfection at the end of the eighteenth century, when it was in its turn superseded by the "great industry" of our own time.

(2) Another, and perhaps more fundamental, definition of the principle (see p. 22) underlying civilised as against that underlying primitive or barbaric society, is that while the former is based on *things* or *property* (in its initial stages chiefly on *land*), the latter is based on *persons* conceived as members of a *related group* (*gens*, *tribe*, or *people*) which owns property in common for its collective *uses*. When once the principle of private or individual property has definitely superseded that of *kinship*-possession as the basis of society, you are bound before long to have a rich and *exploiting* and a poor and *exploited* class in mutual opposition within the community. And this has been the characteristic of the whole history of civilisation.

(3) With reference to the Individualistic influence of Christianity (p. 6), I may quote as illustrating one aspect of this influence a passage in Sir Henry Maine. "I am myself persuaded," says that eminent scholar, "that the influence of the Christian Church on law has been very generally sought for in a wrong quarter, and that historians of law have too much overlooked its share in diffusing the conceptions of free contract, individual property, and testamentary succession, through the regions beyond the Roman Empire, which were peopled by communities held together by the primitive tie of consanguinity" ("Early History of Institutions," p. 104).

(4) A joint-stock company (see p. 46) is an economic unit; it is a unit in the competitive system quite as much as the individual capitalist. The number or size of the shares which compose it does not affect the matter in the least. As an illustration of the effect of competition by such an "aggregate of small capitals", let us suppose a man hitherto making a fair income out of a business finds his trade going or gone from him owing to the competition of a neighboring joint-stock store company. He is persuaded, after shutting up his shop, to invest the couple of hundred pounds he has left in this mammoth concern, with the chance of receiving his 3, 4, or 5 per cent. He does so. He *was* a small capitalist. He *is* a small capitalist. There is only one slight difference in his position. Whereas before his small capital combined with his labor availed him for a decent independent livelihood, he is now thrown on the labor-market and subject to all its conditions, notwithstanding his £200 invested in the joint-stock company. That little difference is just the fly in the amber of the small investor's bliss.

11th Edition—March, 1895.

CATALOGUE

OF

PUBLICATIONS.

N.B.—This edition cancels all previous issues.

LONDON:

A. AND H. BRADLAUGH BONNER,

63 FLEET STREET, E.C.

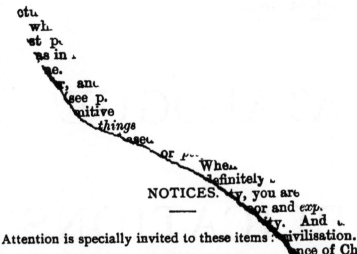

NOTICES.
——

Attention is specially invited to these items :

New volumes of Mr. Bradlaugh's Essays, pp.
Complete sets, thereby obtainable, p. 16.
Second Edition of " Collected Speeches ", p. 7.
Edition in cloth of " Doubts in Dialogue ", p. 13.
New volume of Colonel Ingersoll's lectures, p. 24.
Re-issues at reduced prices of " Genesis " (14), Know
  Trial (16), Buechner and Haeckel (20), and Soury
  Perot (25).

——

For Index of Authors, see p. 31.

——

Orders of 1s. *and upwards sent post free.*
Cheques and P.O.'s crossed ———— *& Co.*

SECOND EDITION.

2 *vols.*, 860 *pp.*, *Demy 8vo.* 10 *Portraits, etc.*
Price 21s.

CHARLES BRADLAUGH:

A RECORD OF HIS LIFE.

BY HIS DAUGHTER.

HYPATIA BRADLAUGH BONNER.

WITH AN ACCOUNT OF HIS PARLIAMENTARY STRUGGLE, POLITICS, AND TEACHINGS,

By JOHN M. ROBERTSON.

PRESS NOTICES.

"The chapters in the earlier volume which describe his beginnings are among the most interesting of the book. Mrs. Bonner is here clear, concise, terse ...... and the picture of the poor lad's home, surroundings, and troubles would have been worth the writing even if it had not been part of the life-story of a noble and notable man..........Mrs. Bonner has been at great pains (and rightly) to confute in detail the many calumnies by which his name was assailed at one time and another, but for many of us her task (which she has performed with perfect success and excellent taste) was fortunately no longer necessary........ .. We recommend our readers to make his acquaintance more completely in the pages of his daughter's book, which, with all its faults, is eminently worth reading. We shall be mistaken if they do not find in it the portrait of an Englishman of whom his countrymen may be proud."—*Saturday Review.*

"Mrs. Bonner has really performed a difficult task after a noble fashion, and in a truly pious spirit. Her father's life was a melancholy one, and it became her duty as his biographer to break a silence on painful subjects about which he had preferred to say nothing. His reticence was a manly reticence ; though a highly sensitive mortal, he preferred to put up with calumny rather than lay bare family sorrows and shame. His daughter, though compelled to break this silence, has done so in a manner full of dignity and feeling."—MR. AUGUSTINE BIRRELL, Q.C., M.P., in *Nineteenth Century.*

"The writers of this book have good excuse for, as they say, going 'more into detail' and making it 'more controversial than is usual or generally desirable with biographies.' In his lifetime Mr. Bradlaugh was misunderstood by many who meant him no injustice, and much maligned by others, and it was only right that pains should be taken to correct false statements about him which are still current..........Of permanent value as a contribution to constitutional history." —*Athenæum.*

"Apart from the excess of detail, Mrs. Bonner's portion of the biography deserves nothing but praise. Candour and breadth of view characterise it throughout....... Mrs. Bonner conceals nothing essential to a full insight into Mr. Bradlaugh's character and career ; and she has the judgment and skill to arrange her facts in due proportion."—*Academy.*

"In two large handsome volumes, beautifully printed, and stoutly bound in buckram, Mrs. Bradlaugh Bonner has at last given us the long and eagerly looked forward to account of the life of her father. It has been the fate of few men to be so misrepresented and maligned as was Charles Bradlaugh. To his daughter the task of writing his life has been a labor of love, for it has given her the opportunity of vindicating her father's character and refuting some of those bitter calumnies of which he had been the object. She has done her work well."—*Weekly Sun.*

"The one predominant thought with which we put down the two volumes of Mr. Bradlaugh's Biography by his daughter, Mrs. Bradlaugh Bonner, is that it is a story of which every Christian apologist ought to be ashamed..........No Christian supported by his faith ever showed a more remarkable courage in face of misfortune. .... Mr. Robertson tells the story of his great Parliamentary battle on the oaths question with great spirit, and he does no more than justice to his remarkable abilities as a speaker and to the extraordinary legal talent which he displayed both then and at all stages in his career."—*Westminster Gazette.*

"It is the story of a life of controversy, yet with a strong element of deep human interest running all through it, and a certain poetical appropriateness in the emergence of its hero into general appreciation at its close........... His daughter's biography is his not unfitting literary monument."—*Daily News.*

"Of the most intensely interesting character, exhibits no little skill in arranging details around the main facts in the life of the subject of the narrative, and is particularly full with regard to the incidents of his parliamentary career. . . . Mrs. Bonner inherits much of her father's literary ability and power of forcible argument. Great taste is manifested in not trenching on any debatable religious topics, so that the most sensitive on these matters will not be offended. On its merits the book must be regarded as one of the most interesting of the season."—*Liberal.*

"This deeply interesting record of the life of a most remarkable man will find a wide circle of eager readers. . .... .Mrs. Bradlaugh Bonner has in the main done her work well ; that is to say, she has managed to convey a living picture of her father... ... Mrs. Bradlaugh Bonner has not only successfully defended her father's memory, but has reared to that memory a worthy monument."—*Daily Chronicle.*

"Mrs. Bradlaugh Bonner has performed her task with painstaking zeal and discrimination. .... Mr. Robertson ... ... gives a very clear and interesting account of 'the Parliamentary struggle ', and an estimate of Bradlaugh's character which people who knew him will endorse. . ... Mr. Bradlaugh's life is in two handsome volumes, with portraits of him at different ages, and is a valuable addition to national biography."—*Star.*

"Something more than the story of the life of an eminent public man. It is, besides, a chapter in the long dreary story of persecution for opinion."—*Echo.*

"The book of the week..........A painful record of the miserable devices successfully employed by professedly religious people to bound a pure-minded, lion-hearted, and absolutely unselfish man into a premature grave."—*Book and News Trades Gazette.*

"'He was ever a fighter'—that would be a fit epitaph for Charles Bradlaugh, whose life has just been traced with loving loyalty by his daughter. Probably in the last half-century there never has been so striking a reversal of popular opinion as in the case of the man who goes proudly down to history as ' Member for Northampton '. With his later years in public life the public is well acquainted. His struggle into the House of Commons, followed by his useful services as a member thereof, is part of the political 'history of our own times'......... Hardly anyone, except Bradlaugh and Bright, really covered themselves with honor in that strange muddle. All the more remarkable is his wonderful success in St. Stephen's during the five years he was allowed to discharge his Parliamentary duties . ... The writer was struck by the constant arrival of Mr. Bradlaugh in the lobby in those busy days, in response to the cards 'sent by all sorts and conditions of men '. No member was in greater request; no man was more courteous in responding to inquiries."—*Sketch.*

"Exceedingly interesting and well got up. No political library will be complete without them."—*Personal Rights.*

"Bradlaugh's Life being written, the only question is whether and in what measure the work has been well done. If, with his daughter's book before us, we had to answer that question in a sentence, we should say that a distinctly successful result is achieved .. .. We have a very clear conception of Charles Bradlaugh .. .... A convincing and lasting picture of a really remarkable man. .... Though Mrs. Bonner's account of her father is professedly defensive and controversial, she fairly allows us to see his weakness as well as his strength."—*Pall Mall Gazette.*

"Now that, three years after his decease, the world is able to look back calmly on the tempestuous career of Charles Bradlaugh, it cannot fail to be recognised that his was one of the remarkable political figures of modern times .. The present biography is of considerable interest as illustrating the struggle of a dauntless man against ceaseless, and often perfectly well-founded opposition, from the lowest rung of the ladder to a prominent place in public life."—*Morning Post*

"Will be read with the deepest interest."—*Evening News and Post.*

"It certainly has a good deal of personal interest, both in what it has to tell us about Mr. Bradlaugh's early life and in the occasional light it throws upon the careers of certain of his contemporaries."—*Globe.*

"We shall not be misunderstood, in the use of the phrase, if we say that this work is a monument of beautiful filial piety. Charles Bradlaugh was worthy of his daughter's devotion; and no more practical evidence of the depth and power of that devotion could be given than in this life .... In spite of the advantage it would undoubtedly have been to obtain the story of Mr. Bradlaugh's life from his own lips, it is difficult to see how the story of his life could have been better told than in the two volumes which lie before us .. .. As far as the book covers events of which we are cognisant, we can speak confidently of its accuracy; and from that portion we may fairly judge the rest .. Of Mr. Robertson's share in the work, we will only say it is an able and wholly admirable picture of the man and of his opinions, and a very complete historical survey of the great struggle of which the man was the hero. The work has been well done."—*Northampton Guardian.*

"Of the daughter's share in the work we can only say that it is written with what, in the circumstances, must be described as wonderful good taste and restraint. Though she could not possibly criticise as an outsider might the father whose achievements fairly justified her filial admiration, she shows comparatively little of that bitterness towards his opponents which might have been expected; and she passes over much difficult ground with a reticence which at the same time is not timidity, and which might be commended as an example to denouncers of certain of Mr. Bradlaugh's opinions . . Mr. J. M. Robertson's portion of the book, we need hardly say, is ably done, and may very well serve as the basis of any future discussions upon questions some of which, at all events, were practically closed by Mr. Bradlaugh himself."—*Bradford Observer.*

"The book of the hour..... Nor is the picture, although drawn by an affectionate and partial hand, either exaggerated or incorrect, as I can myself testify from a somewhat close and personal friendship of many years duration."—*Newcastle Weekly Chronicle.*

"The portion of the work contributed by Mr. Robertson is written with a strong bias in Bradlaugh's favor, a bias naturally produced by an admiration of his sterling honesty, and by the shameful and hypocritical action of the Tory party ... Mr Robertson has very industriously collected and arranged his materials, and so done a public service."—*Sheffield Independent.*

"Controversial frequently and vigorous always."—*North British Daily Mail.*

"Cannot do better than read this life. Upon the whole, it is marked by self-restraint; but, of course, it is not an impartial work."—*Yorkshire Daily Post.*

"Contains a great deal of really interesting matter, and the illustrations are excellent."—*Nottingham Guardian.*

"Mrs. Bonner has accomplished her difficult task very creditably ... ... Many readers will turn with interest to the second part of this biography."—*Dundee Advertiser.*

"Mrs. Bonner has written an exhaustive narrative of her father's eventful career, and corrects many mistakes and misapprehensions current."—*Literary World.*

"The authoress has done her work well....... . A perusal of these volumes will certainly cause an increase of respect for Mr. Bradlaugh's indomitable courage in facing difficulties, and of wonder at the amount of labor, in lecturing, journeying, and writing, which he was able to get through."—*Daily Telegraph.*

"His remarkably varied experiences are recorded with much freshness of interest......... The story of Mr. Bradlaugh's long fight with the law in various forms is given here in elaborate and lucid detail .... These volumes are invaluable as the permanent memorial of a chapter in our constitutional progress. In many other respects they will claim attention for the facts which they contain, and their narrative portion will be found of the most absorbing interest. They form a worthy biography of one to whom even his erstwhile opponents can hardly now deny the title of a great Englishman."—*Birmingham Post.*

"In the main an admirable, though appreciative and affectionate, review of the work of this remarkable man."—*Liverpool Daily Post.*

"His daughter has not spared herself in the task of justifying her father, and her courageous attempt has been successful......... Mr. Robertson has contributed a brilliant and thoughtful account of his political and philosophical work."—*The New Weekly* (Manchester).

"In these closely printed volumes we have the fullest account that Mr. Bradlaugh's warmest admirers could desire of his 'life and work.'........ It was well worth while to give us a full account of the Parliamentary struggle over the taking of the oath, and this—as, indeed, the whole of his portion of the work—Mr. Robertson has done with great ability. These volumes cannot but be acceptable to a numerous class of readers. Mr. Bradlaugh's career as a whole strikes us as eminently pathetic, and there are few who will refuse to him a large amount of admiration and sympathy."—*Manchester Guardian.*

"A kindly, tender-hearted, generous-spirited, even-tempered man was this redoubtable Freethinker and irrepressible Radical. The charges of venality and self-seeking that small spite has levelled against him are blown away as the mist before the morning sun. He stands revealed to us in these pages as a man of strong feeling and of iron will, of inflexible purpose and unshakeable principle, one utterly incapable of anything mean or dishonorable......... These volumes contain a worthy record of a memorable man, who whatever his faults of opinion and errors of judgment, was intellectually head and shoulders above the majority of his critics."—*Glasgow Herald.*

"A work of great interest—an act of filial homage worthily rendered..........It is a very distinctive book, and will serve to perpetuate what is most memorable and striking about a salient personality that played a considerable part in our day. ....It is a faithful record of one of the outstanding men of his time, and as such is of real and lasting value."—*Aberdeen Free Press.*

"There can be no question of its extreme interest to all who in any way concern themselves in the acute theological, political, and social controversies in which Charles Bradlaugh bore so prominent and unfortunate a part."—*World.*

"Mrs. Bonner's record has clearly been a labour of love. A task thus nerved by devotion to her father's memory illumes her pages with a human interest that formal biographies must lack....... Mr. Robertson's part of the book shows nothing less than genius as a polemist and critic. His careful and accurate relation of the Parliamentary struggle is an invaluable contribution to history."—*Halifax Courier.*

"Not only instructive as the biography of a remarkable man, but they are also a useful contribution to the social and political history of our times."—*Western Mercury.*

"Will probably have to be included among the most notable books of the year. · · · Mrs. Bonner, who writes with as much impartiality, perhaps, as the devoted daughter of such a father might be expected to do, has given to the reader an excellent impression of Mr. Bradlaugh's private life."—*Bristol Observer.*

"Der geraden, ehrlichen, ja ritterlichen Natur des grossen Wahrheitskämpfers hat seine Tochter ein schönes Denkmal gesetzt."—*Wiener Tagblatt.*

Now Ready.

SECOND AND ENLARGED EDITION.

Demy 8vo, Cloth, 5s. Post free.

WITH FINE PHOTO (1890) BY ELLIOTT AND FRY.

Collected Speeches of Charles Bradlaugh.

ANNOTATED BY JOHN M. ROBERTSON.

(Uniform with " Labor and Law " and " House of Brunswick.")

CONTENTS.

Preface.

Speeches at the Bar of the House of Commons: June 23rd, 1880; April 26th, 1881; February 7th, 1882; May 4th, 1883.

Speech at Northampton on India, November 19th, 1883.

—— on Capital and Labor, January 7th, 1886.

Speech at New York on Ireland, October 6th, 1873.

Speech in House of Commons on Market Rights and Tolls, April 22nd, 1887.

—— on Second Reading of Affirmation Bill, March 14th, 1888.

—— on the Compulsory Cultivation of Waste Lands, May 11th, 1888.

Before Royal Commission on Market Rights and Tolls, July, 1888.

Speech in House of Commons on Religious Prosecutions Abolition Bill, April 12th, 1889.

—— on Perpetual Pensions, May 16th, 1889.

—— on the Story of a Famine Insurance Fund, August 27th, 1889.

Speech at Bombay to Indian National Congress, December 29th, 1889.

Speech in the House of Commons on the Kashmir Question, July 3rd, 1890.

Closing Addresses at Congresses of the National Secular Society: Newcastle-on-Tyne, June 1st, 1879; London, May 16th, 1880; Bury, June 5th, 1881; International Freethought Conference, London, September 25th, 1881; Edinburgh, May 28th, 1882; Manchester, May 13th, 1883; Plymouth, June 1st, 1884; Birmingham, May 24th, 1885; Glasgow, June 13th, 1886; South Shields, May 20th, 1888.

THE IMPEACHMENT

OF THE

HOUSE OF BRUNSWICK.

TENTH EDITION.

PARTLY REVISED AND RE-WRITTEN BY THE AUTHOR.

160 pp., Demy 8vo.

In neat Paper Boards, cloth back - - **2s.**
(Uniform with " Doubts in Dialogue".)

In Cloth, gilt lettered - - - - **2s. 6d.**
(Uniform with " Speeches " and " Labor and Law ".)

POST FREE.

Press Notices.

" Unquestionably Bradlaugh's political masterpiece. . . . . Mr. Bradlaugh's initial and main contention regarding the Reigning House is constitutional; viz., that Parliament has made it, and that what Parliament has made Parliament can at will unmake."—*Daily Chronicle.*

" A storehouse of facts and statistics, apart from the chief characteristic of the book—a style at once lively, trenchant and severe."—*Liverpool Mercury.*

" As a suggestive review of the events of the last century and a half, it has an historic interest: as an indictment of the follies which it seems impossible to separate from a royal dynasty it deserves the study of every English Liberal."—*Westminster Review.*

" . . . . Without endorsing in full the arguments of Mr. Bradlaugh, we yet recommend the widest circulation of this laborious and suggestive volume."—*Weekly Dispatch.*

" Lord Randolph Churchill's ridiculous parody in 1880 of the historical episode of Burke and the dagger, by dashing to the floor of the House of Commons Mr. Bradlaugh's work ' The Impeachment of the House of Brunswick', concentrated attention on the book. . . . . The book is a powerfully sustained argument against the hereditary fitness of the reigning family. It maintains the supreme authority of Parliament to deal with the Crown, and points out that succession is a right accruing only from statute. It lashes the follies and failings of the four Georges with an unsparing hand ; and there is an appendix dealing with the cost of the Royal Family."—*Halifax Courier.*

" This remarkable *brochure* . . . The present issue will be found pre-eminently valuable to the politician and journalist. It is accompanied by an exceedingly exhaustive and admirably compiled index, which at once enables a person to lay his hand on particulars concerning any of the principal notabilities or chief incidents connected with the history of these islands from 1714 down to a comparatively short time ago."—*Freeman's Journal.*

" This very vigorous political pamphlet . . . . constitutes a scathing and vigorous attack on our reigning dynasty. The four Georges and their misdeeds in particular come in for merciless treatment, and no doubt they deserved it."— *Northern Daily News.*

" The vigorous language in which the late Charles Bradlaugh dealt with political history, past and present, was always enjoyed by Radicals of every shade. The trenchant sarcasm . . . . will be greatly relished by many who are not quite so hostile to the ruling powers as he was."—*Stockton Herald.*

" Contains an appendix of valuable information upon the question of Royal Grants."—*Sunday Sun.*

" Gives very full particulars regarding the cost of Royalty to this country, and its vigorous and trenchant style makes it interesting reading."—*Dundee Weekly News.*

" . . . . Very remarkable book. . . . . His argument is wrought out very carefully and logically. . . . . A very careful examination of his statements has failed to disclose any error of facts ; and, on the whole, his opinions will seem justifiable even to those who do not think that this country is yet ripe for a Republic." —*Dundee Advertiser.*

" Mr. Bradlaugh argues with characteristic force for the repeal of the Act of Settlement, and the exclusion of members of the House of Brunswick from the throne of Great Britain, and passes in review the history of the period that has elapsed since the succession was last settled by Act of Parliament."—*Southampton Times.*

" A strong indictment of the Hanoverian Succession. . . . . Marked by those vigorous and outspoken sentiments so characteristic of the man."—*Wakefield Free Press.*

" Mr. Bradlaugh's lectures on the House of Brunswick will be remembered by all who heard them. Whether we agree with all that he said or not, we must admit that the deceased gentleman was at infinite trouble in preparing his addresses on this subject, and he presented facts as they appeared to him with a power that may not unworthily be compared with Thackeray's trenchant lectures on ' The Four Georges ' ".—*Leicester Chronicle.*

" In this masterly work Mr. Bradlaugh showed up the extravagance of royalty in Great Britain in a way to convince any but a stolid Britisher's mind that the only economical, just, and right thing to do was to abolish the reigning family. He also painted the portraits of the " House of Brunswick " in colors true to history, and held up to his countrymen the long list of dissipated wretches inflicted as rulers upon his countrymen, in all their vicious deformity."—*Boston Investigator, U.S.A.*

. " The present edition is the best that has appeared. . . . . An elegant vol. printed in bold, clear type. . . . . Should be read by all, especially by every Englishman, and we heartily recommend it to our readers."—*Modern Thought* (Bombay).

"LABOR AND LAW."

Being the completed portion of the work on which the Author was engaged up to the time of his fatal illness, with several reprint articles, Two Portraits (taken 1882 and 1890), and a Memoir by J. M. ROBERTSON.

---

282 pp., Demy 8vo, Price 5s.   Post free.

(Uniform with "The Impeachment of the House of Brunswick.")

Press Notices.

"The fragmentary essays on "Labor and Law", which form Mr. Bradlaugh's final contribution to contemporary economics, accentuate the sense of the loss which the House and the country have sustained by the removal of his eminently practical sagacity from the discussion of questions which have now come to the front, and which he had made peculiarly his own.   Mr. Bradlaugh's position as a political philosopher was in some respects unique. . . . It is to his reasonable and temperate attitude as much as to the legal acumen with which he marshals evidence and estimates probabilities, and the courage with which he fights against many of the *ad captandum* schemes which are preferred by the masses to more useful but less attractive measures, that Mr. Bradlaugh's economic writings owe their special value."—*Literary World.*

"A storehouse of facts . . . . an example of Mr. Bradlaugh's wonderful painstaking industry and argumentative ability.   Blue-books, reports of special commissions, Acts of Parliament, law reports, foreign official returns, speeches, newspapers, are all drawn on to sustain his arguments. . . . . The author grapples with the questions which he discusses in a masterly way.   No one else could have have amassed such an array of facts, or driven home his arguments with greater force.   Champion of individualism as he was, Mr. Bradlaugh did more than any modern Parliamentarian to ameliorate the conditions of the people by legislative action.   Mr. Robertson contributes an interesting memoir to the work, which should not be passed over."—*Star.*

"Deserves to be read by all who are taking a practical interest in labor questions."—*Manchester Examiner.*

"This volume, fragmentary as its contents are, will distinctly add to Mr. Bradlaugh's reputation.   The essays show him in the character of the practical politician; and it is as such that his name will longest be remembered."—*Newspaper.*

"A fine work . . . . the contribution of a master mind. No one who pretends to an intelligent interest in the condition of the working class, and the topics which touch it, should be without Mr. Bradlaugh's last, and, in many respects, most important and useful production. . . . These 300 well-printed pages contain a mass of facts and figures, marshalled with the characteristic care and consummate fairness of the compiler, which are simply invaluable to social reformers, even those whose ultimate aims and ideals for social reconstruction widely diverge from his. . . . For a present to a Trades Unionist, a Radical, or even a Social or Tory Democrat, we know no better book than 'Labor and Law'."—*Northampton Mercury.*

"The author's practical bent for dealing with affairs, so markedly displayed Parliament as to earn for him the character of an ideal House of Commons member, is nowhere, in his always clear and unambiguous spoken or written utterances, more strikingly exemplified than in his posthumous work on "Labor and Law". . . . There is but one word to describe Chapter IV, on "Hours of Labor". It is masterly. . . . "Labor and Law" is a most thorough and helpful work, of the highest importance and utility to workers. Its great value lies in the fact that the writer does not merely theorise, but produces a mass of solid substantial fact as basis on which to build his argument. The Trade Councils, workers' clubs, and all labor bodies should obtain the book, and it should be available in the libraries. A freshly treated, incisively written memoir of the author from the pen of Mr. J. M. Robertson, is included."—*Halifax Courier.*

"Consistently impresses one with Mr. Bradlaugh's single-mindedness and earnest desire for the weal of the working class . . . . and it testifies to the laborious way in which he formed and fortified his judgments."—*Daily Chronicle.*

"A valuable memorial of an intrepid and independent politician."—*Co-operative News.*

"Characterised by a strong insight into the questions treated upon. What is equally important is that the insight is so clearly expressed as to be intelligible to the veriest tyro. We exceedingly regret the book was not left us in a finished state. As it is, however, it will well repay perusal by every class of politicians. The facts recorded cannot, in general, be disputed; and the opinions expressed should be widely known."—*Rural World*

"His general views on these questions are well known. He enforces them by powerful historical, as well as logical arguments, and also by a review of what has been tried and experienced in Continental countries. . . . . one chapter is devoted to the question of the hours of labor, and the arguments against State restriction have rarely been more forcibly set forth."—*Scotsman.*

"Mr. Bradlaugh's book has a special interest from its admirably written retrospect of Socialism in Europe, beginning with the insurrection of Babœuf in 1795-6, planned against the French Directory to establish a Communistic Republic. . . . All anxious to follow the drift of recent speculation should read Mr. Bradlaugh's work. The volume is the fruit of exhaustive study, dealing with law and labor in a perspicuous and animated style. It is deeply to be regretted that the author did not live to complete the work. Nevertheless, it is a permanent memorial of his powers."—*Newcastle Daily Chronicle.*

"A legacy of his ripened opinions on questions which are among the most prominent of those now occupying the attention of politicians at home and abroad."—*Morning Post.*

NEW VOLUMES.

Crown 8vo, Cloth, uniform, 2s. 6d. Post free.

Labor Questions and Socialism.

CONTENTS:—The Eight Hours Movement; Debate on do. with H. M. Hyndman; The Employers' Liability Bill; Capital and Labor; Labor's Prayer; Parliament and the Poor: what the Legislature can do and what it ought to do; Some Objections to Socialism; Socialism: its fallacies and dangers; Socialism: For and Against (written discussion with Mrs. Besant); Will Socialism benefit the English People (Two debates, with H. M. Hyndman and E. Belfort Bax).

Crown 8vo, Cloth, uniform, 2s. 6d. Post free.

Political Essays.

CONTENTS:—How are we to Abolish the Lords?; The Radical Programme; Taxation; how it originated, how it is spent, and who bears it; England's Balance Sheet; Royal Grants; Poverty, and its Effects on the Political Condition of the People; Why do Men Starve; The Land, the People, and the Coming Struggle; Compulsory Cultivation of the Land; Real Representation of the People; Mr. Gladstone or Lord Salisbury: which?; Letter to Lord Randolph Churchill, M.P., Chancellor of the Exchequer; The True Story of my Parliamentary Struggle (with Speeches at the Bar of the House); Correspondence with Sir Stafford Northcote; John Churchill, Duke of Marlborough; A Cardinal's Broken Oath (reply to Cardinal Manning).

Demy 8vo, Cloth, 1s. 6d.; Boards, 1s. Post free.

(Uniform with "House of Brunswick", etc.)

Doubts in Dialogue.

Imaginary Discussions, written from time to time for the *National Reformer* during the last few years of Mr. Bradlaugh's life. They "are based upon real doubts, many of them put personally by word of mouth or by letter to Mr. Bradlaugh, or suggested by the reading of certain books."

[CONTENTS: A Christian Priest and an Unbeliever: A Christian Priest and a Sceptic, on Christmastide; A Theist and an Atheist; A Church of England Curate and a Doubter; A Puzzled Enquirer and a Doctor of Divinity; A Respectable Man of the World, reputedly pious, and a Heretic, addicted to the public advocacy of Freethought; A Missionary and an Atheist, on Prophecy as Evidence for Christianity; A Christian Lady and an Infidel; A Christian Missionary and a Sceptic; A Theist and a Monist; An Atheist and a Pantheist; A Liberal Churchman and an Atheist; A Disciple of Herbert Spencer and an Atheist; An Orthodox Christian and a Sceptic, on Jesus.]

Crown 8vo, Cloth, uniform, 2s. 6d. Post free.

The Freethinker's Text Book.

A STANDARD WORK.

CONTENTS.

" The Story of the Origin of Man, as told by the Bible and by Science."

" What is Religion?" " How has it Grown?" "God and Soul."

NEW VOLUME.

Crown 8vo, Cloth, uniform, 3s. Post free.

Theological Essays.

CONTENTS.

Heresy: its Morality and Utility—A Plea and a Justification; Humanity's Gain from Unbelief; Supernatural and Rational Morality?; Has Man a Soul?; Is there a God?; A Plea for Atheism; A Few Words about the Devil; Were Adam and Eve our First Parents?; The New Lives of Abraham, Jacob, Moses, David, and Jonah; Who was Jesus Christ? What did Jesus Teach?; The Twelve Apostles; The Atonement; When were our Gospels Written?; Mr. Gladstone's Reply to Col. Ingersoll on Christianity; A Few Words on the Christian's Creed (Mr. Bradlaugh's first pamphlet).

Crown 8vo, Cloth, Price 3s. 6d.

GENESIS:
ITS AUTHORSHIP AND AUTHENTICITY.

A minute comparison of the many attempts of commentators to make good the historical character of Genesis.

A reliable text-book for those who have neither the leisure nor the means to collect the items for themselves. The object of the work is to show: That the Book of Genesis is unhistoric, and not the work of any one writer, or age; That the narrative is sometimes self-contradictory, and often contradicted by other books of the Bible; That its chronological statements are inaccurate, and overwhelmingly contradicted by history and modern discovery; That the Genesaic teachings on ethnology, geology, astronomy, zoology, and botany, are flatly in opposition to the best knowledge in each of these sciences; And that such teachings of the book as relate to morality would be destructive of human happiness, if generally adopted.

Crown 8vo, Cloth, uniform. Post free.

DEBATES IN THEOLOGY,

BETWEEN

CHARLES BRADLAUGH

AND

ACCREDITED REPRESENTATIVES OF CHRISTIANITY.

VOLUME I. Price 3s. CONTENTS:

GOD, MAN, AND THE BIBLE (With Dr. Baylee, at Liverpool);
WHAT DOES CHRISTIAN THEISM TEACH? (Rev. A. J. Harrison, London);
DOES THE CHURCH OF ENGLAND TEACH ETERNAL TORMENT? (Rev. J. Lightfoot. Written debate);
IS IT REASONABLE TO WORSHIP GOD (Rev. R. A. Armstrong, Nottingham);
CHRISTIANITY IN RELATION TO FREETHOUGHT, SCEPTICISM, AND FAITH: Three Discussions delivered at Norwich by the Bishop of Peterborough, with special replies by Mr. Bradlaugh.

VOLUME II. Price 3s. 6d. CONTENTS:

HAS MAN A SOUL? (Rev. W. M. Westerby, Burnley);
SECULARISM UNPHILOSOPHICAL, UNSOUND, AND IMMORAL. (Rev. Dr. McCann, London);
HAS HUMANITY GAINED FROM UNBELIEF? (Rev. Marsden Gibson, M.A., Newcastle.) Together with the pamphlet of same Title.
NOTES ON CHRISTIAN EVIDENCES. In reply to the Oxford House Papers; with rejoinders by Rev. E. S. Talbot, M.A., Rev. Francis Paget, D.D., W. Lock, M.A., T. B. Strong, B.A., Rev. V. S. S. Coles, M.A.

[These volumes form a storehouse of arguments on both sides, and are valuable aids to the inquirer and student.]

Crown 8vo, Cloth, uniform, 2s. 6d.

Miscellanies.

Comprising Autobiography; Cromwell and Washington, a Contrast; Five Dead Men whom I knew when living (Sketches of Robert Owen, Joseph Mazzini, John Stuart Mill, Charles Sumner, and Ledru Rollin); Freemasonry: what it is, has been, and ought to be; The Channel Tunnel: ought the Democracy to support or oppose it?; Four Lectures on Anthropology; The Laws *re* Blasphemy and Heresy; and Hints to Emigrants to the United States.

Crown 8vo, Cloth, uniform, 3s. 6d.

THE QUEEN AGAINST BRADLAUGH AND BESANT.

Verbatim Report of the Trial of Mr. Bradlaugh and Mrs. Besant for publishing Dr. Knowlton's pamphlet " Fruits of Philosophy: an Essay on the Population Question ". With Portraits and Autographs of the two Defendants. Second Edition, with Appendix, containing the Judgments of Lords Justices Bramwell, Brett, and Cotton.

Charles Bradlaugh's Works.

Complete Sets are supplied as follows :—

Demy 8vo, cloth, uniform—
  Labor and Law, Collected Speeches, House of Brunswick, Doubts in Dialogue.

Crown 8vo, cloth, uniform—
  Genesis, Freethinker's Text Book, Theological Essays, Theological Debates (2), Political Essays, Labor Questions and Socialism, Miscellanies.
  Together with Report of Knowlton Trial. and the Biography by A. S. Headingly.
  In all 14 vols.

For 37s. 6d., carriage paid in United Kingdom.

For 40s. post or carriage paid to any part of the world.

[See also pp. 26 to 29.]

Photographs of Charles Bradlaugh.

Taken by MESSRS. ELLIOTT AND FRY, September, 1890.

Cabinets: 1. Profile; 2. Full Face; 3. Do. With Hat; 4. Half length; 5. Do. With Hat. With signature, each 2s. Any 3 for 5s., or the set of five for 7s. 6d.
Carte-de-visite, 1s.

Large Photo (date 1882), 23½ by 18½, 4s.

By CHARLES BRADLAUGH and others.

Crown 8vo. 224 pp., Cloth, 2s.

Thursday Lectures at the Hall of Science.

(Complete edition : 28 lectures) containing—

Anthropology, By Charles Bradlaugh.

| The Chemistry of Home } By Mrs. H. Bradlaugh
| The Slave Struggle in America } Bonner.

The Physiology of Home } By Annie Besant.
Electricity }

The Plays of Shakspeare } By E. B. Aveling, D.Sc.
Macbeth }

By ADOLPHE S. HEADINGLEY.

Crown 8vo, 208 pp., Cloth, 1s. 6d.

Biography of Charles Bradlaugh.

[To 1880.] With Photograph. Appendix [to 1883] by W. Mawer.

[The best biography published, prior to the appearance of " Charles Bradlaugh, a Record of his Life."]

By HYPATIA BRADLAUGH BONNER.

Crown 8vo, Cloth, 1s.

PRINCESS VERA, and other Stories.

Contains :—Princess Vera ; A Day's Adventures ; How the World was Made ; Tommy and I ; A Children's Picnic.

[See also " Charles Bradlaugh," p. 3, and " Pamphlets," p. 27.]

Crown 8vo, Cloth, 6s.

POEMS, ESSAYS, AND FRAGMENTS.

EDITED, WITH PREFACE, BY JOHN M. ROBERTSON.

With Portrait of Thomson, hitherto unpublished.

POEMS.

The Dead Year—The Dawn of Love—Love Song—Sonnet—Versicles—L'Envoy—Sunday, 14/2/69; Lilah, Alice, Hypatia—Creeds and Men—Proem—On a Debate between Mr. Bradlaugh and Mr. Thomas Cooper on the Existence of God—A Sergeants' Mess Song —Mr. Maccall at Cleveland Hall—The Pan-Anglican Synod—Epigrams : Iphigenia à la Mode—Love's Logic—A Timely Prayer— Who killed Moses?—Suggested from Southampton—Poor Indeed! —In Exitu Israel—The Successors who do not Succeed—Bless Thee! Thou art Translated—Cross Lines from Goethe—We Croak —In a Christian Churchyard—Our Congratulations on the Recovery of his Royal Highness—Pathetic Epitaph. TRANSLATIONS FROM DE BERANGER : The Good God—The Death of the Devil. TRANSLATIONS FROM HEINE : The Greek Gods—The Gods of Greece (another version)—In Harbour—Philosophy—Hindoo Mythology— Epilogue—Reminiscence of Hammonia.

ESSAYS.

Notes on Emerson—A Few Words about Burns—Shelley—The Poems of William Blake—Walt Whitman—How Heine Forwarned France—The Origin of Evil—The Divan of Goethe—The King's Friends—The *Saturday Review* on "Mr. Bright's Edition of Mr. Bright"—How the Bible Warns against Authorship—On Suicide.

FRAGMENTS.

PRESS NOTICES.

"It is easy to agree with Mr. Henry S. Salt, who in his excellent monograph on ' B.V.' expresses the belief that this uncompromising poet of pessimism is likely hereafter to take rank among the foremost writers of the age in which he lived. It is scarcely too much to say that such rank is accorded him already. Were I asked to select for the use of a class of youthful students of English literature the best critical essays on these three writers [Shelley, Whitman, and Blake], bould certainly point to these monographs of James Thomson. . . . ."

In these essays we are face to face with great thoughts, not little ones. . . . . A magnificently-worded vindication of Blake. . . . . The essay on Walt Whitman is perbaps the best piece of work in the volume. . . . . It is tantalising to have to deal with a book like this in a perfunctory manner. Incisive, brilliant, convincing, above all splendidly courageous, no real lover of letters is likely to miss the opportunity of becoming its possessor."—JAS. STANLEY LITTLE, in *Literary World* of Feb. 10th.

"'The Dead Year' is a fine and sombre conception, embodied in sonorous verse. . . . . The beautiful 'Proem' stands out from among the poems by its stately music and delicate finish of line, its harmonious completeness of form, while expressing feelings which too often induce the poet to run riot in chaotic metres and images. Artistically speaking, it seems to us very nearly, if not quite perfect. . . . . This volume contains, as the conclusion to the essay on Blake, one of the loviest of Thomson's lyric gems. We had previously seen it in 'A Voice from the Nile, and other Poems', where it somehow seemed out of place among its surroundings."—*Speaker.*

"The style of his essays is always easy and virile, with that air of distinction which is so nameless and yet so unmistakeable, and also without the awkwardness that not seldom damages his verse. . , . His verse, partly from the intrinsic quality of its theme, no doubt, and partly from the sombre and more than Dantesque melancholy which it reveals in its author, must always be his best known work, as we dare say it is his most characteristic."—*Scottish Leader.*

"We can but thank Mr. Robertson for compiling these fugitive fragments into a compact form, and trust that they will give a better conception of James Thomson's wonderful power and splendid poetic gifts."—*Daily Chronicle.*

"His translations of Heine are extremely clever. . . . . His 'Lines on the Debate between Mr. Bradlaugh and Mr. Thomas Cooper on the Existence of God' deserve to be widely known as the best available satire on the Egoist's conception of 'My God.' . . . . He has much to say of Emerson, Blake, and Walt Whitman, and much of what he says is outspoken common-sense. Mrs. Browning's 'Aurora Leigh' is well-described. . . . . A well-written argument in favor of suicide is too obvious to be convincing."—*National Observer.*

"The essays are vigorous and thoughtful, and are decidedly worth reading."—*Halifax Evening Courier.*

"Thomson's versions from Heine are among the best of the many attempts that have been made to get both the music and the meaning of the German into English. . . . . Thomson was a writer of genius."—*Scotsman.*

"There is always a sort of solemn sincerity, an impressive accent, about the least fragment of his writing. On the whole, Mr. Robertson is probably right in thinking him more mature as a prose than a verse writer. His prose has always an authority, the authority of perfect utterance, which his verse sometimes lacks. . . . . His charming comment on the little baby-poem of 'Infant Joy' (Blake) is the best I have seen."—*Star.*

"Vigorous and stimulating work. . . . . The prose is, without doubt, very strong and individual."—*Newcastle Daily Leader.*

"The translations from Heine, especially 'In Harbour' and 'Reminiscences of Hammonia' are remarkably clever. . . . . Some of the essays are well worth reading for their fine critical insight and original judgment, and Scotchmen ought to be more than satisfied with the enthusiastic praise of their poet in 'A Few Words About Burns'. . . . . The paper on Blake treats the subject from a decidedly fresh point of view, and to some at least the estimate of Tennyson contained in it will have an attraction.'—*Glasgow Herald.*

"The essays on Blake and Walt Whitman are, considering that the one was written in 1863 and the other in 1874, remarkable pieces of appreciative criticism, and fine examples of Thomson's style and command of language."—*Weekly Dispatch.*

"Those who know him already will be genuinely glad of this book if only for the literary essays which form the latter and more important part of it. . . . . It is certainly a book which the man who cares for letters will do well to place on his shelves."—*Eastern and Western Review.*

By Professor LUDWIG BUECHNER, M.D.

Author of " Force and Matter ", " Man, and his Place in Nature ", etc.

Crown 8vo, 360 pp., cloth, 3s. 6d.

Mind in Animals.

Prof. Buechner's own investigations and observations in this most interesting and important subject. A valuable contribution.

WITH PHOTOGRAPH OF AUTHOR.

CONTENTS.

INTRODUCTION : Historical Review ; Intelligence and Instinct.

ANTS AND ANT LIFE : General Characteristics ; Ants in History ; Ant Architecture ; Road-Making ; Harvesting Ants ; Cattle and Milking ; Intelligence and Language ; Slavery ; Friendship and Enmities ; Wars and Battles.

THE TERMITES OR WHITE ANTS : Termites at Home ; Termites Abroad.

THE BEE NATION. Royalty ; Swarming ; Domestic Work ; Activity Abroad ; Monarchy, Socialism and Instinct ; Cell-Building ; Other Species of Bees.

THE WASPS : General Details ; Various Species of Wasps.

THE SPIDERS : General Details ; Various Species of Spiders.

THE BEETLES : Beetle Intellect.

[See also " Tracts ", p. 28.]

By PROF. ERNST HAECKEL.

Crown 8vo, 360 pp., Cloth, uniform, 3s. 6d.

The Pedigree of Man

AND OTHER ESSAYS.

WITH 80 ILLUSTRATIONS, AND INDEX.

CONTENTS.

PART I : The Pedigree of Man ; The Darwinian Theory ; The Origin of the Human Race ; The Division of Labor in the Life of Nature and of Man ; Cell-Souls and Soul-Cells.

PART II : The Progress and Work of Zoology ; The Development of Life-Particles and the Perigenesis of the Plastidule ; The Proofs of Evolution ; The Present Position of Evolution in Relation to Science ; The Origin and the Development of the Sense-Organs.

Crown 8vo, Cloth, 2s. 6d., or boards, 2s.

CHRIST AND KRISHNA.

Reprinted from the *National Reformer* with many important Additions and Corrections, and with an analytical table of contents and a copious index.

SECTION HEADINGS :—Preamble; Question of Priority; Age of Indian Documents; The Special Documents; The Krishna Legend; The Christian Argument; The Central Disproof; Antiquity of Krishnaism; Invalid Evidence; Weber's Theory; The Solar-Child Myth; The Stable and Manger; The "Christophoros" Legend; Indian and Christian Religious Drama; The Seven Myth; The Descent into Hell; Examination of the Krishna Myth; Krishnaite and Christian Doctrine: The "White Island"; Summary of Results.

Crown 8vo, Cloth, limp, 1s. 6d.

ESSAYS IN HISTORY AND POLITICS.

Comprising: The Perversion of Scotland; Royalism; Toryism and Barbarism; Socialism and Malthusianism; Over-population.

Demy 8vo, Cloth, limp, 1s. 6d.

DISCOURSES ON LIFE AND LETTERS.

Comprising lectures delivered at South Place Institute on The Pleasures of Malignity, Culture and Action, Equality, Emotion in History, and The Religion of Shakspere; also "The Upshot of Hamlet, by Arthur Gigadibs".

Crown 8vo, Cloth, limp, 9d.

THE PERVERSION OF SCOTLAND

(SINS OF THE SCOTCH CHURCH).
A booklet in favor of Disestablishment.

[See also "Pamphlets," p. 27 ; and " Tracts, ' p. 29.]

Crown 8vo, 216 pp., Cloth, limp, 2s.

Fourteen Orations.

CHEAP EDITION.

Comprising, Take a Road of your own; Divine Vivisection, or Hell; The Christian Religion; The Ghosts; Law, not God, or the Message of Humboldt; Is all of the Bible Inspired?; The Mistakes of Moses; Saviors of the World; How Man Makes Gods; Thomas Paine, the Republican; What must I do to be Saved?; The Spirit of the Age; Human Liberty, or Intellectual Development; Which Way?

Crown 8vo, 112 pp., Cloth, 1s. 6d.

Five Orations.

Comprising, On the Gods; Thomas Paine; Humboldt; Heretics and Heresies; The Arraignment of the Church.

[See also " Pamphlets," p. 27 ; and " Tracts," pp. 28-9.]

By LOGAN MITCHELL.

Crown 8vo, 220 pp., Cloth, 2s. 6d.

RELIGION IN THE HEAVENS,

OR

MYTHOLOGY UNVEILED.

CONTENTS.

On Miracles, Christian Supernaturalism, The Christian Fathers, Pagan Allegories, Christian Superstition and its effects, Physiology and Theology.

PAMPHLETS.

Crown 8vo, paper covers.

By CHARLES BRADLAUGH.

THEOLOGICAL.

DEBATES—All Verbatim Reports.

God, Man, and the Bible. Three nights' discussion with the Rev. Dr. BAYLEE. (Liverpool, 1860.) 6d.

Christianity in Relation to Freethought, Scepticism, and Faith. Three Discourses by the Bishop of Peterborough, with special replies by Charles Bradlaugh. (1871.) 6d.

What does Christian Theism Teach? Two nights' public debate with the Rev. A. J. HARRISON. (London, 1872.) 6d.

Does the Church of England Teach Eternal Torment? Written debate with the Rev. J. LIGHTFOOT. (1875.) 6d.

Is it Reasonable to Worship God? Two nights' debate with the Rev. R. A. ARMSTRONG. (Nottingham, 1878.) 1s.

Has Man a Soul? Two nights' debate with the Rev. W. M. WESTERBY. (Burnley, 1879.) 1s.

Secularism Unphilosophical, Unsocial, and Immoral. Three nights' debate with the Rev. Dr. McCANN. (London, 1881.) 1s.

Has Humanity Gained from Unbelief? Two nights' debate with Rev. MARSDEN GIBSON, M.A. (Newcastle, 1889.) Together with the pamphlet of same Title. 1s.

Notes on Christian Evidences. In reply to the Oxford House Papers; with rejoinders by Rev. E. S. Talbot, M.A., Rev. Francis Paget, D.D., W. Lock, M.A., T. B. Strong, B.A., Rev. V. S. S. Coles, M.A. 6d.

When were our Gospels Written? 6d.

The Laws relating to Blasphemy and Heresy, 6d.

Heresy; its Morality and Utility. A Plea and a Justification, 9d.

A Plea for Atheism, 3d.

A Few Words on the Christian's Creed (Mr. Bradlaugh's First Pamphlet, 1850), 2d.

POLITICAL, ETC.

Socialism. Containing the written Debates with Annie Besant and E. Belfort Bax, and "Socialism: its fallacies and dangers". 1s.

Socialism: For and Against. Written debate with Mrs. Besant, 4d.

Will Socialism benefit the English People? Written debate with E. Belfort Bax, 6d.

The Eight Hours' Movement. One nights' debate with H. M. Hyndman, 6d.

The True Story of my Parliamentary Struggle. Containing
a Verbatim Report of the proceedings before the Select
Committee of the House of Commons; Mr. Bradlaugh's
Three Speeches at the Bar of the House,.etc., 6d.

Taxation : how it originated, how it is spent, and who bears
it. Second Edition, 6d.

Cromwell and Washington : a Contrast, 6d.

Five Dead Men whom I knew when living. Sketches of
Robert Owen, Joseph Mazzini, John Stuart Mill, Charles
Sumner, and Ledru Rollin, 4d.

Autobiography. Reprinted, with portrait. 36 pp., 4d.

Anthropology (4 Lectures), 4d.

By H. BRADLAUGH BONNER.

The Chemistry of Home (four lectures), 4d.

The Slave Struggle in America (four lectures), 4d.

By J. M. ROBERTSON.

The Upshot of Hamlet, 6d. (*Demy 8vo.*)

Thomas Paine ; an Investigation, 4d.

Royalism, 4d.

By Col. R. G. INGERSOLL.

The Liberty of Man, Woman, and Child, 6d.

The Gods, 6d.

Heretics and Heresies, 4d.

Thomas Paine, 3d.

The Mistakes of Moses, 3d.

Humboldt, 2d.

Arraignment of the Church, 2d.

ORATIONS, Cheap Edition, 6d. each.

Series I : Take a Road of your own ; Divine Vivisection, or
Hell ; The Christian Religion ; The Ghosts ; Law, not God.

Series II : Is all of the Bible Inspired ? Mistakes of Moses ;
Saviors of the World ; How Man Makes Gods ; Thomas
Paine, the Republican.

Series III : What Must I do to be Saved ? The Spirit of the
Age ; Human Liberty, or Intellectual Development ; Which
Way ?

Series I and II in one Book, 1s.

By ROBERT COOPER.

The Holy Scriptures Analysed. With Life of Cooper written
by C. Bradlaugh. 6d.

By DAVID HUME.

On Miracles (The famous Essay). Edited by J. M. Wheeler. 3d.

TRACTS.

Crown 8vo, 3d. each.

By CHARLES BRADLAUGH.

Will Socialism Benefit the English People (Verbatim Report of Debate with H. M. Hyndman).
The Employers Liability Bill (A Letter to Thomas Burt, M.P.)
The Compulsory Cultivation of Waste Lands.
A Plea for Atheism.

By DAVID HUME.

The Famous Essay " On Miracles ".

By Col. R. G. INGERSOLL.

The Mistakes of Moses.
Thomas Paine.

2d. each, or 10s. per 100 for distribution.

By CHARLES BRADLAUGH.

Socialism : its Fallacies and Dangers.
The Eight Hours' Movement.
Parliament and the Poor : What the Legislature can do; what it ought to do.
Capital and Labor.
The Real Representation of the People.
The Radical Programme.
Northampton and the House of Commons (Correspondence between Charles Bradlaugh, M.P., and the Right Hon. Sir Stafford Northcote, M.P.).
John Churchill, Duke of Marlborough (" Mob, Scum, and Dregs ").
The Channel Tunnel : ought the Democracy to support or oppose it ?
What Freemasonry is, what it has been, and what it ought to be.
Humanity's Gain from Unbelief.
Has Man a Soul ?
The New Life of David.
A Few Words on the Christian's Creed (A reproduction of Mr. Bradlaugh's first pamphlet).

By Prof. LUDWIG BUECHNER.

The Influence of Heredity on Free Will.

By Prof. H. D. GARRISON.
The Absence of Design in Nature.

By Col. R. G. INGERSOLL.
The Ghosts.
Is all of the Bible Inspired ?
What Must I Do to be Saved ?
Human Liberty ; or, Intellectual Development.

By J. M. ROBERTSON.
Socialism and Malthusianism.
Toryism and Barbarism.
Blunders of Faith.

By A. MAJOR.
A Few Objections to Spiritualism.

1d. each, or 6s. per 100 for distribution.

By CHARLES BRADLAUGH.
How are we to Abolish the Lords ?
Poverty, and its Effects on the Political Condition of the
    People.
Why do Men Starve ?
A Cardinal's Broken Oath (Reply to Cardinal Manning).
Labor's Prayer.
Supernatural and Rational Morality.   Mr. Gladstone's
    Reply to Col. Ingersoll on Christianity.
Were Adam and Eve our First Parents ?
A Few Words about the Devil.
Is there a God ?
Who was Jesus Christ ?
What did Jesus Teach ?
The Twelve Apostles.
The Atonement.
The New Life of Jacob.
The New Life of Abraham.
The New Life of Moses.
The New Life of Jonah.

By ALICE BRADLAUGH.
Mind considered as a Bodily Function, 16 pp., 1d.

By Col. R. G. INGERSOLL.
Take a Road of Your Own ; Divine Vivisection, or Hell ;
    The Christian Religion ; Thomas Paine the Republi-
    can ; Saviors of the World ; How Man makes Gods ;
    Law, not God, or The Message of Humboldt ; The
    Spirit of the Age ; Which Way ?

THE
FREE REVIEW,
A MONTHLY MAGAZINE.
EDITED BY JOHN M. ROBERTSON.

Price 1/-; or 14/- per annum post free to any part of the world.
(Trade supplied by Swan Sonnenschein and Co.)

Some Recent Press Opinions.

" Original, fresh, daring, exceptionally well written. . . . . De-cidedly piquant throughout."—*Sun.*

" Fully maintains its reputation for uncompromising vigour and piquancy."—*Glasgow Evening News.*

" Bears the same relationship towards the ordinary monthlies as do the quarterly reviews to their minor brethren. What dis-tinguishes the FREE REVIEW from magazines like the *Nineteenth Century* is that the latter are filled merely with lengthy leading articles, written in a prosaic style by men whose chief claim to being afforded publicity is their social or other notoriety, while the former bears a monthly packet of thought to its readers."—*Reynolds'.*

" The FREE REVIEW is solid, sensible, and severe as usual. . . . . Subjects of deep interest are discussed with a freedom and frankness which is thoroughly invigorating. This magazine is doing valuable service by its treatment of social and political problems."—*Arbroath Herald.*

" The FREE REVIEW is as bold in its opinions as it is able in its advocacy of them."—*Weekly Sun.*

" All these matters are dealt with in a straightforward way, in accord with modern thought, and in language which predicts and foreshadows the inevitable. They are subjects which it has been for years the practice to shut out of the field of practical discussion. But the spread of education and the extension of higher education, will ere long put the defenders of many long accepted doctrines to the test."—*Folkestone Express.*

" Keeps up its high standard of excellence."—*Somerset Express.*

INDEX TO AUTHORS, &c.